T0330459

Finance, Investment and
Economic Fluctuations

To Sophie and Solène, and to my parents.

Finance, Investment and Economic Fluctuations

An Analysis in the Tradition of
Hyman P. Minsky

Eric Nasica
Lecturer in Economics
University of Nice-Sophia Antipolis, France

Translated by Cécile Dangel
With a Foreword by Jan A. Kregel

Edward Elgar
Cheltenham, UK • Northampton, MA, USA

Published by
Edward Elgar Publishing Limited
Glensanda House
Montpellier Parade
Cheltenham
Glos GL50 1UA
UK

Edward Elgar Publishing, Inc.
136 West Street
Suite 202
Northampton
Massachusetts 01060
USA

A catalogue record for this book
is available from the British Library

Library of Congress Cataloguing in Publication Data

Nasica, Eric, 1967–
     Finance, investment and economic fluctuations: an analysis in the tradition of Hyman P. Minsky / Eric Nasica; translated by C. Dangel with a foreword by Jan A. Kregel.
     Includes index.
          1. Financial crises—Mathematical models. 2. Business cycles—Mathematical models. 3. Uncertainty—Mathematical models. 4. Endogenous growth (Economics)—Mathematical models. 5. Minsky, Hyman P. I. Minsky, Hyman P. II. Title.

HB3722.N37 2000
332—dc21   99–087210

ISBN 1 85898 896 9

Contents

List of Figures and Table

FIGURES

TABLE

Foreword

There have been a number of events honouring Hyman Minsky since his death in 1996. However, none of these contributions to these events has presented as serious and honest an evaluation of Minsky's work as this book. It is a real tribute, for it not only looks backwards in assessment, but also forward to new developments, developments that Minsky himself considered promising. Nasica's exposition has managed to grasp both the ambiguous and eclectic nature of Minsky's financial fragility hypothesis, noting the originality of what Nasica calls the 'financial theory of investment'. But, he also notes the central importance of the institutional furnishing of the theory, and in particular the centrality of banks in Minsky's system. Minsky was the Cassandra of financial instability, best known for his financial fragility hypothesis. As with other original thinkers, his theories are often reduced to simplifications which eventually lose all contact with the rich underpinnings of theory and history that produced them. Nasica reminds the reader of the heterodox mix of constituent elements that went into the development of Minsky's approach.

During his lifetime, there were many examples of financial breakdown 'near misses', and this did not surprise Minsky. His work was well known in financial circles, precisely because it explained how the near misses had come to take place. The increasing frequency of financial crises in the years since his death make a full understanding of Minsky's theory even more imperative both for economists and for financial markets participants. Although Minsky was close to the post-Keynesian tradition, his insistence on endogenous dynamics of the interaction between finance and investment, and consequently the importance of decision-making in financial institutions, set him apart, and indeed often created frictions with other economists working in that broad tradition. Amongst these factors was Minsky's attempt to find a bridge to mainstream theory as well as to the new developments in non-linear dynamics. Nasica's book first sites Minsky's theory within the broad post-Keynesian tradition, providing one of the best presentations of what might be called the 'American Keynesian' monetary tradition. He then turns to confront Minsky's approach with both the new Keynesians and what, for want a better description might be called 'dynamical post-Keynesian' theories, distinguishing their affinity to Minsky by the way they have managed to capture the institutional elements of financial markets and the operation of financial institutions that were crucial to Minsky's position. These are developments of post-Keynesian theory that are often overlooked, and deserve wider dissemination. They are also developments that have attempted to formalize Minsky's work in an attempt to make it more accessible to mainstream theorists. This was clearly Minsky's desire, and Nasica shows both the limitations and the potential of such developments, as well as the directions in which research must be developed to fulfill Minsky's desire of being understood by all school of economists. Minsky could not have a better memorial to his work.

Jan Kregel

Acknowledgements

First of all, I should like to express my thanks to Cécile Dangel. This book would not exist without the faultless work of translation she made. I also thank Jan A. Kregel and Richard Arena warmly for their encouragement and suggestions. Finally, I acknowledge the Laboratoire d'Analyse et de Techniques Economiques (LATEC, UMR 5601 of the CNRS) which funded a great part of this work.

Introduction

Once the standard reference in macroeconomics, what is known today as the 'neoclassical synthesis' has gradually become less influential over the past twenty years. The erosion of the predominance of Keynesian orthodoxy coincided for some time with the rise of a new school of thought, the new classical school, whose achievements are now considered standard in macroeconomic analysis.

Two features are characteristic of the models developed within the latter approach. The first is the secondary role ascribed to financial factors in the explanation it offers of economic fluctuations. The second is the exogenous conception of economic instability developed by the authors belonging to this family of economists. In the theoretical setting used by the new classical school competitive market mechanisms are powerful enough to drive the economy, in the absence of any external disruption, towards an equilibrium, that is, a position where the plans of all individual agents are made mutually compatible. All forms of observable instability are therefore to be exclusively attributed to the exogenous shocks – monetary shocks for the theory of equilibrium cycles or technological shocks for the real business cycle theory – that might arise and disturb the natural equilibrium of the system.

There are many reasons for questioning the relevance of the explanation of economic fluctuations that the new classical economists propose and, more generally, the validity of an approach that completely disregards the role played by financial structure in the emergence and development of business cycles.

The first reason is empirical. It has to do with the inability of these theories of business cycles to explain both the recurrence and the acuteness of the financial instability that we have been witnessing in the past twenty years. The best example of this phenomenon is offered by the American economy and the numerous financial crises it has experienced since World War II: the 1966 credit crunch, the collapse of Penn Central in 1970, the failure of Franklin National Bank in 1974, the liquidity crisis of 1980, the stock market crash of October 1987 and the problems brought about by the bailing out of the Savings and Loans Associations in 1990–91.[1]

More recently the slowdown in growth to which one OECD country after another was subjected at the beginning of the nineties appears, to a large extent, to be related to the evolution of financial structure in the previous decade. During the 1980s the accumulation of debt created financial fragility which remained unapparent as long as assets generated capital gains, while it made borrowers more vulnerable to unforeseen shocks. In particular the sharp rise in interest rates, which occurred at the end of the 1980s in a context of financial fragility had a much more spectacular impact (causing a collapse of asset prices and an increase in repayment defaults) than it would have had it concerned agents with robust capital structures. The efforts firms made then to raise their self-finance ratio well above one hundred per cent, with a view to reducing their indebtedness, entailed a pronounced and lasting decrease in productive investment. The central role played by these financial adjustments thus appears to have been one of the important aspects of the slowdown in economic activity at the beginning of the 1990s.

Beyond these empirical considerations another reason for considering the role of capital structure is related to the dissatisfactory treatment of financial relations within the real business cycle theory. Certainly the boundaries of this school of thought have become increasingly blurred. In particular, in the attempt to make up for the lack of financial factors in the initial basic model, a nominal dimension was later incorporated so as to reintroduce the role played by money in generating economic fluctuations.[2] However the different routes real business cycle theorists have taken in order to make room for monetary relations are still, at present, far from convincing.[3]

It is therefore necessary to examine how financial factors could be more appropriately introduced into the analysis of economic fluctuations. In this perspective the line of research initiated by Hyman P. Minsky at the end of the 1950s is relevant. Minsky, who died in 1996, developed an approach where one could recognize the main themes developed by the Keynesian fundamentalists: the role of uncertainty and the behaviours it generates, the dynamic instability of market economies, the role of money and the role of liquidity preference. However undeniable the influence of the ideas he inherited from Keynes, Minsky was an economist it is difficult to classify. Indeed other theoretical schools and other individual authors (such as Fisher, Kalecki and Schumpeter) also left their mark on his writings.

This mixed background prompted Minsky to construct an original business cycle theory, sometimes qualified as the 'financial instability hypothesis', sometimes as the 'Wall Street paradigm'.[4] Minsky's contribution to contemporary macroeconomics is, as we shall see, quite essential. He proposes a truly explanatory model of the way contemporary market economies work. His approach rests upon an endogenous and financial conception of economic fluctuations, which is completely at odds with the vision of the harmonious, self-regulating and constantly-in-equilibrium economy depicted by the new classical economists. It is analysed in Part One of this book.

However, the complexity and the richness of Minsky's analysis, associated with an almost total lack of formalization, have not facilitated the understanding of his approach, which explains to a large extent the comparative disregard with which his theory of fluctuations has been considered up till recently. Notwithstanding this, in the past ten years or so, a still small but increasing number of economists have set out to rehabilitate the endogenous and financial vision of economic fluctuations focused upon by Minsky. The models that underpin their analyses are examined in Part Two. They present two key features.

First, they benefited during the 1980s from the development and the diffusion among economists of the qualitative and numerical methods of analysis developed in the mathematics of non-linear dynamical systems. The objective pursued by economists taking up this lead was to abandon the paradigm of equilibrium and stability endorsed by the proponents of the exogenous approach, while avoiding coming up against the explanatory deficiencies associated with linear business cycle models. The theoretical contribution of these various works should not be neglected, if only because cycles appear in non-linear models for a very large set of parameters and also because, whatever the initial conditions, 'resistant' fluctuations arise in the form of an 'attractor', the limit cycle, towards which all trajectories tend. Moreover, for the study of dynamic phenomena, non-linear modelling of business cycles has benefited in recent years from the discovery of a new analytical tool, deterministic chaos. The essential characteristic of chaotic processes is to generate deterministic and erratic (i.e. acyclical) trajectories featuring considerable and entirely unstable irregularities. These irregularities strongly resemble those created by stochastic processes. However, in contrast to what is obtained within the exogenous approach, where only random shocks can account for the irregularity of economic movement, reasoning in terms of deterministic trajectories of the chaotic kind gives rise to irregular dynamics generated by the structure of the model *per se*. New analytical perspectives are thus open to the analysts of economic fluctuations eager to break away from the methodology adopted by the new classical economists. We shall see, in particular, that this type of formalization accounts quite faithfully for the endogenous process that creates financial fragility and instability within the economy that Minsky analyses.

Second, these models are an attempt to reinterpret the results Minsky obtains by using tools borrowed from new-Keynesian economics. In the latter, disequilibria appear in the form of rationing in financial markets and are explained in an endogenous fashion, that is, as a consequence of the behaviour of economic agents alone. Disequilibria occur for an economy where information is distributed asymmetrically and where problems of adverse selection and moral hazard prevail. Above all, as in Minsky's, these works offer an endogenous and financial explanation of such phenomena as self-amplification and persistence of economic instability. In short, in these new Keynesian models of financial instability, as in Minsky's works, the origin of disequilibria and of fluctuations is to be found in the normal functioning of the market economy and not in the rigidities that characterize the neoclassical synthesis model nor in the shocks, be they real or monetary, which are a main feature of the new classical model.

Thus the research in macroeconomics, whose initial result was to undermine the authority of Keynesian orthodoxy gave rise at the end of the 1990s to an extraordinarily rich array of hypotheses and theories. These theories, with the help of new analytical and mathematical tools, provide results akin to those obtained in an essentially literary fashion by Minsky. This quite naturally raises the question of to what extent the emergence and development of these new Keynesian non-linear models challenge the specificity of Minsky's theory.

This question is addressed in Part Three of this book. It requires examining two aspects of Minsky's analysis that are often neglected. The first one concerns the problem of rationality and of how expectations are formed in a situation of uncertainty. It will thus be interesting to compare Minsky's approach to this problem with the one provided by the more recent analyses of fluctuations and capital markets in terms of asymmetric information and sunspots. The second aspect refers to the role of institutional factors. This institutional dimension of economic fluctuations is central to Minsky's analysis of the dynamics of contemporary economies, yet it is completely overlooked even in the latest works of authors seeking to formalize the financial instability hypothesis. Our aim will then be to examine how, in addition to taking into account the real and financial forms of the dynamics characterizing market economies, considering its institutional form leads to findings that differ from those obtained by both traditional and more recent macroeconomic approaches.

NOTES

1. For a detailed theoretical and empirical analysis of the phenomena of financial instability, the reader can refer to the books by Aglietta (1995) and Wolfson (1994).
2. This applies in particular to the contributions of King and Plosser (1984) and Williamson (1987).
3. See Stadler (1994).
4. See Dymski and Pollin (1992).

PART ONE

Minsky's Endogenous and Financial Cycles

1. The Post-Keynesian Legacy

1 INTRODUCTION

Minsky's propositions reveal his constant desire to depart from theories of neoclassical inspiration, such as those developed by the Keynesian neoclassical synthesis and the new classical school. Small wonder, then, that his analysis contains themes akin to those developed within the post-Keynesian approach.

The post-Keynesian theory rejects three axioms considered as fundamental to and characteristic of new classical economics. The first axiom is that decisions are made in an environment best described as one where agents are subject to probabilistic risk. This is rejected by the post-Keynesians, whose analytical construct revives the definition of radical uncertainty spelled out initially by Keynes. As a result they discard theories of decision-making where analysis of uncertainty relies on the standard theory of probabilities, whether they be objective or subjective. This does not mean that the post-Keynesian economists rule out all utilizations of probability tools. Rather they consider that the cases where such use is possible are few. It is therefore not appropriate to base a general approach on such grounds. More general foundations are thus required, ones that rest upon the notion of 'true' or 'fundamental' uncertainty.

The second axiom is that the rationality of economic agents is best represented by the rational expectations hypothesis. According to Lucas, economic analysis only applies to a world where uncertainty in the strong sense has been excluded: 'In situations of risk, the hypothesis of rational behavior on the part of agents will have usable content, so that behavior may be explainable in terms of economic theory. In such situations, expectations are rational in Muth's sense. In cases of uncertainty, economic reasoning will be of no value' (1977, p. 15). Such a point of view is not acceptable to the post-Keynesians. Though it is true that in an environment where fundamental uncertainty has no place 'rational, fully-informed equilibrium is excluded [and] expectation is not rational' (Shackle, 1972, Preface) in the sense of the new classical school, it remains possible to build a concept of a form of 'rationality' that does not emulate that of the 'decision-making robot' of the rational expectations theory. Doing so requires returning to Keynes's works on probabilities and to 'individual rationality of a conventional type'.

In this chapter we do not dwell on these two important ideas, so typical of post-Keynesian theory. For reasons that will become obvious to the reader as he or she moves forward, we have chosen to examine them in more detail in Part Three. For the time being, we shall focus on the third axiom of new classical economics, namely the neutrality of money.

Neutrality of money is something that is unconditionally asserted by the traditional quantity theory and at least partially (that is, at least in the long run) reaffirmed by the neo-quantitative and monetarist approaches. In contrast, statements such as 'money is important' and 'money is not neutral even in the long run' are frequently found in post-Keynesian literature.[1] They must however not be considered as the opposite of assertions such as 'money is not important' and 'money is neutral' put forward by some economists. On the one hand, when the Radcliffe Report (1959) claims that 'money is not important', it means that the nominal stock of money has either no or only a small causal independent effect on the economy, thereby contradicting Milton Friedman's statement that 'money is important', which implies that variations in the nominal stock of money play an important role by triggering fluctuations of production and employment (in the short term) and by determining the inflation rate (in the medium and long term) (1968). On the other hand, 'neutrality of money', in its modern mainstream acceptance, refers to the idea that exogenous variations in the nominal stock of money have only temporary effects on real variables, so that long-run reactions to such shocks merely take the form of nominal readjustments. Accordingly 'non-neutrality of money' signifies that exogenous changes in the monetary stock have effects on the real variables that are persistent in the long run: such shocks are not entirely absorbed in the form of nominal readjustments. This is a vision usually associated with the idea that some obstacle (some 'friction') prevents the realization of these readjustments.

When the post-Keynesians contend that 'money is important', they neither reject the concept contained in the Radcliffe Report, nor support the same position as Friedman. Nor is it true, when they claim that 'money is non-neutral', that they generally consider that exogenous variations in the money supply have real permanent effects. As we shall see, these two affirmations simply mean that monetary holdings, monetary transactions, monetary prices, appraisals made in monetary terms and the financing of production by means of money are typical of a capitalist economy. This contrasts with the view that to analyse a modern economy it is possible to consider it as if it was basically a system of barter where all decisions are expressed in terms of real goods and where money operates as a veil – as a simple *numéraire*. For the post-Keynesians, it is the mere existence of money that is 'non-neutral' and not the variations of its quantity. An economy embodying genuine money behaves in a way that differs radically from that of a barter economy, one that relies on some *numéraire* called 'money', selected in some arbitrary way.

This places the post-Keynesian conception within the 'monetary analysis' tradition, as opposed to the 'real analysis' tradition, to use a distinction introduced by Schumpeter (1954) and recently revived by Rogers (1989). It is thus an approach that stands in clear opposition to the different varieties of neoclassical theory. Such characterization of post-Keynesian analysis remains very general, however. Authors such as Hayek and Marx – whose respective ideas strongly differed in other respects, and also sharply diverged from those of Keynes – belong to monetary analysis. It is therefore necessary to examine in more detail the way the post-Keynesians develop the theme of monetary analysis.

Building on Keynes's ideas, the post-Keynesian economists have sought to explain why the market economy is not a self-regulating system. Thus their main goals have been to produce an analysis contrasting with the traditional Keynesian IS-LM model and to show that economic disequilibrium does not only result from obstacles hindering the market adjustment process, such as imperfect flexibility of prices or institutional factors. In the post-Keynesian approach, the economy is subject to macroeconomic disequilibrium because of factors that have nothing to do with the existence of rigidities. They relate to aspects introduced originally by Keynes: the long-term demand for liquidity; the need to form expectations in a situation of uncertainty; the 'essential properties' of money. It is these three aspects and their influence on the way the economy behaves that will be examined next.

2 THE LONG-RUN DEMAND FOR LIQUIDITY

In post-Keynesian theory the existence of long-run legally enforceable contracts, denominated in monetary terms, is what makes the monetary environment a non-neutral one, even in the long run.[2] Post-Keynesians insist that money is not merely a *numéraire* chosen arbitrarily or just some accounting device. It also permits all legal contractual obligations to be fulfilled. The holding of money provides cash, that is, the capacity to honour contractual commitments at their redemption date. Moreover, in an uncertain economic environment where commitments can only be specified and made enforceable in monetary terms, 'the holding of money is a valuable choice' (Davidson, 1991, p. 139).[3] In other words, the existence of market institutions that allow (and encourage) agents to enter into contracts involving payments at some future date creates the need for money and liquidity. Post-Keynesians thus share Keynes's belief that: 'It is however, interesting to consider how far those characteristics of money as we know it ... are bound up with money being the standard in which debts and wages are usually fixed ... The convenience of holding assets in the same standard as that in which future liabilities may fall due ... is obvious' (Keynes, CW VII, 1973, pp. 236–7). As further specified by Davidson, 'this is an essential feature of the performance of all real word market-oriented monetary economies, where production activity awaits the remorseless passage of calendar time' (1980a, p. 299).

For post-Keynesian economists, liquid assets also provide economic agents with a safe haven that avoids committing funds to the acquisition of manufactured goods or monetary claims paying distant and uncertain incomes.[4] Accordingly, when facing the uncertainty that is characteristic of future events, agents will tend to adopt an attitude that consists in waiting – including in the long run, as we shall see. They will thus be induced to diminish their demand for manufactured goods and will turn instead to an additional demand for liquidity. As emphasized by Davidson, 'only in an unpredictable environment does it make sense to defer expenditures in this way, as opposed to spending all one's earnings on the various products of industry being traded in free markets' (1991, pp. 139–40).

The analytic foundations of the post-Keynesian concept of liquidity might appear, to some extent, akin to those underlying the conception developed by certain general equilibrium theorists. In particular, the notion of 'waiting', put forward recently by Kreps, suggests that at some near-future date, when settlement takes place, all agents will receive 'information about which state will prevail' (1988, p. 142). However more careful scrutiny leads us to reject any possible connection between these two notions. In fact, post-Keynesians, after Keynes, insist that the decision not to purchase goods (that is, to adopt an attitude of saving and waiting) does 'not necessitate a decision to have dinner or to buy a pair of boots a week hence or to consume any specified thing at any specified date ... It is not a substitution of future consumption demand for current consumption demand – it is a net diminution of such demand' (Keynes, CW VII, 1973, p. 218). In other words, concepts of neoclassical inspiration such as Kreps's waiting option, founded on intertemporal substitution of consumption goods, are not compatible with the Keynesian decisional environment. For Keynes intertemporal choices are not what necessarily occurs when agents decide to 'wait' and therefore to hold savings in the form of liquid assets.[5] In the long run, in an environment of true uncertainty, people may very well desire to remain in a liquid position, a view supported by certain empirical results, such as those obtained by Danzinger *et al.* (1982–3). These authors show that, though existence becomes more uncertain over the years, the elderly continue to wait, instead of spending their incomes or their resources. Such behaviour is inconsonant with Kreps's notion of waiting, which is embedded in a probabilistic framework and can only explain the existence of a momentary (or short-run) need to postpone spending. Therefore, as Davidson puts it, 'unless one is willing to admit that even in the long run "information about which state will prevail" may not exist, and some economic decisions are made under a state of true uncertainty,' such behaviour seems irrational within the limits of standard theory (1991, p. 141). The behaviour underlying the long-run demand for liquidity is however altogether rational in an environment of uncertainty. Its mere existence, as underlined in Keynesian analysis, is likely to drive the economy towards a long-period equilibrium characterized by durable unemployment.[6]

3 EXPECTATIONS, NOMINAL WAGES AND SAY'S LAW

Understanding the theoretical implications associated with the 'monetary production economy' concept requires the careful examination of the works Keynes presented in his Cambridge lectures, during the period separating the publication of the *Treatise* from that of *The General Theory*.[7] At that time a fundamental evolution in Keynes's analysis was taking place. It consisted in rejecting Say's law and in introducing the distinction between expected and realized values, which appears in the November 1933 lectures. The aim of this distinction was to show that the decision to save does not produce the market signals that induce entrepreneurs to make the proper amount of investments, those that would give rise to the future consumption represented by current savings. Therefore, Keynes's purpose was to bring to light the 'real-world' factors that prevent the existence of such market signals. Why saving 'does not create demand for more future consumption' or a corresponding amount of investment is because, as Kregel observes, 'producers can't know what consumers will want to buy because consumers themselves don't know'.[8] In other words the absence of information allowing income and spending always to coincide is due to the uncertainty surrounding households' future consumption expenditure. Keynes's position thus sharply conflicts with the one, defended by the classical school, that 'saving [is] considered ... as a distribution of income through time'.[9]

The explicit taking into account of uncertainty and therefore of expectations within his analysis, which he associates with economic decision-making, thus enables Keynes to show that there exists no automatic tendency towards full employment. It is this vision of the economy that is retained by post-Keynesian economists for whom 'the system fails, not because of operational or institutional malfunction, nor because uncertainty leads to perverse buyer behavior, but because there is no market capable of linking future consumption decisions to present expenditures decisions if the former do not exist when the latter must be undertaken' (Kregel, 1980, p. 37).

In addition, as stressed by Keynes and the post-Keynesians, the monetary economy of production is also a 'money-wage' or 'entrepreneur' economy: incomes are not paid in kind or out of the output produced by the worker. In this economy the 'psychological law' applies. It relates variations of consumption to variations of income and leads to a positive amount of saving out of wage-earnings: current expenses can therefore differ from current income at the individual level, i.e. for every consumer or investor.

Keynes was nevertheless aware that his characterization of the monetary economy of production was still incomplete. What was needed was to demonstrate that the savings made out of money wages were not automatically transformed into an equivalent amount of investment. Had they been so, the economy would have been self-regulating: disequilibria between income and expenditure at the individual level would have coexisted with full-employment equilibrium in the aggregate, the interest rate bringing investment and saving into equality. In other words Keynes needed to show that 'an act of saving does nothing to improve prospective yield' and therefore 'does nothing to stimulate investment' because it produces no present signal concerning the future market (Keynes, CW VII, 1973, p. 212). Accordingly, Keynes set out to introduce into his analysis an aspect he considered typical of a monetary economy of production, namely the presence of a store of value allowing the purchasing power of current income to be preserved.

4   FROM   THE   'ESSENTIAL   PROPERTIES'   TO MACROECONOMIC DISEQUILIBRIUM

In Chapter 17 of the *General Theory*, Keynes investigates the theoretical implications associated with the existence of such a store of value. He begins by assuming that the kind of money to which we are accustomed has 'special characteristics' or 'essential properties' that prevent the system from converging towards a full-employment equilibrium (Keynes, CW VII, 1973, p. 229). This assumption having been made, Keynes proceeds to study the 'essential properties of interest'.

In order to prove the existence of a discrepancy between aggregate incomes and expenses and thereby to invalidate Say's law, Keynes needs to explain that some share of current income, whether saved or hoarded, gives rise to no current spending in the market for new and labour-produced goods. To provide a store of purchasing power, savings must be converted into something durable. However, even if all durable assets can by definition serve as a store of value, the saver does not necessarily want 'a capital asset *as such*... [W]hat he really desires is its *prospective yield*' (ibid., p. 212). Therefore, to determine the one that will be acquired by savers, Keynes suggests classifying all potential stores of value according to their expected returns.

With this aim in view, Keynes divides the yield of a durable asset into three components: its net yield, q, generated by holding it or by using it productively; its carrying cost, c, resulting from the need to maintain it as time goes by; its liquidity premium, l, determined by the variability of its value in terms of other goods and by the ease and convenience with which it can be converted into other goods at some future date. Accordingly all durable goods can be classified in terms of their total return, $(q-c) + l$, which determines their ability to play the role of store of value. Keynes labels this return the 'marginal efficiency of assets'.[10]

These assumptions having been made, what is it that induces agents to hold money, i.e. a durable good whose production requires no labour and whose yield, $q-c$, is small if not equal to zero? To address this question Keynes begins by noting that the expected returns of non-monetary durable assets are not, in general, independent of savers' demand for them. In the short run, the net yield of these assets – their marginal efficiency – is inversely related to demand.[11] Therefore savers will continue demanding the non-monetary durable asset whose expected return is highest, in order to hold it as a store of value, until the expansion of its supply has caused its expected return to fall and reach the return of the asset that ranks immediately below it within the above-mentioned classification. This process will continue until the $[(q-c)+l]$s of all potential stores of value have become equal.

In an economy where no durable asset possesses money's specific features, this process of equating net returns will continue until: (1) assets all have the same expected yields; (2) the quantity of all durable goods has been increased to the point where demand for newly produced durable goods equals current net savings. As noted by Kregel, such an outcome would be 'the formal equivalent to Say's law, for current income is always spent on current output whether it is "consumed" or "saved" and used to purchase stores of value' (1980, p. 41). In contrast, if in the system some durable asset possesses the essential properties of money, the equating process could very well come to an end before full employment has been reached. Indeed the durable asset called 'money' provides a specific store of value whose expected return does not decrease when demand rises, because it is not affected by technological conditions of production. Rather its expected return solely consists of the third component, the liquidity premium, which proves to be independent of the variations in the supply of money and dependent instead on the influence of the psychology, the 'liquidity preference' of the public. When the liquidity premium of this asset has therefore risen above a certain level, savers will prefer to store their wealth in the form of money. Then the demand for newly-produced, non-monetary durable stores of value will fall below the value representing the amount of full-employment savings. The gap between these magnitudes thus corresponds to the demand for money held as a store of value. Under these conditions it is the 'marginal efficiency' of money, the rate of interest, that 'rules the roost' because it puts a brake on the investors' demand for stores of value in the form of capital goods, before the demand for investment reaches the level equal to full employment savings (Keynes, CW VII, 1973, p. 223).

Keynes devotes the rest of Chapter 17 to analysing the 'special characteristics' that make money a 'bottomless sink for purchasing power' (Keynes, CW VII, 1973, p. 231). The two essential properties of money (and of all other liquid assets) are, on the one hand, 'a zero, or at any rate very small, elasticity of production' and, on the other hand, an elasticity of substitution equal, or nearly equal, to zero' (Keynes, CW VII, 1973, pp. 230–1). Many works of post-Keynesian economists have developed this aspect of Keynes's analysis, because it allows them to establish the link between macroeconomic disequilibrium and money.[12] Thus, as Davidson emphasizes, for a commodity to have a positive elasticity of production simply requires that a rise in the demand for this commodity induces suppliers to produce more of it and hire more workers. Under these conditions 'to say that money has an elasticity of production of zero is merely to state in the language of the economist the old adage that money "does not grow on trees"' (1980b, p. 168). A zero elasticity of production does not therefore mean that the supply of money is invariable. It only implies that growth of the money demand will not lead to a proportional rise in the demand for labour in order to 'produce' more money.

On the other hand, for a good to exhibit a positive elasticity of substitution, an increase in its price must divert a fraction of its demand towards one or several other goods, qualified as 'substitutes'. Gross substitution – which prevails when every good in the economy is a substitute for some other good – is, as shown in particular by Arrow and Hahn, one of the fundamental axioms of neoclassical theory. These authors indeed remind us that gross substitution is the sufficient condition predominantly assumed by neoclassical economists to prove the existence, the uniqueness and the stability of a solution to a general equilibrium system (1971, pp. 15, 127, 215 and 305). In the absence of gross substitution certain excess-demand functions may not exhibit downward-sloping shapes; therefore, there may be no price vector permitting all markets to clear simultaneously. Besides Arrow and Hahn demonstrate that, even if such a price vector existed, a sequential price adjustment mechanism that would not rely on the axiom of gross substitution might not converge towards general equilibrium at all (1971, p. 305).

Thus, in an economy where money is not merely considered as the $(n+1)^{th}$ good of the system but as possessing the characters identified previously, the normal operation of demand and supply at the aggregate level can cause macroeconomic disequilibrium and unemployment to arise. A conclusion of this kind undermines the consistency of the neoclassical analysis of market economies and has not left those economists who are attached to general equilibrium theory indifferent. Hahn, in particular, recognizes that 'to many economists, Keynesian economics deals with important relevant problems and

General Equilibrium Theory deals with no relevant problems at all. This view [...] has, alas, an element of truth' (1977, p. 25). Nonetheless Hahn has also striven to preserve the relevance of the research programme embedded in the general equilibrium framework. With this in mind he has introduced the zero-elasticity-of-production property of money into a general equilibrium model, while taking care to dissociate this property from its link with money. His conclusion is that the mere presence in the economy of some non-reproducible asset (not necessarily money), in which agents can hold their savings, can lead to an equilibrium where unemployment prevails (1977, pp. 27 and 31).

However, according to the Keynesian approach, non-reproducibility of money is not the only cause of disequilibrium in the real world. As mentioned earlier, a second property characterizing money, zero elasticity of substitution, prevents Say's law from applying, but admitting this second property would have driven Hahn to violate the axiom of gross substitution, fundamental to general equilibrium analysis and its logical consistency. Consequently, this is something he has not done and, from this point of view, his analysis of equilibrium is open to the criticism of post-Keynesian economists. In the words of Davidson, 'there is an elemental logical incompatibility between the "serious monetary theory" advanced by Keynes and the neoclassical general equilibrium analysis of Hahn' (1980, p. 305).

The incompatibility between Keynesian analysis and approaches of neoclassical inspiration extends far beyond the divergence in opinion concerning the elasticity properties of money. It is the manifestation of two radically differing visions of the way market economies operate. Accordingly insistence upon the 'essential properties' allows Keynesian economists to stand apart from their neoclassical counterparts and to deny both the self-regulating character of the economic system and the natural tendency of market economies to move towards full employment.

The specific features of money in the Keynesian analytic setting imply small or zero elasticities of production and substitution. Saving that is then transformed into demand for money as a store of value does not 'involve the placing of any specific forward order for consumption, [and] thereby the cancellation of a present order. Thus, since the expectation of consumption is the only *raison d'être* of employment, there should be nothing paradoxical in the conclusion that a diminished propensity to consume has, *ceteris paribus,* a depressing effect on employment' (Keynes, CW VII, 1973 p. 211). Here the neoclassical conception of how markets work is strongly called into question, since the demand for money as a store of value conveys no signal to producers who are observing consumers indicating what the latter's future spending decisions might be. As Kregel notes, 'such demand is undefined (or ineffective) demand for a still to be determined product, at an as yet to be determined time. It gives no "information" upon which to base a rational decision on investment in productive capacity' (1980, p. 44).

Such reasoning implies that in post-Keynesian theory it is no longer assumed, as in neoclassical analysis, that equilibrium can only occur in a situation of full employment or that unemployment should be considered as a mere 'accident' explainable by the frictions that exist in an otherwise perfectly working competitive system. The removal of restrictions to the free operation of markets, even if it were possible, would not prevent such an accident in any way, even in the long run. The analysis of liquidity and of 'essential properties' and the rejection of the universality of the gross substitutability axiom lead to the conclusion that unemployment is the fundamental problem of the monetary economy of production. Once these questions are clarified, the relation between macroeconomic disequilibrium and money can be dealt with adequately. It is then possible to show why, independently of the occurrence of any market failure or rigidity, an equilibrium may arise where unemployment prevails because savings maybe used for the acquisition of a durable asset with zero elasticities of production and substitution, in other words, for the procurement of money.

By relating the occurrence of unemployment equilibria explicitly to the existence of money as a store of value, the post-Keynesian theory strongly diverges from the Keynesian synthesis and from new classical economics. This central idea of post-Keynesian fundamentalism will form, as we shall see, one of the key elements of Minsky's theory. The fact that they share a certain number of common ideas does not, however, mean that Minsky entirely supports the post-Keynesianism of Kregel or Davidson. As early as 1974, in the review he wrote of Paul Davidson's book, *Money and the Real World*, shortly after his own book, *John Maynard Keynes* had been published, Minsky took the opportunity to point out several limitations inherent in the post-Keynesian approach. In particular he blamed Davidson, and post-Keynesian theorists in general, for attaching too much importance to the ideas contained in Chapter 17 of *The General Theory*. Qualifying the methodology underlying the chapter as 'obscure because [Keynes] slips, almost as if by second nature, back into the world of the classical economy', Minsky is particularly critical of the way Keynes describes the accumulation process and his too great reliance on decreasing factor productivity (1975, p. 79). His conclusion is that 'in this chapter Keynes reverted to a classical equilibrium growth and accumulation view of the economic process' (1975, p. 80). Minsky considers this shortcoming to be an illustration of the fact that 'as Joan Robinson suggested, Keynes was a like a snake shedding his skin as he was writing *The General Theory* and the book was written when the old skin – the classical view – was not fully off' (1975, p. 129).

Instead, Chapter 12 of *The General Theory* and the *Quarterly Journal of Economics* 1937 article are what afford the indispensable, Minsky believes, theoretical underpinnings for the building of a genuinely Keynesian analysis of fluctuations. These works embody Keynes's essential idea that 'the proximate cause of the transitory nature of each cyclical state is the instability of investment; but the deeper cause of business cycles in an economy with the financial institutions of capitalism is the instability of portfolios and of financial interrelations' (1975, p. 57). An important aspect of Minsky's thought appears implicitly here, which will never be called into question in his later writings. In Minsky's opinion the 'traditional' post-Keynesian approach, interesting as it may be, proves to be sterile because of two important limitations. On the one hand, it does not make any use of the theoretical foundations underlying its critique of new classical economics, although it could have done so in order to build an entirely different business cycle theory. On the other hand, it takes insufficient account of the links between financial structure and economic instability, upon the acute and recurrent character of which we have insisted.

One of the main goals of the approach developed by Minsky will be to remedy these two important deficiencies of post-Keynesian theory. Influenced by authors belonging to very different schools of thought, he will develop a genuine, original and complex analysis of business cycles, which we examine next.

NOTES

1. See for instance the title *Money Matters* of the post-Keynesian book edited by Dow and Earl (1982).
2. See Davidson (1988).
3. This is also the opinion articulated by Keynes in Chapter 17 of *The General Theory* (CW VII, 1973 pp. 236–7).
4. This is akin to Keynes's analysis of the precautionary and speculative motives. See Keynes (CW VII, 1973) p. 168 and pp. 196–204.
5. Davidson (1991) states that the same conclusion applies to Grandmont and Laroque's option demand for money (1976).
6. For a more detailed analysis of rationality within an uncertain environment, see Part Three.
7. On this point, see Kregel (1980) from which the present argument draws extensively.
8. Keynes, *Bryce's Lecture Notes*, 11 November 1933.
9. Keynes, *Bryce's Lecture Notes*, 11 November 1933 and Kregel (1980, p. 38).
10. This concept is to be found originally in Keynes's earlier works on the 'parity of interest rates' and in Sraffa's analysis of 'own rates of interest.' For a more detailed analysis, see Kregel (1982, 1988).
11. Keynes refers to the same argument of decreasing returns when he explains the decreasing scope of the marginal efficiency of capital curve. See Keynes (CW VII, 1973, p. 228).
12. In particular, see Davidson Chapters 6–9; Davidson (1980a, 1980b, as well as Kregel (1980, 1982).

2.   The Financial Theory of Investment

1 INTRODUCTION

In *The General Theory*, Keynes emphasized the central role played by investment in the theory of aggregate production and employment. His ideas contrasted with the traditional approaches of his day, and with the analysis still prevailing today, for two main reasons. First, the importance of investment did not only result from its long-term effect on capital growth, but also and chiefly from the crucial role it plays in the determination of aggregate demand and short-term fluctuations of economic activity. Second, Keynes rejected the microeconomic foundations of investment that were exclusively related to the technological conditions underlying the productivity of capital. Instead he placed emphasis on uncertainty, finance and monetary factors, which he considered as the fundamental determinants of investment.

One of Keynes's main objectives was to examine the circumstances under which 'money', defined in a broad sense, influenced real macroeconomic dynamics. This goal is clearly apparent in his theory of investment where financial and monetary conditions are decisive in determining the capital outlays of firms. Keynes's insights have bred an abundant theoretical and empirical literature during the decades following the publication of *The General Theory*. What could be labelled 'financial Keynesianism' has developed, the aim of which has been to underscore the essential role played by finance.[1] According to this approach investment cannot be understood if its financial determinants are ignored.

These ideas have however been strongly disputed. In particular, economists belonging to the neoclassical tradition have raised doubts about purely financial factors being able to influence real phenomena such as investment. Such influence would be irreconcilable with the microeconomic foundations of decision-making that characterize the neoclassical approach. In this area the most important works are associated with the names of Jorgenson and co-authors.[2] As desired accumulation of capital, and thus optimal investment, are only grounded on fundamentals, namely the preferences and technology that characterize the economy, purely financial factors do not affect investment. In fact Jorgenson bases his results on the

Modigliani-Miller theorem (1958) and the demonstration that, under certain conditions, real decisions are independent of financial choices.

This conception strongly contributed to the emergence of a synthesis between Keynesian macroeconomics and neoclassical microeconomic foundations. In the 1960s and 1970s this synthesis led to the rise and development of the neo-Keynesian approach. The great majority of the economists belonging to this school of thought made no allowances for most of the aggregate demand volatility predicted by Keynes. Concepts like 'animal spirits' that are difficult to model no longer played a critical role in the understanding of macroeconomic fluctuations. In the Keynesian neoclassical synthesis, investment is basically determined by stable preferences and unchanging technology, implying that fluctuations in aggregate demand are on the whole predictable and easily handled by appropriate stabilization policy.

It is precisely the will to reconstruct the Keynesian theory of investment by doing away with the investment function of the neoclassical synthesis model that guided Minsky into the building of his theory of investment. In his analysis financial factors have their place in the investment process and play an essential part through two main channels:

1. the 'two-price' approach;
2. the explicit taking into account of financial structure.

2 THE 'TWO-PRICE' APPROACH

First, we review the origin and the evolution of models based on this kind of approach, before examining Minsky's own interpretation.

2.1. Origins and Evolution of the 'Two-Price' Analyses of Fluctuations[3]

The origin of the 'two-price' model for the study of cyclical fluctuations is not recent. Models of this kind are present, for instance, in the works of Fisher (1907, Chapters 5 and 14; 1911, Chapter 4) and support a large share of Keynes's own works.[4] Fisher attributes the increase in the price level of outputs – in proportion to the rise in the price level of financial assets, expressed by the interest rate – to the growth of the money supply. As higher prices involve greater profits for projects financed with borrowed funds, greater investments follow and more bank credit is granted until the point is reached where the interest rate has increased to such an extent that the situation reverts to what it was initially.

At the time he was beginning to develop his own approach of monetary problems and of macroeconomic fluctuations, Keynes was well acquainted with these contributions. He felt no affinity, though, with the mechanistic conception behind Fisher's equation of exchange. Instead he thought an adequate explanation of the process – through which an increase in the money supply brings about a rise in prices – was to be found in the analysis of the working of the banking system. He developed this view in 'How Far Are Bankers Responsible for the Alternations of Crises and Depressions?', written in 1913 after reading Robertson's *Study on Industrial Fluctuation*. In the simple model he describes, income is either spent on consumption goods, saved and kept in the form of financial assets, or held in the form of current accounts to serve as 'free resources to be spent or saved according as future circumstances may determine' (Keynes, C W XI, 1983, p. 5). In their attempt to maximize their returns, banks lend these resources, thereby enabling entrepreneurs to finance the acquisition of capital goods. Consequently, realized investment exceeds the economic agents' planned purchases of financial assets, as materialized by the proportion of their income allocated to savings. Acting in this fashion, banks thus use what the public believes to be 'free resources' in order to finance fixed capital investments. When the time comes for 'take-out' finance (sales of financial assets to agents) to be set up, however, planned savings turn out to be insufficient and 'bankers as a whole suddenly find that what looked like liquid assets has turned into assets that are very far from liquid indeed' (ibid.). As the resulting situation is likely to create difficulties, insofar as the liquidity of the banks' assets will deteriorate, current loans will be curtailed and a reduction of funds available for new investment projects will ensue (ibid., pp. 9–11). During the adjustment process prices of goods will have risen as an effect of the boom induced by the excess of investments over savings. Thus, as early as 1913, the idea was clearly taking shape in Keynes's mind that banks could create a wedge between households' planned savings and entrepreneurs' realized investments, thereby contributing to changes in commodity prices and fluctuations in investment.

In Keynes's 1913 article there is however no direct recognition of the link between the interest rate, the price of capital assets and investment. This appears for the first time in *A Tract on Monetary Reform*, a book in which Keynes continues to seek an interpretation of the relationship between money and prices that differs from Fisher's analysis. The formulation of the parity of interest rates theorem that the book also contains provides a clear outline for the explanation of how interest rates influence capital asset prices and therefore investment decisions.[5]

Keynes pursues the analysis of the dynamic determination of prices in *A Treatise on Money*. In this book Keynes proposes replacing the quantity theory equation of exchange by a 'fundamental equation' measuring the price level of consumption goods in terms of unit costs of production and excess demand (the divergence between investment and savings already present in the 1913 essay). At a second stage Keynes obtains a second fundamental equation defining the overall price level by combining this price with the price of capital assets determined on the basis of 'a different set of considerations' (Keynes, CW V, 1971, p. 123). In fact the price of capital assets, or the rate of interest, results from the confrontation between the 'bearishness' of agents (their demand for savings deposits) and the supply of deposits determined by the behaviour of the banking system.

The origin of Keynes's 'two-price theory' is also to be found in a set of writings published in 1931, often considered as of secondary importance, notwithstanding the better understanding they provide of the role played by money and financial relations in Keynes's theory of prices. These writings reflect the observations and discussions that took place during Keynes's visit to the United States where he was asked to participate in the Harris Foundation Conferences. Keynes's strong reaction to the banking crisis of 1931 is obvious in these writings. In particular he takes up a theme already present in his analysis of the August 1914 London Stock Exchange crash: the divergence between 'productivity' or the real value of capital assets and their nominal or money values, as represented by their financial market prices. In 1914 Keynes had already noted that the 'destruction of paper values', due to the threat of war, conveyed an impression that was misleading, since the capacity to produce capital assets was in fact intact. He wrote: '[w]ith a ... fall in the value of securities, we learn not, as with the destruction of Liège or Louvain, of a loss in the world's real wealth, but only of the financial world's extreme urgency for money ... . We experience, therefore, a sudden and violent change in our relative valuation of present and future income' (Keynes, CW XI, 1983, p. 268).

Reacting likewise to the 1929 crash and the 1931 banking crisis, Keynes found it important to emphasize that many of the assets composing capital wealth were obtained through money borrowings. According to him the financial activities of the modern banking system (in particular the provision of guarantees) placed a 'veil of money' between capital assets and their nominal owners and obscured the question of real wealth and its holding (Keynes, CW IX, 1972, p. 151).

Keynes's analysis became more elaborate as he set out to study the effect of a reduction in the money value of real assets – for unchanged marginal productivity – by a percentage that was greater than the conventional 'margin'.[6] Even when there is no reason for panic, he argued, the realization by banks that their 'margins' have 'run off' is likely to have

> a very adverse effect on new business ... . For the banks, being aware that many of their advances are in fact 'frozen' and involve a larger latent risk than they would voluntarily carry, become particularly anxious that the remainder of their assets should be as liquid and as free from risk as it is possible to make them...[i]t means

that the banks are less willing than they would normally be to finance any project which may involve a lock-up of their resources' (Keynes, CW IX, 1972, pp. 153–4).

Here it is the banks' 'urgency for money' that is identified as crucial. However the analysis developed by Keynes in 1931 goes one step further. He specifies that 'a decline in money values so severe as that which we are now experiencing threatens the solidarity of the whole financial structure' (ibid., p. 156). Besides 'nothing on earth can put the banks in good shape or save them from ultimate default except a general recovery in prices and money-values' (ibid., p. 157). Consequently, a reduction in the value of capital assets that is substantial enough to exceed normal margins of safety will diminish confidence in banks' liabilities and, in the end, result in a drop in their value that will lead to a bank panic and to a collapse of the system. Eighteen months later, in February 1933, a breakdown of the banking system occurred.

An important feature of the Keynesian theory of fluctuations is that the stability of financial structure depends on the relation between two prices, the price of real capital goods and the price of financial liabilities. The distinction between these two price categories has its correspondence in *The General Theory*. In this book 'liquidity preference' allows Keynes to take into account the influence of agents' expectations with regard to the prices of debt instruments, and 'marginal efficiency of capital' enables him to consider the effect of entrepreneurs' expectations concerning the prices of capital assets (Keynes, CW VII, 1973, p. 173). This new opposition results from the differences between *The General Theory* and the *Treatise*, in particular the definition of income. To that effect, savings and investment are always brought into equality by variations in the level of income determined by the multiplier. Nonetheless, one of Keynes's main goals being to clarify the impact of money on prices, he makes a careful distinction between how the price of debt instruments is set and how the price of capital goods is established, the interest rate or the price of debt being determined by liquidity preference, marginal efficiency of capital being what establishes the price of capital assets. The separation between the determinants of prices of capital assets and of debt instruments, in the form of the distinction between the marginal efficiency of capital and liquidity preference, is thus to be considered as one of the fundamental innovations contained in *The General Theory*.[7]

On these grounds anticipated sales or expected profits on anticipated sales of non-monetary goods (effective demand) explain the value of capital assets, their demand price, that is to say, their present value, determined by the future incomes they are expected to generate, and discounted on the basis of the interest rate applied to competing financial assets. The sudden drop in the monetary values of assets and liabilities that takes place independently of any change in their underlying productive potential can now be explained by shifts in the liquidity preference of agents, by the transformation of their holdings of financial instruments into more liquid assets. This spills over onto firms' liabilities which are also banks' assets, inducing the latter to become less accommodating in an attempt to restore the liquidity of their balance sheets. The resulting rise in the interest rate brings about a reduction in the discounted value of anticipated profits, as well as a general downward reappraisal of expectations. A decline in the prices of capital assets follows, leading to a reduction of the marginal efficiency of capital, which causes investment outlays to diminish.

The previous account helps understand why, in Chapter 11 of *The General Theory*, Keynes qualifies his theory of investment as a 'two-rate' or 'two-price' theory. It also substantiates the contrast between Keynes's theory of investment and the interpretation retained by the Keynesian neoclassical synthesis. For the economists belonging to this school of thought a positive divergence between the marginal efficiency of capital and the interest rate entails an increase in investment, brought into equality with the greater savings generated by the expansion of output. A simple quantity adjustment process is thus what takes place within the framework of neoclassical Keynesianism. However, a second type of interpretation, the one favoured by post-Keynesian economists, consists in underscoring the existence of a price adjustment process.[8] There are in fact two ways of considering this process. In the wording of the *Treatise* a discrepancy exists between the demand price of capital goods and the supply price or the price of current output of capital goods. In *The General Theory* Keynes defines this process as an adjustment between the prices of capital assets and those of debt instruments: investment continues until the price of assets has dropped to the level reached by the prices of liabilities, in particular the price of money. Thus the multiplier does not only affect the quantity of output. It also causes changes that 'modify the money prices of other capital assets in such a way as to equalize the attraction of holding them and of holding cash' (Keynes, CW XIV, 1973, p. 213). In equilibrium demand and supply prices of capital goods are equal and so are the prices of assets and debts. As emphasized by Kregel (1985), this demonstrates that there is unity in the adjustment process of prices and quantities in *The General Theory*, a unity that later disappeared in the expositions in terms of fixed prices or fixed quantities.

2.2. Minsky's Interpretation

Minsky's analysis of macroeconomic fluctuations is clearly based upon the Keynesian 'two-price' approach. On the one hand, Minsky retains the distinction made in Keynes's *Treatise* between the prices of current output and of capital goods output. On the other, he also refers to the difference which appears in Keynes's writings of 1931, and is developed in *The General Theory*, between the prices of new and existing capital assets and the prices of new and existing financial liabilities.

The distinction between current production and capital goods prices suffices, as will be demonstrated hereafter, to account for the tendency of financial instability to arise endogenously. As for the difference between the prices of capital assets and those of financial debts, it is what enables Minsky to build his financial theory of investment, also based on the idea that agents try to keep 'margins of safety.' Moreover, it allows a comprehensive analysis of the way price drops of the assets held by firms exhibiting high levels of indebtedness affect the value of and thus the confidence in bank liabilities and are likely to lead to panics and financial crises. Accordingly, in line with Keynes's approach, Minsky writes:

> There are really two systems of prices in a capitalist economy – one for current output and the other for capital assets. When the price level of capital assets is high relative to the price level of current output, conditions are favorable for investment; when the price level of capital assets is low relative to the price level of current output, then conditions are not favorable for investment, and a recession – or a depression – is indicated (1986a, p. 143).

The first price system, that of current production, is not directly related to money but is determined by the interactions between supply of and demand for output and labour in the context of particular institutional arrangements. In accordance with the post-Keynesian theory of the determination of output prices, price levels cover costs and make allowance for profits. In the aggregate, the main out-of-pocket costs that need to be recovered are wage costs. Thus, as a first approximation, the price level of current output is determined by money wage rates.[9]

The second price system concerns the prices of capital assets and of debts issued by firms and reflects the views of agents dealing in such assets with regard to the levels of gross profit flows. These assets are either debts of other agents or equities, namely protected or residual claims on profits flows. For Minsky current prices of capital assets and financial instruments reflect the expectations of market participants about the future of the economy, the future achievements of its various actors and the future performance of financial markets. In contrast with the assumptions made within neoclassical financial theory, such future conditions are uncertain and cannot be appraised in terms of probabilistic risk. As a result, current asset prices, given that the price of the money asset is always one, mirror both portfolio managers' views on the future evolution of aggregate profits and the margins of safety they require.

Three fundamental consequences follow from Minsky's theory of investment. First, the price level of capital assets is not tied down in any precise way to current production costs of investment output. Second, the endogenously determined stream of aggregate profits is critical in determining the viability of any liability structure. Third, changing market valuations of the liquidity of the various assets making up a portfolio (that is, their ability to be transformed into cash without their holder incurring the risk of making capital losses) also affects their price.

This last consequence is obviously related to the special nature of money, as a result of the institutional arrangement according to which debts are denominated in money: the subjective yield of money (somewhat similar to the protection provided by an insurance policy) sets a floor for the returns of assets that do not possess the properties of money. In particular, if circumstances are such that this subjective yield increases (as an effect of an increase in liquidity preference, as analysed by Keynes), nominal prices of assets whose value rests upon the money income they are expected to earn will fall. Such a drop will also involve a reduction in the prices of capital assets relative to those of investment goods. Thus, the discrepancy between the money prices of assets and the current supply price of investment goods is, as has been underlined, a main determinant of investment. Consequently, a shift in portfolio preferences towards greater holdings of money will bring about a reduction in investment and therefore in income and profits.

The clarification by Minsky of the Keynesian price theory is an essential feature of his model of financial instability. This aspect alone reflects Minsky's originality and contrasts with the view of other economists for whom no price theory is to be found in Keynes's works.[10] Minsky's analysis thus departs considerably from the neo-Keynesian interpretations of *The General Theory* in terms of sticky interest rates (the horizontal portion of the LM curve), sticky wages (the horizontal portion of the supply of labour curve), and of sticky prices. However Minsky did not limit himself to identifying and elucidating Keynes's two-price theory. He enriched Keynes's original approach substantially by adding a certain number of fundamental traits to the general outline provided by the author of *The General Theory*.

3 THE INTRODUCTION OF FINANCIAL STRUCTURE

Left to itself the adjustment process between the two prices generates instability. The introduction of the two-price system is therefore an important stage in Minsky's analysis of financial instability. Instability principally concerns the investment function, as determined by the ratio of the 'objective' variable P_I (the current supply price of investment) to the 'subjective' variable P_K (the price of capital assets). Subjectivity interferes since, as was shown above, uncertainty with regard to profit flows, the expected degree of liquidity and the interest rate applied to loans can be considered as factors causing fluctuations of investment and of the economic system.

This stage having been achieved, Minsky's approach could – quite rightly – have been interpreted as a simple updating of Keynes's analysis of macroeconomic instability. Besides strong similarities appear with Tobin's more orthodox, albeit Keynesian, 'q' theory.[11] Tobin also distinguishes between two prices: the production price of currently produced capital goods on the one hand; the market price of pre-existing capital goods, on the other. Thus q is simply the ratio of the market price to the production price. When q is greater than 1, investment takes place, since any good already in existence is overrated by the capital market. On this basis Tobin constructs a deterministic equilibrium model where agents are budget constrained – but not by financial resources – and expected returns are identically stochastically valued by and known to all agents. This apparent similarity between the two analyses has led Tobin to consider Minsky's formulation as identical to his: 'Minsky's excellent account of asset pricing and investment decisions is separable from his theory of prices, wages and profits. It sounds like "q" theory to me' (1989, p. 106). Such a comparison does not however really hold. Minsky's approach is more original, compared with Tobin's and that of the neoclassical synthesis, but also with Keynes's and that of the post-Keynesian economists. Indeed, at this point of his analysis, Minsky's theory of investment (and of fluctuations) is quite incomplete, in that he does not 'close' the model at this stage. What is lacking is an essential ingredient: the way investment projects are financed.

The introduction of financial relations into Minsky's theory of investment involves a more complex determination of the prices of capital assets. So far we have insisted upon the importance of variables such as the quantity of money, income and liquidity preferences for the explanation of how asset prices are set. We have also seen that asset prices govern the demand price of the various investment goods. However, according to Minsky, demand prices for capital goods are not sufficient to determine the pace of investment. Even the existence of a market price for capital assets and of a demand price for comparable investments does not necessarily imply that there is an effective demand for investment. Effective demand must be backed by finance. Three potential sources of finance are available: cash and financial assets in hand, internal funds (gross profits after taxes and dividends) and external funds (borrowings and share issues).

Within this context, when setting up an investment project the investor is confronted with two sets of interlocking decisions. The first involves the expected incomes as well as the investment costs associated with the use of a particular capital asset in the production process. In the framework chosen by Minsky the cost of financing the production of investment is as much part of the supply price as are wages and input costs. The fact that a firm has to borrow to pay wages raises the effective costs by the interest payments on the loans it takes out. The supply price of investment goods therefore includes the financial costs (interest charges) incurred throughout the gestation period. Finance for production purposes being typically short-term, its usual form is bank loans.

The second set of decisions concerns financing the acquisition of the capital asset. This take-out or 'permanent' finance is presumably long-term. The funds used in take-out finance may be obtained either from the sales of bonds, mortgages, new-equity issues, or from corporate retained earnings. Choosing a form of permanent finance therefore necessarily implies trying to forecast the size of future retained earnings and the conditions that will prevail in capital markets when the financial arrangement is put together.

As a result the decision to invest involves: (1) a supply function of investment that depends upon labour costs and on short-term interest rates; (2) a demand function for investment, as determined by the price of capital assets; and (3) the anticipated financial structure and the financial conditions that will be applied in the future. As indicated, the financial structure is anticipated on the basis of expected flows of internal and external finance, on the mix of internal and external financing that will be needed, this proportion depending on the extent to which finance for investment goods will be forthcoming from profit flows. Obviously these flows will be influenced by the evolution of the economic situation between the date at which investment is decided and the date at which it is completed. An additional element of uncertainty is thus introduced by Minsky into the investment decision-making process, which is entirely neglected by the approaches previously examined. A sign of such uncertainty appears in the willingness of agents to lever or debt-finance positions in inherited capital assets, financial assets and newly produced capital assets.

Choosing the adequate financial structure falls upon two sets of decision-makers: the owners of capital assets and the financial community. Both will require 'margins of safety', as Keynes explained in his 1931 writings and in *The General Theory*. Minsky considers that in an economy characterized by a system of borrowing and lending, these margins influence the size of external finance, which means that the ratio of external to internal financing that is acceptable changes over time and reflects the experience of economic agents. If recent experience is that outstanding debts are easily serviced, then they will be inclined to allow higher debt ratios; if recent experience includes episodes in which debt-servicing has been a burden and representative units have not fulfilled debt contracts, then acceptable debt ratios will decrease. In sum current investment decisions reflect past – in particular recent past – experience which influences expectations regarding future outcomes. A series of business successes will tend to diminish safety margins and may well be associated with an increase in investment. A series of failures will lead to the opposite result. This is what is meant by Minsky when he repeatedly asserts that investment is essentially a financial phenomenon.

The way the different factors (asset prices, financial conditions, income flows) that influence the pace of investment and the way the different arguments of the investment function are interrelated is illustrated in Figure 2.1.

Minsky's investment function displays particular features. First, it appeals explicitly to the borrower's risk and the lender's risk, two notions introduced by Keynes:[12]

Two types of risk affect the volume of investment which have not commonly been distinguished, but which it is important to distinguish. The first is the entrepreneur's or borrower's risk and arises out of doubts in his own mind as to the probability of his actually earning the prospective yield for which he hopes. If the man is venturing his own money, this is the only risk that is relevant. But where a system of borrowing and lending exists, by which I mean the granting of loans with a margin of real or personal security, a second type of risk is relevant which we may call the lender's risk. This may be due either to moral hazard, i.e. voluntary default or other means of escape, possibly lawful, from the fulfilment of the obligation, or to the possible insufficiency of the margin of security, i.e. voluntary default due to the disappointment of expectation' (Keynes, CW VII, 1973, p. 144).

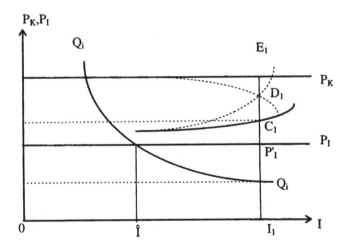

Figure 2.1 Minsky's investment function

In Minsky's version of the investment function, the borrower's risk has two facets; the first concerns asset diversification insofar as the capitalization factor assigned to each type of capital asset employed in a particular sector diminishes as its amount increases. The second is related to the fact that, because financial commitments associated with debt are certain, any increase in the debt-to-investment ratio reduces the borrower's safety margin. This implies an increase in the discount rate that the borrower applies to his expected returns or quasi-rents.

To finance an amount of investment that is greater than his own resources, the borrower is then confronted with the following options: to run down his holdings of financial assets or to engage in external finance. However, a reduction in financial asset holdings diminishes the margin of safety for managers and equity owners. If, instead, new issues of common shares are undertaken, the issue price will need to be attractive, which may mean that existing shareholders will feel their equity interest is being diluted. Finally, if the firm resorts to issuing debt – in the form of bonds, bank loans or short-term securities – the share of future cash flows devoted to reimbursements will increase, which will diminish the security margins of managers and shareholders. Consequently, whatever choice is made – running down financial assets, issuing new common shares or borrowing – the borrower's risk will increase as the weight of external or liquidity-diminishing finance increases.

The rectangular hyperbola, Qi-Qi, represents the level of investment that it is possible to self-finance, with Qi, the anticipated internal flows. The intersection between the hyperbola and supply price, P_I, of investment determines $\hat{I}$, the amount of investment that can be realized thanks to anticipated internal resources. The decreasing dotted line illustrates the effect of the borrower's risk on the demand price, P_K, of capital assets. The price thus diminishes in proportion to the market price, and the greater the commitment to this particular type of asset and the greater the ratio of borrowed funds, the steeper the decline. This decrease of P_K generally occurs to the right of $\hat{I}$ but, as will be seen later, it can in certain circumstances take place before.

The investment goods supply curve, represented by P_I, increases beyond a certain level of investment. This occurs for technological reasons, since the existing stock of capital assets and of labour specialized in the production of investment goods sets a limit on the capacity to produce them. Furthermore, and more fundamentally, the lender's risk creates a deterioration in supply conditions of capital assets that are independent of any technological consideration and are related instead to the harsher financial conditions set by bankers. In loan and bond contracts the lender's risk takes different forms: increases in the interest rate, shortenings of maturity or greater demands for guarantees. In addition, covenants and codicils restrain dividend payments, limit further debt or restrict sales of assets.

The intersection between the demand for investment curve, modified in order to take into account the borrower's risk, and the investment supply schedule, which reflects the lender's risk, determines the level of investment, I_l, at price P_l. Total investment expenditure $OP_lP'_lI_l$ will be financed partly through internal finance (OAA_lI_l), partly through external finance $(AP_lP'_lA_l)$.

As Minsky indicates, this representation in the form of a diagram can only serve as an illustration, insofar as it cannot account for the entirety of Minsky's investment theory. In particular it is obvious that an accurate measure of the reduction of P_K is not within reach. In Minsky's analysis this diminution depends, as has been underlined, on the borrower's indebtedness, on the way external finance influences his assessment of the return and risk of his project, and on the borrowing conditions he is offered. It is thus clear that, although the demand price of capital assets diminishes as asset acquisitions are increasingly financed by debt, the size of this drop will be indeterminate. In a similar way, although the lender's risk corresponding to a particular investment project 'does appear on signed contracts', its true magnitude is, as with the borrower's risk, also indeterminate (1975, p. 110). Consequently, in Minsky's schema, investment takes place when P_K and P_I are equal, but only after P_K and P_I have been affected in some imprecise fashion, by the borrower's risk and by the lender's risk respectively. The main outcome of the previous analysis is, however, clear: the pace of investment will change as the borrower's and the lender's risks vary. This feature of Minsky's analysis is what contributes to distinguish it from Tobin's. Indeed reliance on both the borrower's and the lender's risks enables Minsky to incorporate two essential aspects of Keynes's theory – fundamental uncertainty and the pivotal role played by financial relations – and to show they are essential determinants of investment decision-making.

However Minsky's financial theory of investment differs in some respects from the approach developed by Keynes in *The General Theory*. Keynes's reference to the borrower's and the lender's risks mainly relates to investment decision-making and to long-run expectations. Minsky's analysis is also based upon the works devoted by Kalecki to the 'principle of increasing risk', and, according to this principle, the marginal risk of investing in fixed capital goods increases with the size of their acquisition. Kalecki gives two reasons for this increase. First, the more he invests, the greater the risk of failure to which the entrepreneur's wealth is exposed. The second reason relates to the illiquidity risk that arises when increasing quantities of capital are invested in industrial facilities that cannot be readily reconverted into liquidity without generating capital losses.

Another distinctive feature of Minsky's approach, compared to the one contained in *The General Theory*, concerns bank finance. Keynes's demand for money depends on the interest rate, but is subject to no quantity constraint. Thus, the banking system plays a somewhat passive role in the determination of the quantity of money. In contrast, there is a quantity constraint affecting Minsky's demand for money, in addition to the effect of the interest rate. This constraint derives from the lender's risk, which induces banks to limit the availability of finance once loans have reached a certain amount, thereby creating a form of credit rationing.[13]

The essential point to be retained from the above analysis is that investment is typically, in Minsky's theory, a financial phenomenon. Basically the author's approach is organized around a model of negotiation between banks and businessmen, the driving force of which is the dynamic interaction between expectations and financial structure. In this model emphasis is placed primarily on the structural form taken by financial arrangements. What Minsky is saying implicitly is that the interest rate, which plays an essential role in the neoclassical synthesis, is on the whole of secondary importance. The fundamental financial variables of the model are rather: (1) the cash flows generated by economic activity; (2) the internal finance these cash flows potentially give rise to; and (3) their ability to validate (a) prior payment commitments that result from the complex structure of financial interrelations and instruments and (b) the prices paid for the acquisition of capital assets and investment output.

It is precisely the evolution of these financial variables that causes fluctuations and instability. This relation between finance and instability, which is at the heart of Minsky's financial instability hypothesis, is what we deal with next.

NOTES

1. Among the most significant contributions to be cited are those of Gurley and Shaw (1955) and Meyer and Kuh (1957).
2. Famous papers include Jorgenson (1963) and Hall and Jorgenson (1967).
3. This analysis draws extensively from an article by Kregel (1992).
4. See also Wicksell (1898), for whom the discrepancy between the natural rate of interest and the money rate of interest (set by the banking system) is at the root of a cumulative process.
5. On this point, see Kregel (1982).
6. Since, according to Keynes, banks 'will only lend [the borrower] money up to a certain proportion of the value of the asset which is the "security" offered by the borrower to the lender' (*The Collected Writings*, IX, 1972, p. 152).
7. In particular, compared with *A Treatise on Money*. See Kregel (1988), pp. 63–4.
8. See in particular, Kregel (1985) pp. 233–9.
9. A more complete explanation of prices adds a mark-up, determined by aggregate profits, to wage costs. On this point, see Minsky (1986a) Chapter 7, 'Prices and Profits in a Capitalist Economy', and Ferri and Minsky (1984).
10. Rymes, in *Keynes's Lectures, 1923-35* (1989, p. 10) has recently noted that the fact that 'Keynes was fundamentally rewriting the theory of value' was not generally acknowledged even by his students. An in-depth analysis of the two-price approach has been provided by Kregel (1982, 1985 and 1988).

11. Tobin (1969). These similarities are underscored in particular by Silipo (1987), pp. 144–5 and by Dymski and Pollin (1992) pp. 36–7.
12. As noted by Minsky himself (1975, p. 106 and 1986a, p. 190).
13. This point will be developed in more detail in Part Three.

3. The 'Incoherence' of Market Economies

1 INTRODUCTION

Arrow and Hahn have been right in placing emphasis on the fact that mainstream economics has, since Adam Smith, 'sought to show that a decentralized economy motivated by self-interest and guided by price signals would be compatible with a coherent disposition of economic resources' (1971, pp. vi, vii). Contemporary analyses of neoclassical inspiration are still attempting to make this demonstration by studying the characteristics of an abstract exchange process. However the validity of this theory depends on its capacity to show that the property of 'coherence' exhibited by the exchange process can be preserved when the model is modified in order to take into consideration the ingredients that enter today's financially sophisticated economies.

Minsky's theory incorporates these different elements explicitly, as it focuses on the interactions between factors such as the creation of money, financial structure as well as the valuation of assets and investment which accompany the evolution of the economy. These interactions give rise to a system where the profit-seeking behaviour of economic agents will tend to destroy the previous coherence and create an unstable environment. This central aspect of Minsky's model rests upon two distinct features:

1. The inherent tendency for the economy to transform itself into an unstable 'financially fragile' system, through the simple interplay of the profit-seeking behaviours of rational agents.
2. The propensity of the same agents to respond to disequilibrium by creating even more disequilibrating forces.

Before investigating these two important aspects of Minsky's dynamic theory, it is necessary to examine how the author defines the overall financial fragility of an economy.

29

2 CHARACTERIZING THE FINANCIAL FRAGILITY OF AN ECONOMY

In Minsky's theory, firms are considered as 'packages' of investment projects. At each point in time, a given firm will have a certain number of projects, expected to give rise to both cash flows and debts, while actual net returns of projects may either confirm or disappoint expectations, or even be negative. As a result, the financial fragility of a firm depends negatively on the cash flows generated by each of its investment projects, weighted by its size within the firm's portfolio of assets, and positively on the financial commitments associated with each of the items composing its liabilities.

Minsky proposed characterizing financial fragility by separating firms into three categories. He distinguished between 'hedge', 'speculative' and 'Ponzi' finance.[1] Hedge finance is a situation where, in each period, debt repayments are smaller than expected profits. Thus the net value of firms engaged in hedge finance is always positive, whatever the discount rate, and their liabilities are essentially composed of shares and long-term debts, although they may rely on short-term loans to finance current expenditures. Money balances required for current spending and short-run financial commitments are generally small. The viability of firms engaged in hedge finance does not depend on the prevailing financial market conditions, but only on the generation of cash flows by the normal operation of the goods and factors markets.

Firms that resort to speculative finance generate proceeds that allow for the payment of short-term interest charges, but which are sometimes lower than the corresponding total debt repayment costs (principal and interest). This means that firms engaged in speculative finance must accumulate liquid reserves and sometimes roll over their debts in order to meet their financial commitments. As a result, the solvency of such firms, as opposed to that of firms committed to hedge finance, depends on financial market – in addition to goods and labour markets – conditions. Should a firm need to borrow at a time when actual interest rates exceed expected interest rates, this will affect its present value negatively and it will become insolvent.

The third kind of financial behaviour depicted by Minsky is Ponzi finance. For businesses engaged in Ponzi finance, even repayment of interest is impossible without reliance on additional debt. This kind of finance is reminiscent of pyramiding schemes. It should however be borne in mind that a firm endowed with an investment project whose gestation period is very long can be impelled to engage in this kind of finance. Ponzi firms are strongly dependent on the uninterrupted issuance of debt and are, consequently, even more exposed than speculative firms to the fluctuations of money markets. They must therefore, with yet greater reason, hold a large amount of liquid assets, enabling them to raise money, should it become difficult to do so on the money market.

Identification of the category to which a firm belongs permits the measurement of its individual financial fragility. Classification of the firms making up the economy allows us to assess global financial fragility at a particular point in time. Obviously, the larger the proportion of firms engaged in speculative and Ponzi finance, the greater is the fragility. The demand for external resources by such firms is inelastic and their solvency is related inextricably to the evolution of money markets. The viability of these economic agents is thus seriously threatened by increases in interest rates. Concurrently the inelasticity of their demand for external resources exerts upwards pressure on interest rates. Another way for these firms to obtain funds is to utilize their liquid reserves or to sell off other assets. But, as will be shown later, simultaneous sales of assets by a large number of firms when interest rates are high cause the prices of these assets to fall. In addition, sales of income-generating resources by speculative firms can transform them into Ponzi firms.

In sum, Minsky's static model of financial fragility simply states the fact that the larger the proportion of agents engaged in speculative and Ponzi finance, the more fragile is the economy. Fragility is greater because the economy loses its shock-absorbing ability. Shocks are then more likely to lead to a financial crisis and to initiate a debt-deflation process: 'The stability of a financial system depends on the weight of hedge finance in the total private financial structure. The smaller the weight of hedge finance (the greater the weight of speculative and Ponzi finance), the greater the possibility of a financial crisis, because the greater the likelihood that rising interest rates will lead to present-value reversals' (1982b, p. 26).

What needs to be explained now is the process that determines the proportions of agents engaged in hedge, speculative and Ponzi finance and, thus, the degree of overall financial fragility.

3   PROFITS, INVESTMENT AND INDEBTEDNESS

Our next step is to examine Minsky's explanation of the transition causing a robust financial structure to become more fragile. This aspect of his construct is of particular importance, as it is critical for the analytical consistency of his model. Having shown that the increase in interest rates has a cumulative impact, but only on an economy characterized by speculative or Ponzi finance, Minsky needs to demonstrate that the natural trend for an economy is to develop speculative-type behaviour.

Over the years Minsky tried to improve his description of the nature of the mechanism underlying financial fragility. As early as 1977 he defined it as follows: 'Over a period in which the economy does well, views about acceptable debt structure change. In the deal-making that goes on between banks, investment bankers, and businessmen, the acceptable amount of debt to use in financing various types of activity and positions increases' (1982a, pp. 65–6).

The evolution of financial structure during a Minsky-like business cycle is best understood by beginning with the analysis of what happens immediately after a financial crisis. During this period economic agents (bankers and entrepreneurs) who have incurred losses avoid engaging in speculative or Ponzi finance. Moreover, in the wake of a financial crisis affecting an economy, income, employment and profits are sustained by government deficits. As a result corporate profits increase in proportion to investments, and the weight of external finance diminishes in comparison with purchases of assets. Concurrently, refinancing at post-crisis lower interest rates allows consolidation of short-term debts and their transformation into equity or long-term debt. At the same time, because of the budget deficit, the weight of government securities increases within the portfolios of banks and other institutions. Consequently, exposure of the banking and financial system to default risk decreases. In other words, the financial crisis results in the economy emerging from the preceding recession with greater robustness.

Following an economic crisis the interest rate structure creates profit opportunities, those created by acquiring capital assets with short-term debt, as we explain now. Balance sheets display large amounts of liquid assets and cash, so liquidity is not highly valued. Besides, the government deficit generates quasi-rents that are large compared with current outlays for capital assets. Consequently short-run interest rates on riskless instruments are substantially lower than capital returns. In addition interest and principal repayments for long-term debt appear to be small in comparison with expected quasi-rents. Therefore, the interest rate utilized to capitalize financial commitments of a firm engaged in hedge finance will be lower than the interest rate used to capitalize the quasi-rents of capital assets. Finally, the interest rate on short-term debt issued by firms and financial institutions will be lower than the long-term interest rate applied in the hedge financing of capital assets. On the whole the interest rate structure prevailing after a crisis offers two sets of profit opportunities: those associated with the financing of capital assets with long-term and short-term debt; those connected with the financing of long-term financial assets with short-term debt.

The expansionary phase of economic activity can then begin. The main idea Minsky develops is that, during this stage, the economy will experience a simultaneous increase of investment, profits and indebtedness. A simple way of understanding how growth and financial fragility are related is to refer to Figure 3.1, depicting Minsky's financial theory of investment.

However, the previous analysis underlying it must be modified and made more elaborate, in three respects. First, it applies to the aggregate economy and no longer to the individual firm. Second, it focuses on what happens when current profits vary (and when the internal resources curve shifts). Third more details are given showing how the balance sheets of firms are affected

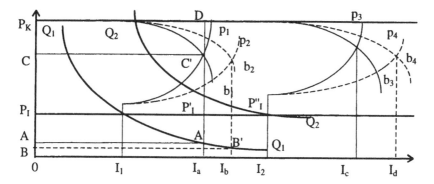

Figure 3.1 Growth and financial fragility

during the expansionary phase.

The diagram presented in Figure 3.1 allows us to understand the development of an investment boom and the ensuing increase in indebtedness. It illustrates the different configurations that arise, depending on how effective outcomes compare with agents' expectations and affect aggregate investment.[2] To begin with, we assume that the internal flows realized at the aggregate level are at least equal to expected internal flows. This situation corresponds to two cases that we examine in succession.

First, let us consider the case where the realized cash flows, Q_l-Q_l, are just equal to expected cash flows. In this case the value of firms is OP_KDI_a. This value corresponds to the capitalized value of the firms' future cash flows, that is, to the capitalized value of their gross future incomes minus the capitalized value of their financial commitments. In the diagram the size of these financial commitments is represented by rectangle $ACC'A'$. Its size is a function of the lender's risk, which determines both the discount rate applied to these financial commitments and their amount. As previously $OAA'I_a$ is equal to the quantity of equity finance and $AP_lP_l'A'$ to that of debt finance.

The main outcome of this process is the capital gain realized by shareholders: their initial wealth, $OAA'I_l$, is now worth $OAA'I_l + CP_KDC'$. Generating this capital gain affects the behaviour of both borrowers and lenders. It will cause a reduction of the borrowers' appraisal of the risk they incur, which will result in a rightwards shift of curve P_K from b_l to b_2. For lenders the realization of these expected profits diminishes the fear that borrowers might default. The rate at which lenders discount future repayments is then likely to decline and they will be prone to accept a greater indebtedness on the part of their borrowers. Accordingly curve P_l, augmented by the lender's risk, shift rightwards from p_1 to p_2.

What is the overall outcome of this dynamic interactive process, which involves expectations, investment and indebtedness? At a first stage investment increases, moving from I_a (initial investment) to I_b (desired investment). Next, if the desired investment is undertaken and if the then realized cash flows remain equal to Q_1, not only does the level of indebtedness augment, but so does the indebtedness (the debt to equity ratio), shifting from $AA'P_l'P_l$ / $OAA'I_a$ to $BB'P_l''P_l$ / $OBB'I_b$. This has a very important consequence: in a economy where expectations are merely realized, unstable dynamics arise and develop endogenously. It takes the form of an increase in investment and in indebtedness, accompanied by greater fragility of the financial structure of the economy.

This raises the question of whether these conclusions remain valid when actual cash flows are greater than expected ones. In this case the internal resources curve shifts from Q_1-Q_1 to Q_2-Q_2. This 'overrealization' of profits substantially modifies the behaviour of agents and curves P_K and P_I are subject to several changes: (1) they become flatter (curves b_1 and p_1 convert into curves b_3 and p_3); (2) they level off even more than in the previous case (stretching out from b_3 to b_4 and from p_3 to p_4). Indeed actual leverage of the aggregate balance sheet structure will be smaller than expected. Consequently investors will come upon sounder balance sheets than predicted, meaning that there will be an 'unused borrowing power', and subsequent financing conditions will become more favourable (1986a, p. 194).

A final modification – not represented in our graph – is also to be noted. It relates to the fact that a change in aggregate gross profits (quasi-rents), as compared with those that were expected, influences not only the way investment weighs on firms' balance sheets but also how it affects the level of capital asset prices. In particular, if actual quasi-rents are greater than expected, the surplus of actual profits, in proportion to expected profits, will cause P_K to increase, which will in turn increase the discrepancy between P_K and P_I. Thus, for any inflexion of the curve due to the borrower's risk, the new level of the demand price, P_K, will be higher for all levels of production.

The graph shows that the effects on indebtedness and investment are amplified, in contrast to the case where expectations are merely realized. Here a sort of acceleration effect appears in that, the greater the difference between actual and expected cash flows, the greater the investment and the level of the economy's indebtedness, leading to an investment boom and an upsurge in indebtedness.

Nonetheless, an important point needs to be stressed here. Some authors claim to have detected a weakness or at least a certain looseness in this part of Minsky's theory. The question they raise is whether an increase in financial fragility is likely to occur. Criticisms are mainly of two sorts:

1. According to some commentators Minsky's model is inconsistent insofar as, while and even though agents might consider a depression or a financial crisis to be in the offing, the way they compose their portfolios actually tends to increase the likelihood of the crisis. In particular, for Friedman and Laibson, 'some element of myopia is a crucial ingredient here as well' (1989, p. 169). A similar point of view is voiced by Tobin who, commenting on Minsky's approach, writes 'rational expectations adherents will doubtless object that the alleged cycle would vanish as soon as borrowers and lenders understood it' (1989, p. 106).
2. A second critique is that, even if indebtedness increases, even very rapidly, there is no reason why *a priori* the economy's financial structure should deteriorate.[3] Referring to the graph, one observes that, depending on the size of the increase in profits (that is, the amplitude of the rightwards shift of the internal resources curve), the debt to equity ratio may either increase, remain stable or even diminish during the economy's expansionary phase.

Let us begin by examining the validity of the first objection: is the endemic fragility underscored by Minsky at odds with the existence of 'rational' behaviour? Is it true that Minsky's model would lack a convincing explanation of why 'rational expectations' would not prevent behaviour that makes the system more fragile? Careful reading of Minsky's writings leads us to answer these queries in the negative. To begin with, as Dymski and Pollin argue, the financial instability hypothesis actually refers to economic behaviour resulting from two phenomena, a 'fallacy of composition' and an 'asymmetric structure of rewards'.[4] Let us specify these two concepts in succession.

Consider first, 'fallacy of composition'. If an individual firm finds it is worthwhile to rely on increased indebtedness, the fragility of the system, taken as a whole, will not increase as long as the majority of firms continue to engage in hedge finance. However, it is reasonable to assume, whenever economic information and its circulation are not perfect, that the individual firm will lack information as to the financial situation of the other firms. In addition, notwithstanding the substantial improvement in the circulation of information, there is no evidence that today's better informed agents are able to reckon what level of indebtedness (their own and/or that of other agents) transforms a robust financial structure into a fragile one. In other words increased fragility of the economy is not the consequence of lack of rationality on the part of the individual firm.

Another argument put forward by Dymski and Pollin is that, whatever the quality of the information relative to indebtedness and whatever the 'lessons of history', it is not at all certain that firms will use all available information as best they can (that is, from the viewpoint of the welfare and stability of the economy as a whole). All that agents can do is interpret past financial crises and adapt their behaviour accordingly. They do not have sufficient information at their disposal to allow them to understand (let alone construct) the Minsky model. In this model what creates the conditions for an outburst of a financial crisis is the process of financial fragilization of the economy. However, for the economic agents themselves, things appear quite differently. In their eyes the crisis is caused by a 'shock' (in particular by an increase in the interest rate) that triggers the crisis and in no way by the risky financial techniques that may, among other things, have been applied. For the agents 'the lesson of history may be that their financial posture was reasonable, but that a onetime shock, for which they bore no responsibility, brought the system, and themselves, to a crisis' (Dymski and Pollin, 1992, p. 44). Accordingly, the lack of recognition of his or her own responsibility explains in part why, in particular during phases of prosperity, each agent contributes to intensifying the economy's financial fragility at the aggregate level and thus to undermining his or her own situation and that of the other agents.

Let us imagine now that, despite the highly improbable character of such an occurrence, our agents come a little closer to becoming omniscient and acquire a perfect knowledge of Minsky's theory. Agents will then be perfectly aware of the consequences their actions inflict on the aggregate stability of the system and know that a financial crisis is to occur sooner or later. Even in this extreme case, though, one variable remains unknown, namely the exact moment at which the financial crisis will actually break out. Now this variable is a crucial one, inasmuch as today's market economies are characterized by an 'asymmetric reward structure'. This means that for the individual firm it is in no way profitable to engage in hedge finance during an economic boom. In fact, a firm that would not make use of all available leverage would run the risk of seeing its market value drop (since, among other reasons, it would distribute fewer dividends than other, more indebted, firms). Moreover, in the long run, it would not be able to remain competitive. As a result, when prosperity wanes, aggressive managers will already have been rewarded, while hedge managers, if they have not been eliminated, will have made lower profits. In addition, during a crisis many aggressive managers default, so that the responsibility of financial distress falls on no one in particular, in sharp contrast to the situation prevailing during the boom where exaggerately cautious agents find themselves in an isolated position. For Dymski and Pollin, this is the essence of the asymmetric reward structure: 'aggressive behaviour is rewarded more and punished less than cautious behaviour, even though the "lessons of history" should promote a well-honed sense of caution' (ibid., p. 45). The same idea was expressed by Keynes many years ago, in Chapter 12 of the *General Theory*: 'worldly wisdom teaches that it is better for reputation to fail conventionally than to succeed unconventionally' (Keynes, CW VII, 1973, p. 158).

This discussion clearly establishes that Minsky's agent is neither irrational nor myopic. Simply, he must form expectations and make decisions in an economy characterized by fallacy of composition and by an asymmetrical reward structure. As a result, financial fragility builds up endogenously in the expansionary phase because it is then individually rational for firms to issue more debt and for banks to make more loans. Notwithstanding the opinion of Friedman and Laibson, Minsky's idea that 'even as agents note the unfavourable objective circumstances, their significance for today is discounted' (Minsky, 1989, p. 181) is not based upon 'behavioural underpinnings [that] have remained vague' (Friedman and Laibson, 1989, p. 161). Minsky's agent is fully rational. He or she is, however, subject to a particular form of rationality. As we shall see in Part Three, Minsky-type rationality seems more suitable for depicting the behaviours found in contemporary financially sophisticated economies than the one implied by the usual rational expectations hypothesis.

Let us examine now the second critique to which Minsky's process of financial fragilization is subjected. Why does the indebtedness ratio increase during phases of prosperity? Before answering this question, it should be noted that Minsky himself recognized that the existence of profit-making opportunities did not necessarily imply the immediate emergence of fragile financial structures: the borrower and the lender's risks set limits to the pace at which the opportunities provided by the management of liabilities might be exploited. In much the same way, he also underlined that banks are unlikely to endorse the optimistic profit expectations of firms.[5] In fact their attitude tends to delay the financial fragilization process. There is thus clearly, in Minsky's analysis, a sort of 'orthodox financial barrier'. We return to this point more extensively in Part Three, but we can already indicate that during booms, the 'barrier' to financial innovations will be gradually lowered, whereas during slumps financial distress will tend to raise it.

In addition it should be stressed that greater profits (and thus the apparent capacity to support more indebtedness), far from weakening Minsky's theory, are on the contrary the manifestation of an essential characteristic of the financial instability hypothesis: once the move towards external funding and speculative finance has begun, reactions on the part of the market validate the decisions to engage in such financial structure, at least at a first stage, which intensifies the cumulative indebtedness process.

More fundamentally Minsky proposes a rationale of the reduction in aggregate profits during the business cycle.[6] The explanation he proposes in many of his works rests upon Kalecki's 'equation of profits' where aggregate profits are directly proportional to the volume of investment. The variations of investment then become the key to the solution: 'in the simplest Kalecki case, where aggregate gross profits (aggregate Q) equals aggregate investment, the shortfall of realized profits below anticipated profits requires a logically prior shortfall of investment. This leaves the generation of financial crises and deep depressions essentially unexplained, for it is the decline of investment that has to be explained' (1982b, p. 25). Among the various factors that are likely to influence the level of investment, there is one on which Minsky focuses his attention more particularly - the rate of interest, or rather the variations in the rate of interest during the business cycle. The analysis of the determination of the rate of interest is one of the most original, but also one of the most complex, aspects of Minsky's theory. It cannot be dealt with in just a few lines, as it requires an examination of the author's detailed analysis of the behaviour of banks. In fact Minsky's theory of the rate of interest brings into play several actors (the central bank, the different financial institutions and the borrowers) and various markets (the monetary market and the market for loans, in particular). A thorough presentation of how the interest rate is determined is provided in Part Three, where we study the institutional dynamics of the financial instability hypothesis.

Anticipating what follows, we can however already point out that the analysis of the institutional dimension of the financial instability hypothesis enables Minsky to establish that the rate of interest is a procyclical variable. Within the framework of our present discussion, procyclicity of the interest rate has a direct and fundamental implication: because of the increase in the interest rate brought about by the boom, investment will tend to slow down and aggregate profits to drop. It is then highly probable that the debt-to-equity ratio of the economy will augment since the increase of the interest rate affects its numerator positively and its denominator negatively. Referring to the previous graph, we can notice that the investment and indebtedness 'accelerator' will act in exactly the opposite direction: the shortfall of actual cash flows below expected cash flows implies that the amount of external finance will be greater than its expected amount. As a result, actual aggregate leverage will be higher than anticipated. Consequently, investors will come across more fragile balance sheets than expected and subsequent financing conditions will become less favourable.

The increase in the rate of interest thus reinforces and accelerates the financial fragility of the economy. However, in Minsky's analysis variations of the interest rate have other consequences that are as harmful to economic activity, since they influence the demand price of capital assets and the supply price of investment goods. Let us consider first the influence of the short-term interest rates that prevail in the loans market. We saw earlier that these rates strongly condition the supply price of investment goods. According to Minsky an 'inelastic demand for finance' exists in the market for credit, since some capital assets (such as power plants, pipelines, etc.) have no value until they have been completed and begin to operate (1986a, p. 195). Furthermore, this demand rises throughout the process during which suppliers deliver the components for complex installations. Meanwhile, for a variety of reasons related both to actions of the central bank and to the limited amount of equity of commercial banks, the supply of finance from banks eventually becomes less than infinitely inelastic.[7] Consequently, after some time has elapsed, the cost of financing investment goods in the process of being produced tends to rise. This increase causes a rapid augmentation of short-term interest rates. As a result the supply price of investment goods grows sharply.

In addition Minsky reminds us that short-term financing is used in modern stock markets to finance positions in equities and bonds. Therefore, in financially sophisticated economies, a frequent effect of quickly augmenting short-term interest rates will be a brutal increase in long-term interest rates, implying a fall in the prices of shares and bonds. However, rising short-term and long-term interest rates have opposite effects on the demand price of capital assets and on the supply price of investment. The former falls when long-term interest rates increase, while the latter rises when short-term interest rates become higher. The differential between the two prices underlying the demand for investment goods tends thereby to be dissipated. In addition, it is entirely possible (as we show below) to witness present value reversals, characterized in particular by values of P_K becoming lower than those of P_I, causing abrupt interruption of investment. Nevertheless the variations in investment activity are not limited to this extreme case. In fact 'it is enough that the margin between the price of capital assets and the supply price of investment varies inversely with interest rates' (1986a, p. 195).

From this discussion it is possible to retain the two essential features of Minsky's analysis of the relationship between debt structure and the unfolding of the cycle. First, Minsky's model places emphasis on the predominance of destabilizing forces that are embedded in any economic system incorporating financial markets, which influence the investment process, as we have seen. Second, although the relationship between investment and the interest rate can in fact be represented by a decreasing function, no analogy should be drawn between this feature and the orthodox Keynesian theory of the neoclassical synthesis. In fact, the relationship established by Minsky between the variations in the borrower's and the lender's risks, on the one hand, and the overall behaviour of the economy, on the other, as well as the analysis of the way investment determines profits and thus the actual amount of borrowings, imply that the decreasing relation between investment and the interest rate can in no way be interpreted as a simple corollary of the decreasing technical productivity of capital assets. Minsky's investment function is in fact subject to a complex cluster of influences that combine technical, commercial as well as financial aspects. It is thus dynamically unstable, all the more because the actual trajectory of the system modifies current expectations with regard to the subsequent evolution of the economy.

We now go on to complete Minsky's view of dynamic and endogenous instability, by showing that the deflationary pressure resulting from a slowdown in aggregate activity is not necessarily stabilizing.

4 DEBT-DEFLATION OR THE FINANCIAL AMPLIFICATION OF THE MINSKY CRISIS

In this section we study an important factor of macroeconomic instability contained in Minsky's theory, namely the existence of a downward cumulative process which might worsen the state of disequilibrium initially reached by the economy. According to Minsky, when expectations of current profits induce a level of investment that is insufficient for the maintenance of full-employment, the reactions of agents will cause expectations to deteriorate and investment to diminish even more. More precisely his approach to this problem rests upon the theory of debt-deflation that he embeds within a framework where expectations interact dynamically with financial structure. The main idea underlying his analysis is that the economy generates harmful disruptive forces created by a generalized flight to liquidity and by the development of deflation.

As was seen in the previous section, Minsky identifies a 'natural tendency' for agents to engage in speculative activities. Speculation takes three forms. First, the holders of capital assets speculate by debt-financing both the investment process and the purchases of capital assets. Second, banks and other financial institutions speculate by modifying their mix of assets and liabilities. Third, firms and households speculate by choosing which financial assets to hold and how to finance such holdings. During a boom the speculative demand for money declines and portfolios become more heavily weighted in capital assets financed by debt. For holders of capital assets this means that increasing proportions of expected cash flows are allotted to the payment of financial commitments. Banks increase their lending activity to the detriment of their holdings of (mainly Government) securities. In addition they increase the scale of their operations although, thanks to an active management of their liabilities, the amount of their liquid reserves remains unchanged. Finally, households and firms replace money with non-monetary financial assets which, from there on, serve as liquid reserves.

When an agent who does not own enough liquid assets is required to honour his or her payment commitments, an increase in monetary interest rates and/or a lack of operating income can persuade him to sell (or to pledge) illiquid assets.[8] However 'the making of position by selling position may be feasible as an isolated incident, but any generalized attempt to make position by selling out position leads to a collapse of asset values' (Minsky, 1991a, p. 162). In reality, according to Minsky, the likelihood of an extensive sale of assets during a depression is high. Indeed increases in the interest rate that signal the incipiency of a crisis lead to less investment and thus to reductions in the aggregate flow of profits. In this context expected profits continue to diminish while liquidity preference increases. A situation of this kind can lead to a liquidity run: firms that cannot meet their payment commitments either from their proceeds or through borrowings must sell off part of their assets.[9] Such sales cause asset prices to collapse, which might turn a recession into an economic depression.[10]

This part of Minsky's theory displays a strong affinity with the approach developed by Irving Fisher in his 1933 article entitled 'The Debt-Deflation Theory of Great Depressions'. This article represents so great a break from Fisher's previous theories that it is not even mentioned by Mark Blaug, whereas Schumpeter valued it highly.[11] In Fisher's article money exerts a strong influence on the dynamics of the main macroeconomic variables, namely production, employment and the rate of profits. This can be explained by the historical context that prevailed in the 1930s. In fact, Fisher's *aggiornamento* is not unrelated to his total surprise at the harshness of the open crisis of 1929. In addition, the measures taken by Roosevelt in the area of banking had proved, by then, to be broadly effective, thereby contradicting the allegations expressed by the supporters of laissez-faire for whom the economy would depart spontaneously from depression, once imbalances had been eliminated. Consequently, Fisher's attempts to integrate monetary and real variables in some of his previous writings became the central theme in a book he published in 1932, of which the 1933 article provides a synthesis, updated in the light of the ongoing recovery.[12]

Fisher's theory can be usefully summed up with the aid of two propositions outlining, first, the reasons for and, second, the consequences of over-indebtedness. As for the first proposition, Fisher adopts a position that is reminiscent of Schumpeter's in the *Theory of Economic Development* (1912). At the outset of the boom there are new investment opportunities (inventions, new products, new markets and new resources) that raise prospects of greater profits. Businesses will then resort extensively to debt issues whenever return rates are greater than the interest rate applied by banks (point 44 of the 1933 article). The resulting over-indebtedness can, however, cause readjustments of over-optimistic expectations, either because of stock exchange scandals (point 47) or as an effect of changes in attitude on the part of claimholders or borrowers (point 24).

More importantly, Fisher's article deals with the sequence that begins with the perception by economic agents of their over-indebtedness. Among the intertwining factors distinguished by Fisher (points 22 to 27) there are several whose interactions may lead to a cumulative depression. At a first stage firms will try to reinstate the structure of their balance sheet by paying back their debts. They will thereby be driven to sell their assets, even at reduced prices, in order to meet their payment commitments and to cover their financial costs. If markets are competitive and all firms adopt a strategy of this kind, prices will actually decline. As a result, notwithstanding the efforts made to diminish the nominal amount of debt, its volume measured in real terms is more likely to increase rather than to decrease: hence a series of new disaster sales by firms striving to meet their commitments – of unchanged nominal value but of greater real value – and to restore their liquidity position. Impressed by the events that took place between 1929 and 1933, Fisher believed this process to be cumulative, rather than self-regulating, in spite of what many authors thought in those days.[13]

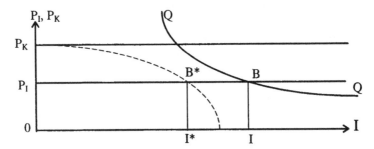

Figure 3.2 Reinstatement of balance sheets (optimistic scenario)

Minsky is one of the first authors to have unearthed this text. Later he constantly referred to it and updated its contents, by taking into account the evolutions he was observing (1975, Chapter 6). According to Minsky, the debt-deflation process Fisher describes is characteristic of two situations (1975, p. 126). In the first one, represented in Figure 3.2, the demand price of capital assets, as determined by the market capitalization of expected profits, is greater than their supply price, but the borrower's risk is so great that investment, OI^*, is lower than the amount permitted by internal funds.

This situation arises from borrowers beginning to view their liability

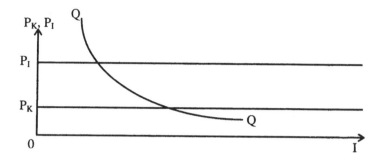

Figure 3.3 The debt deflation (pessimistic scenario)

structures as too risky. Thus the amount of anticipated internal funds, Q-Q, will be used in part to finance investment (OP_IB*I*) and in part to repay outstanding debt or to acquire financial assets ($I*B*BI$). But if the level of investment $I*$ is insufficient to generate the internal flow of funds corresponding to expectations, desired balance sheet reinstatements will not be achieved. Consequently, a deflationary cumulative process will be triggered (ibid.). The diagram in Figure 3.3 illustrates this situation. The depreciation of capital assets is then such that it causes their demand price to fall below their supply price. Investment in this case will tend to zero. All internal funds will serve for repayment of debt, as the main aim of firms and banks will be to clean up their balance sheets.

In the two above-mentioned situations, firms often repay their short-term debt by issuing long-term debts to replace maturing short-term debts (ibid.). In this way the share of their near-term liabilities is reduced, but this funding may tend to maintain, if not increase, long-term rates while short rates may be decreasing. Minsky's conclusion for the economic situations illustrated by the previous diagram is: 'we are in a debt-deflation process. A feedback from the purely financial developments to the demand-for-investment output, and by way of the multiplier to the demand-for-consumption output, takes place. Unemployment and a depression result' (ibid.). In other words, as long as asset prices continue to drop and firms keep on incurring losses, there is no market mechanism that is able to eliminate the imbalances that are instead reinforced.

An interesting aspect of Minsky's approach to macroeconomic fluctuations is that it allows us to distinguish clearly between simple situations of investment slowdown and much more damaging cases of debt-deflation. For Minsky it is the stability or instability of long-term profit expectations and of acceptable liability structures that determine both the degree of seriousness of an economic setback and whether a recession will turn into a depression.

Thus as we saw in Figure 3.1, which depicts a simple setback, shifts in the curves representing the supply price and demand price of investment reflect changes in the variables affecting aggregate supply and demand. However, variables determining long-run expectations remain unaltered. This means that, in spite of variations in realized profits and financial conditions, there are no modifications in current expectations concerning longer-run profits, interest rates and acceptable financial structures. In this case a leftwards shift in the diagram representing the supply and demand curves can be offset by minor changes in the money market conditions, in fiscal policy or in monetary wage rates.

In contrast, in the next two diagrams, the positions of the demand and supply curves reflect the variations in the long-run profit expectations and in the desirable financial structure. Changes in profits, market interest rates, money wages and fiscal policy could sustain income and full employment but would have no immediate effect on supply and demand for investment goods. As Minsky remarks, these two diagrams can be considered as an illustration of the liquidity trap (1975, p. 116). However, the lack of effectiveness of monetary policy described here does not require that the interest rate remain constant when the money supply increases. As was shown previously, even if the interest rate on financial assets continues to fall as the money supply rises, the increase in the capitalization rate applied to capital assets may be insufficient to stimulate investment.

By developing this reasoning, Minsky is in fact questioning the traditionally established market laws. Indeed 'whereas variation in market variables that are determined by "supply and demand" conditions in product, labor, and money markets are effective governors of the rate of investment when long-run expectations are conducive to investment, variations in these same variables are not effective governors of investment once the shift in long-run expectations that occurs with and after a financial crisis has taken place' (1982a, p. 108). Here again approaches assuming endogenous self-regulation of the economic system are those directly targeted by Minsky. The question raised is whether market adjustments induced by a situation of unemployment can affect long-run expectations and create a demand for investment that is great enough to ensure the return to full employment. But 'framing the question in this way demonstrates the impossibility of a definitive answer' (1980, p. 29). Indeed diminishing monetary wages and the interest rate can favour the return to optimistic long-run expectations and thereby to an increase in the demand for investment. Nonetheless, wage and price flexibility in a period of underemployment can also have the reverse effect and increase unemployment. This can occur because deflation, associated with a corresponding decline in realized and expected long-term profits, has a negative effect on investment. It weakens the safety margins of existing financial structures and long-run profit expectations. Consequently, Minsky argues, 'unless we can predict how expectations will be affected, there can be no a priori answer' concerning the reaction of the market to a situation of unemployment (ibid.).

5 CONCLUSION TO PART ONE

Minsky's analysis of financial dynamics leads to three important results. First, Minsky offers analytical support to the position developed by Arrow and Hahn in Chapter 14 of *General Competitive Analysis* (1971). For these authors the proposition, according to which the working of decentralized markets yields a coherent result, has not been demonstrated for an economy where money is represented by contracts created through banking operations and where the purchase of costly and durable assets requires a reliance on profit-seeking financial arrangements. One of the merits of Minsky's approach is precisely to highlight the fact that only an analysis of fluctuations placing money and finance at the forefront of reasoning can explain why the financing of capital assets acquisitions can disturb, from time to time, the 'coherence' of the system.

Second, in contrast to the neoclassical synthesis and to the new classical school, Minsky provides a 'rational theory of macroeconomic incoherence'. Accordingly, when the economy becomes or is in the process of becoming chaotic, the signals received and interpreted by the economy's rational agents – notably entrepreneurs and banks – behave in strange ways.[14] In addition, rational responses (that is, consistent with experience) of agents to market signals create even more incoherence. The financial instability hypothesis makes it clear that nowhere is such behaviour more devastating to the coherence of the economy than in financial markets. This is so because in these markets today's views concerning tomorrow determine payment commitments that fall due both today and tomorrow. That the economic system may be self-regulating is thus an idea that vanishes instantaneously. Smith's invisible hand, to which the neoclassicists are so attached, no longer holds in Minsky's setting where the dynamics of the economy appears to be a multi-dimensional and a non-linear process where past, present and future events are related to each other. In his approach no agent responding to signals by 'intend[ing] only his own gain' acts so as to contribute to 'rendering the annual revenue of the society as great as he can' (Smith, 1776, Book 4, chapter 2). Quite the contrary, as has been underlined, it is very likely that the behaviour of agents may drive the economy towards a situation of even greater instability.

Finally, Minsky's analysis of 'rational incoherence' also opens the way to new approaches to the relations between macroeconomic evolution, economic institutions and economic policy. The most striking implication of the foregoing analysis is the possibility that the processes involved in the natural adjustment of a market economy may be insufficient to counterbalance destabilizing forces. However, notwithstanding his insistence on the highly probable existence of unstable adjustments, Minsky does not in any way predict the disintegration or the complete and definitive collapse of market economies. Rather he suggests that the explanation of the overall stability of post-war market economies requires considering matters that go beyond the price and quantity adjustment process focused upon by the neoclassical synthesis. It is in fact more than likely that other aspects of the economy, which we have not been considered so far, may check the potential dynamics identified by Minsky. In particular, intervention of government and monetary authorities can, as is shown in Part Three, set limits to the endogenous instability of the system.

NOTES

1. The most significant articles are Minsky, 'The Financial Instability Hypothesis: A Restatement' (1978) in *Can It Happen Again? Essays on Instability and Finance* (1982a, pp. 90–116); Minsky (1982b); Chapter 9 of Minsky (1986a). All these works develop ideas already contained in his earlier writings, in particular Minsky (1977). For a more formalized version of the different types of financing structures, see Minsky, (1986, Appendix, pp. 335–41).
2. This diagram draws from Minsky (1975, 1986) and Brossard (1998).
3. See for instance Lavoie (1983, 1985).
4. Dymski and Pollin (1992). See also Crotty (1986 and 1990).
5. In *The General Theory*, Keynes also observes that entrepreneurs' disposition to borrow in the wake of a financial crisis precedes banks' willingness to lend.
6. Minsky (1982a and 1982b, 1986a).
7. See Part Three.
8. That is, the assets that form the 'position' of an agent. Such assets generate an income but are not very marketable. They comprise both the capital assets that firms need in order to produce and the assets held by financial institutions, the market of which is narrow. For a more detailed analysis, see Minsky (1975, pp. 124–7).
9. While the demand for credit may be satisfied when financial institutions increase supply, the demand for cash cannot be satisfied because banks are also searching for cash. Like speculative or Ponzi firms, banks also try to sell off their assets and to borrow reserves. See Minsky (1986a, pp. 216–7 and 1988, pp. 22–8).
10. See Minsky (1975, pp. 124–30). For the time being, we neglect the 'stabilizing' effects of public deficits and the interventions of the role of lender of last resort played by the central bank. This is developed in Part Three.
11. See Blaug (1978). In this book, Blaug provides a careful account of Fisher's contributions to the area of utility theory, interest rates and money. See Schumpeter (1954).
12. See Fisher (1932).

13. We allude, in particular, to Hawtrey (1919, 1928).
14. And also, as we shall see in Part Three, central bankers and government officials.

PART TWO

Modelling the Financial Instability Hypothesis

4. Linear and Non-Linear Models

1 INTRODUCTION

The complexity and the richness of Minsky's analysis, associated with an almost total lack of formalization of the financial instability hypothesis, have not facilitated the understanding of his approach, which largely explains the comparative disregard with which his theory of fluctuations has been considered until recently. As Tobin underlines, 'Minsky does not provide a rigorous formal model, and without one readers cannot judge whether an undamped endogenous cycle follows from the assumptions or not' (1989, p. 106). The emphasis placed on the institutional aspects of economic activity and the utilization of phrases such as 'financial fragility', which economists consider as vague or unclear, have raised the question of whether Minsky's analytical construct is well founded and has led it to be considered as 'beyond the reach of mere algebra'.[1] Admittedly the absence of modelling has sometimes made the consistency of Minsky's arguments seem difficult to check. Indeed, the implications of the interaction that takes place between real and financial factors are closely dependent on the specification of the dynamic structure of Minsky's 'financially sophisticated economies', the shapes of the functions and the values of the parameters describing them, all aspects that appear difficult to take into account without the support of at least some sort of formalization.

In the past ten years some economists have sized up the problem and have endeavoured to propose formalized interpretations of the financial instability hypothesis. The first authors who attempt to do so had a specific aim: to provide a rationale for the potentially destabilizing role of financial variables, thus opposing the position both of the Keynesian synthesis and new classical economics.[2] The essentially pedagogical results of these pioneer works have not been negligible in terms of the clarification they have offered of Minsky's approach. They remain nonetheless open to criticism, owing in particular to the linear nature of the models from which they derive. However, this shortcoming has been considerably overcome with the emergence of the second wave of models, founded on non-linear relations, developed at the end of the 1980s. As we shall see, this second wave of models affords a reinterpretation of the financial instability hypothesis, more in accordance with Minsky's initial text.

2 THE LINEAR MODELS

In the middle of the 1980s a first set of models appeared, aiming to give a formal representation of the financial instability hypothesis. These models exhibit two main features: 1) they highlight the role of monetary and financial variables in the emergence and development of economic fluctuations; 2) their structure is linear.

The model built by Taylor and O'Connel (1985) is the first attempt to formalize the financial instability hypothesis. It has remained a reference for all the subsequent contributions on the subject. As such it deserves particular attention. The analysis of the authors is carried out in two main stages. The first consists in showing how equilibrium is reached in both the market for goods and the market for money. Their main assumptions are the following: 1) businesses rely exclusively on external sources of finance, namely bank loans and share issues; 2) savings are transferred by the banking system towards businesses, in a Kaleckian mode; 3) there exists a strong substitutability between money and shares that governs agents' portfolio choices. This last assumption is crucial.

It is then possible to obtain two IS and LM-type relations: the demands both for investment goods and for money are functions of the interest rate, the current profit rate and the expected profit rate, which represents here the 'state of confidence' prevailing among economic agents. The essential difference with traditional IS-LM models is in the existence of a decreasing LM curve (as modelled in the interest rate - rate of profit diagram) implied by the third assumption of strong substitutability.

The second phase of the analysis consists in bringing to light a 'Minsky crisis'. For this the authors use a system of two linear equations. The first defines the evolution over time of the state of confidence, negatively related to the discrepancy between the current and the 'normal' level of the long-term interest rate. The second one describes the evolution of the money supply to government debt ratio. The dynamical properties of the model then depend crucially on the value of one main parameter: the elasticity of the interest rate in terms of the state of confidence. Mathematically, when this parameter is weakly negative, the linear system of equations depicting the evolution of the economy is globally stable: in particular the trace and determinant of the associated Jacobian matrix are respectively negative and positive. However, if the interest rate elasticity is strongly negative, the trace of the Jacobian can become positive and the system globally unstable. This occurs when substitutability between assets is strong. In economic terms, what we obtain is a cumulative decreasing process of the debt-deflation kind. It takes place in the following way: deterioration in the state of confidence leads to an increase in the interest rate and to a reduction in the rate of profit. Portfolio choices then result in greater holdings of money, which has the effect of accentuating the rise in the interest rate and the fall of the rate of expected profits (and correlatively the drop in prices of capital assets and of shares). And so on.

In contrast to the traditional IS-LM presentations, this model shows that unstable macroeconomic dynamics can emerge, owing to the interaction between the markets for both real and financial assets. More precisely the main contribution of this approach is to highlight an important aspect of the financial instability hypothesis: beyond a certain point (in the present case beyond a certain value of the sensitivity of the interest rate to the state of confidence) the economic system is likely to generate strongly unstable dynamics in the form of debt-deflation and deep depression.

The results of the model thus exhibit an obvious similarity to the findings Minsky obtains in a literary way. However, the model is underpinned by certain assumptions that differ substantially from those formulated by Minsky.[3] In the first place, the linear system of equations defining the dynamics of the model relies on a relationship between the state of confidence and the interest rate that is open to criticism. It is indeed assumed that shifts in confidence depend inversely on the current level of the interest rate. This hypothesis is not clearly grounded, as it seems unlikely that expected profitability might change without agents taking into account the outcomes that have been achieved. In particular, if the interest rate remains at a low and constant level, the model suggests that expected profits are constantly reappraised upwards, since a constant rate of profit will cause the discrepancy between expectations and effective outcomes to always increase further.

The treatment in the model of both the role and the determination of the interest rate is also open to criticism for anyone in search of a formalization of Minsky's analysis. To begin with, the choice of the interest rate as the single and key financial variable seems questionable. It is certain that interest rate variations play no negligible part in triggering a Minsky crisis. Nevertheless, the approach adopted by Taylor and O'Connel consists in replacing Minsky's analysis of the complex process of dynamic interaction between expectations and financial structures with simple interest rate variations. Consequently, the effect on economic instability of the level of businesses' indebtedness and of their payment commitments is not considered. Inevitably this leads to trivialization and greatly impoverishes the analysis, which reduces all the more the capacity of the model to provide a faithful account of Minsky's contribution.

In addition, the increase in the interest rate (at the origin of the change in the state of confidence) is merely assumed; it is given exogenously in the model. As a result, the authors develop a representation that is incompatible with Minsky's analysis of the endogenous money supply, an analysis that lays stress on the active role commercial banks play on both the money and the loans markets, as will be seen later. Thus the Taylor and O'Connel model does not account for an essential aspect of Minsky's approach to financial instability, where not only is the money supply determined endogenously, but the interest rate as well.

To a large extent later works devoted to the modelling of the financial instability hypothesis avoid these criticisms by explicitly taking into account the role Minsky assigns to changes in financial structure and their effects on economic dynamics. The model proposed by Lavoie (1986–87) is one. It aims at specifying the nature of the internal mechanism underlying the financial instability hypothesis. It is essentially formed by three linear equations. The first, drawing from the analyses of Kaldor (1966) and Wood (1975), relates the growth rate of capital positively to the evolution of both the share of profits within national income and the economy-wide indebtedness ratio. Measured by the share of investment financed externally, this ratio is utilized to characterize the degree of vulnerability in the system. The second, borrowed from Weintraub (1978), is an increasing function of the evolution of prices in terms of profits. The third describes a positive link between the nominal interest rate and the inflation rate, resulting from the behaviour both of the rentiers – trying to maintain their purchasing power, and the monetary authorities – reacting to inflationary pressure through increases in the discount rate and open market operations.

The dynamics of this model of financial fragility can be summarized as follows: an investment boom causes an increase in the share of profits and a rise in the indebtedness ratio. As a result the financial system becomes more fragile and inflation accelerates. In turn, greater inflation leads to an increase in the interest rate. Lavoie shows then that higher rates, in a more fragile financial environment, are likely to generate a financial crisis and possibly a debt-deflation process.

The main interest of this very simple model is therefore that it yields two of Minsky's fundamental results: the greater financial fragility of the economy is obtained endogenously as is the concurrent increase in the interest rate. The aim of the model is, however, according to Lavoie himself, an essentially pedagogical one. Obviously it can only provide a reductionist view of Minsky's vision of how financial variables and institutions evolve during the process of increasing fragility. In particular Lavoie attributes the rise in the interest rate to the action of the monetary authorities in response to greater inflation. The undeniable advantage of this explanation is that the increase in the interest rate is no longer an *ad hoc* hypothesis as in the Taylor and O'Connel model. Nevertheless, here again, the analysis of the interest rate centres exclusively on the action of the monetary authorities and remains incomplete with regard to the complexity of the analysis developed by

Minsky. Finally, the analytical setting Lavoie adopts is clearly and basically the same as Taylor and O'Connel's: the explanation of the Minsky crisis is founded on the relation between the rate of profit and the interest rate. This relation is however not crucial for Minsky, since the financial instability hypothesis rests primarily upon the distinction between the price of capital assets and the price of investment goods.

More fundamentally, the main weakness of the Lavoie and the Taylor and O'Connel models stems from the linearity of the equations they contain. As a linear structure precludes the appearance of self-sustained fluctuations, these models do not generate any persistent cycles: trajectories are globally either stable or unstable. As we know, in the absence of exogenous shocks, complex dynamics cannot be obtained in models that do not display non-linearities. Models of this kind thus offer an impoverished view of the conception of economic change developed by Minsky for whom, in contrast, 'the dynamics may lead to explosive growth, implosive decline or complex business cycles rather than sustained exponential growth'.[4]

3 INTRODUCING NON-LINEARITIES AND CHAOS

In the middle of the 1980s economists began formalizing the financial instability hypothesis, using non-linear models and applying the theory of chaos. Ten years or so after the publication of the very first works, the time has come for an examination of these contributions and a comparison with Minsky's research programme. With this in view we start with a brief exposition of the main features of the mathematical analysis of non-linear systems and of the theory of chaos.

3.1 From Non-linearity to Chaos

In 1933 the French physicist, Le Corbeiller, suggested that business cycles might be modelled by means of the non-linear oscillations that physicists had just discovered. However, formal complexity prevented any progress in this area before the 1950s. Only then did some economists – Georgescu-Roegen and Goodwin, in particular – set out to tackle the problem more seriously.

The introduction of non-linearities into macrodynamical models seemed justified from several points of view. In the first place, in linear models regular, self-sustained oscillations appear only for very special values of parameters. For instance, in Samuelson's 1939 model persistent cyclic evolutions (that are neither implosive nor explosive) are only possible for very specific values of the multiplier and the accelerator. In all other cases the model does not have the ability to explain the occurrence of self-sustained fluctuations and to account for the irregular fluctuations found in economic time series where in addition hardly any any damping is observed. This mismatch between empirically observed fluctuations and theoretical results of linear models stems from an unequivocally general property of this type of formalization: its inability to account for persistent fluctuations, i.e. fluctuations that are neither damped nor amplified.

In the second place, in the absence of non-linearities, the instability of a dynamical model is often seen as a shortcoming, for the following reason. In the presence of a locally unstable equilibrium, any small departure from it would be amplified. The system is thus more than likely to become economically non-viable, if only because one or several magnitudes might become negative. Therefore, since we know such phenomena do not occur in the real economy, any model leading to results of this kind should be discarded. There thus exists a well-grounded conviction that unstable equilibria cannot be used to describe economic reality.

When the model is non-linear, the previous reasoning no longer holds. The range of possibilities is richer than simple stability or instability and the model can generate endogenous periodic trajectories. A brief presentation of Goodwin's (1967) model affords a good understanding of the features of the non-linear approach to fluctuations. Drawing from the works of Kaldor, Keynes and Marx, this model is characterized by the great simplicity of its assumptions and the behaviours it portrays. For Goodwin the aim is not to propose a complete and realistic representation of the economy – one that would feature government intervention, money, foreign trade, etc. – but to select two simple, but fundamental, mechanisms of capitalist economies and to show that their interaction is sufficient to yield cycles. With this in mind Goodwin makes a certain number of assumptions: the productivity of workers and their supply of labour increase regularly at constant rates; wage raises are explained by the Phillips curve, that is, they are an increasing function of the rate of employment; workers consume their wages entirely and businesses invest all of their profits.

On these grounds Goodwin obtains a non-linear dynamical system for which the two state variables are the rate of employment (x_t) and the wage share of national income (z_t). The reduced form of the system can then be written as:

$$dz_t /dt = g(x_t, z_t)$$
$$dx_t /dt = h(x_t, z_t)$$

The stationary point of the system, (x^*, z^*), for which there is stability of both the rate of employment $(dx_t /dt = 0)$ and the wage share of national income $(dz_t /dt = 0)$ is such that:

$$x^* = (b + \mu)/a$$

$$z^* = 1 - (\mu + n)v$$

where μ and v are the (constant) growth rates of labour productivity and of labour supply, a and b being two positive constants used to spell out the Phillips relation, assumed here to be linear.

The non-linear system describing the dynamics of the economy can be written as:

$$dz/dt = (x_t - x^*)az_t$$
$$dx/dt = (z^* - z_t)(x_t/v)$$

Thus, depending on the position of x_t with regard to x^* and of z_t with regard to z^*, the share of wages and the rate of employment will vary, positively or negatively, in the positive quadrant of plane (x, z). Starting from some point of the quadrant, the trajectory of the economy has the shape of a single closed orbit around the stationary point, perpetually passing through the starting point, and limited by points (x_{max}, z^*), (x^*, z_{min}), (x_{min}, z^*) and (x^*, z_{max}). The economic interpretation of this cyclical dynamics is very simple. When the share of wages within national income is small, investment, which equates to profits, is large. Therefore growth is strong and the rate of employment high. This evolution is however subject to the constraint of labour resources. Indeed sustained growth will use up the available workforce and the resulting shortage will allow workers to recover their bargaining power over employers. Workers are then in the position to obtain raises. But as the share of wages increases, erosion of investment takes place and growth weakens. A decrease in the rate of employment ensues, while a certain amount of the workforce becomes available. This enables capitalists to pay lower wages, which triggers back the ascending phase of the cycle. Thus the model explains economic fluctuations as resulting from the struggle over income distribution and the confrontation between capitalists and workers.

This model is interesting from a theoretical point of view because the non-linearity of the equations allows cycles to be generated in a completely endogenous fashion. Oscillations here are self-sustained and of constant amplitude. These properties do not require the introduction of repeated exogenous shocks, as in linear models. Besides, equilibrium is unstable, which implies that a disturbance, however small, sets the dynamics into motion. However, despite such instability, the model is realistic: owing to its intrinsic non-linearities, no explosive process occurs but movement is maintained within the limits of an oscillation of constant amplitude (non-obtainable in explosive linear models).

From a more formal standpoint, however, the model is open to criticism. In the first place it is not very robust: relatively small changes in its hypotheses are sufficient to cause the persistence of cycles to vanish. In particular, if decreasing returns are assumed, cycles disappear. Oscillations gradually lose their intensity and the economy moves asymptotically towards a point of stable equilibrium, corresponding mathematically to a node.[5] In the second place, the amplitude of fluctuations depends entirely on the initial position of the economy (i.e., on point of departure (x, z)): once this is known, the economy follows the same closed orbit around the point of equilibrium indefinitely. A corollary is that the economy may not fluctuate at all if, from the beginning, it is in equilibrium. Thus, even if fluctuations are actually endogenous and self-sustained, an element of exogeneity remains in the system, namely the need to set the initial position.

In sum, Goodwinian fluctuations are perpetually on the knife-edge and the introduction of certain behaviours is likely to make the economy sway either towards local stability or local instability. This objection has long since been raised and addressed to models of populations: in this form, they have been judged unsuitable for a realistic description of demographic phenomena. Whatever the merits of the Goodwin model as to its capacity to represent the dialectics of class conflict, its lack of basic stability invests it with the same weakness.

Like biologists, economists have accordingly taken pains to build models that can exhibit 'resistant' fluctuations. The non-linear theory of dynamical systems provides a particularly well-adapted tool, the limit cycle. This is simply a closed orbit towards which all trajectories, coming from all directions, converge, whatever their starting point. Contrary to the Goodwin model which may be qualified as a spurious non-linear model, insofar as it yields qualitatively identical dynamical behaviours whatever the distance separating the starting point from equilibrium, the principle of the limit cycle makes the most of the differences between local and global behaviour caused by non-linearities.

The Poincaré-Bendixson theorem spells out the mathematical conditions for the appearance of a limit cycle.[6] This theorem is very useful in the context of two-dimensional differential equation systems. In a dynamical system of two dimensions (x, y), there will be at least one limit cycle if the following conditions hold: a) the long-run equilibrium is unique and is locally unstable; b) within set (x, y) there exists a closed annular region C that encloses but does not contain the equilibrium point, so that C is not departed from as t increases. To give a rough idea of the intuition underlying this mathematical result, it may be said that the limit cycle results from the confrontation between the attractive great-distance effect of equilibrium and its short-distance repulsive effect. The limit cycle therefore occupies a unique orbit that is not restricted to the immediate neighbourhood of the equilibrium point.

Efforts to analyse economic fluctuations by relying on models exhibiting limit cycles are quite recent. Among the most representative contributions in this area, the Goodwinian models of Jarsulic (1986) and Skott (1989) can be mentioned. Earlier Chang and Smyth had reformulated the Kaldor (1940) model by establishing conditions for local stability and for the existence of limit cycles.[7] Later Torre, Schinasi and Benassy developed models drawing both from Kaldor and from the IS-LM version of Keynes.[8] The cycle they describe is a succession of non-Walrasian equilibria exhibiting labour market disequilibrium. Results are then intuitive enough: if the accelerator is large with regard to the speed of wage adjustment, the model generates a limit cycle. In addition the pace of adjustment and errors in expectations of an adaptive-type also play an important role in the occurrence of endogenous cycles.

The theoretical contribution of these various works, compared with that of previous models, is not to be neglected, not only because cycles appear here for a very large set of parameters (in contrast to the linear models of the Samuelson-type), but also because, whatever the initial conditions, resistant fluctuations arise, whereas they could not in Goodwin's model. These fluctuations are represented by an attractor, the limit cycle, towards which all trajectories are pointing. Yet these models of economic fluctuations are far from giving complete satisfaction. Indeed, asymptotically, the trajectories generated by limit cycle models have shapes that are much too regular. And, as Baumol and Benhabib observed, until quite recently, 'this is pretty much where matters were left, with the work stopping short of introducing explicitly a degree of nonlinearity sufficiently great to generate chaotic behavior' (1989, p. 79).

Consequently, the overt irregularity exhibited by macroeconomic series is still generally attributed to the presence of random shocks disrupting a stable equilibrium. As Sargent notes, only 'if initial conditions of low-order, deterministic linear difference equations are subjected to repeated random shocks of a certain kind', it is possible for 'recurring, somewhat irregular cycles of the kind seemingly infesting economic data' to emerge (1979, pp. 218–9). From this point of view recent business cycle analyses that rely on stochastic processes, such as real business cycles theories, appear undeniably superior to the endogenous approaches. Only they have the capacity, so it seems, to account for the observed irregularity of fluctuations, in strong contrast to deterministic periodical (limit cycle) approaches.

The previous discussion has shown that economic theory involving non-linear dynamics, although it allows self-sustained fluctuations to appear in a completely endogenous way, remains nonetheless in line with the traditional deterministic conception of economic change. This conception implies that the knowledge of initial conditions, or of any one of the points along the time path, allows us to rebuild the entire trajectory of an evolution that is governed by a differential system. Given this deficiency of non-linear models, the use by economists of a new formal tool, deterministic chaos, for the analysis of dynamic phenomena has opened new paths. It is worthwhile briefly reviewing the origins of this mathematical concept.

According to Mandelbrot (1983), the theory of chaos draws from two apparently competing approaches developed at the end of the nineteenth century. The first is the theory of bifurcation, where dynamical equilibria split into two similar equilibria, developed initially by Poincaré (1890) in order to explain the qualitative behaviour of planetary movements when three bodies collide. The second is the study and the building of 'monstrous' sets exhibiting non-integer dimensionalities, initiated by Cantor (1883). This twofold origin explains why most non-linear differential equation systems react to the continuous variation of a parameter by undergoing a series of bifurcations of their equilibria – causing each time the periodicity of their oscillations to double – until a point, called a 'strange attractor', is reached where the equilibrium trajectory exhibits oscillations over a 'monstrous' set of a non-integer dimensionality (Mandelbrot speaks in terms of 'fractal' dimensionality).[9]

The scientific study of chaotic dynamics was developed in many different fields before the uniqueness and the common aspects of the phenomena that were being observed were recognized.[10] Among the most significant contributions to be noted we find Van Der Pol's analysis of the oscillator, the modelling of turbulent climatic dynamics by Lorenz and the study of chaotic dynamics of population in ecological systems by May.[11] The essential idea underlying these different analyses is that chaos is a pathological manifestation of deterministic dynamics. Indeed, only an infinitely precise, therefore inaccessible, knowledge of the initial conditions allows access to the whole trajectory of the system. In other words, whereas in 'standard' forms of dynamics neighbouring final states were associated with neighbouring initial conditions, in situation of chaos the smallest departure from initial conditions is irremediably amplified: however close – though not rigorously identical – two initial situations may be, the two trajectories stemming from them will diverge exponentially over time. This phenomenon is not merely some theoretical curiosity; it actually implies real disasters: knowledge of infinite precision is required for the forecast of the behaviour of chaotic dynamics. Its absence leads to predictions impaired by errors that will grow exponentially over time. The signal representing the dynamics is then characterized by a loss of self-memory: however far back in the past we go, the knowledge of previous states of the system does not allow us to determine how it will evolve in the future. Notwithstanding the problem that chaos raises in practice – the impossibility of making predictions – it has a considerable theoretical advantage: disorderly evolutions, which were formerly required to be reproduced by reliance on stochastic terms, can now be determinated deterministically. As Day and Shafer put it, with chaos, 'nonperiodicity, irregularity, erraticness ... or randomness ... emerges from the underlying structure of relationship' (1985, p. 278).

3.2 Chaos and Modelling Macrodynamics

The very recent character of systematic studies of chaotic dynamics is even more obvious for anyone interested in their economic applications, in full swing today.[12] Pioneering works – drawing mainly from May's paper (1976) – only date back to the beginning of the 1980s with the contributions of Stutzer (1980), Pohjola (1981) and Day (1982). The intrusion of deterministic chaos into numerous fields and, in particular, into economics could not have taken place without the considerable progress accomplished in its study in the 1970s. Chaos, it became apparent then, could arise in extremely simple mathematical systems (Lorenz 1963, May 1976, Feigenbaum 1978). The most frequently referred to example is the logistic curve, representing a unidimensional non-linear dynamical equation including a single parameter, w, of the following type:

$$y_{t+1} = wy_t(1 - y_t) \tag{A}$$

with $y_t \in [0,1]$ and $w \in [0, 4]$. As the logistic equation possesses a single extremum, its graph is labelled a one-humped curve.

Increasing parameter w stretches the graph of the logistic equation upwards. For all $w \in [0,4]$, interval $[0,1]$ of the state variable y is mapped onto itself. Two examples of the logistic equation for different values of w are provided by Figures 4.1a and 4.1b.

The stationary equilibria (or fixed points) of (A), i.e. the values of state variable y for which $y_{t-1} = y_t = y_{t+1} \forall t$, are determined by the intersection of the graph of (A) and the 45° ray. In addition to the origin, the trivial equilibrium point (point y_0), a second stationary equilibrium exists for $y_1 = 1 - (1/w)$.

The questions to be raised then are whether these equilibria are stable and whether the time paths that lead to them are convergent. It is possible to show that the properties of stability and convergence depend on the value taken by parameter w.

For $0 < w \leq 1$, the phase curve lies entirely below the 45° ray in the positive quadrant. Point y_0 is the only equilibrium and it is stable.[13] The phase diagram (i.e. the representation of the dynamics in plane (y_t, y_{t+1})) shows that, in this interval, the dynamics takes the form of a regular contraction of y_t that finally vanishes.

For 1 <$w \leq 3$, y_0 is unstable and y_1 is stable. In fact the dynamics converges towards stationary point y_1, in a regular way (for 1 <$w \leq 2$) or in an oscillatory fashion (for 2 < $w \leq 3$). Beyond $w = 3$, Feigenbaum (1978) shows the existence of a series of critical values for parameter w. For each of these values, a bifurcation occurs that modifies the nature of the attractors of the dynamics. For $w_1 = 3$, stationary state y_1 divides into a stable cycle of two periods (a cycle of order two). For $w_2 = 3.449$, the two-period cycle splits into a four-period cycle. Crossing w_n transforms a (2n - 1)-period cycle into a (2n)-period cycle. The process of bifurcation, i.e. of splitting into two, continues until a particular value of parameter w, the Feigenbaum point, is attained, that is, when $w = w_F = 3.5699...$

Thus, until parameter w reaches this particular value, the economy follows three types of evolutions: 1) a monotonous evolution (without fluctuations) towards a value of y that is either zero or a permanent regime value; 2) an oscillating convergence towards the permanent regime value; 3) a stable cycle of 2, 4, 8, 16,..., 2n periods. In the limiting case, a stable cycle of infinite periodicity makes its appearance.

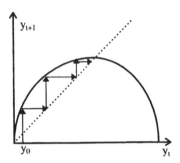 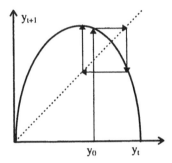

Figure 4.1a Stable dynamics   *Figure 4.1b Unstable dynamics*

Up to this point, however, no chaotic dynamics has emerged (despite the complicated nature of this evolution). Chaos only appears, in the strict sense, beyond the Feigenbaum point. Then the chaotic behaviours that appear for w_F < $w \leq 4$ (beyond this value the study of the function is no longer of any interest) are characterized by the coexistence of cycles of different periods and of 'aperiodic' fluctuations.

As for the chaotic zone, the Li and Yorke theorem shows that for any integer k, there exists an initial condition, y_0, for which a k-period cycle unfolds. Moreover there exists an uncountable and scrambled set S with the following properties: all trajectories with initial conditions in S remain in S; every trajectory in S wanders arbitrarily close to every point in S infinitely often (trajectories are dense in S); no matter how close to each other two distinct trajectories in S come, they eventually wander away (owing to the instability of chaotic trajectories); and every trajectory in S wanders away from any cyclic trajectory, however close it may approximate it for some time (owing to non-periodicity).[14]

In sum, chaos is characterized, for a well-chosen set of initial conditions, by the possible occurrence of cycles of whatever period (including odd-period cycles) and of aperiodic behaviours. It is mainly these results that have given rise to economic applications.

A good illustration of the application of chaotic dynamics to macrodynamical models can be provided by a brief examination of the Day and Shafer model (1985, 1987). This model is generally considered to be the main reference in the application of deterministic chaos to the IS-LM model. The basic idea is to provide an alternative solution to the traditional dynamical analysis where the phase diagram of the differential system takes the form of an IS-LM model. In the latter case the analysis is carried out on the basis of linear or linearized investment and demand for money functions. This amounts to considering only the local properties of equilibrium. Standard results are achieved thus: stability depends on the slopes of the IS and LM curves and the model is stable (unstable) depending on whether the slope of IS is smaller (larger) than that of LM. By contrast, Day and Shafer place emphasis on the non-linear character of the IS-LM model functions. Results do not then depend on some *ad hoc* assumption, applying in particular to the investment function, as with the S-shape function retained by Kaldor (1940). They derive from the nature of the model itself, for given values of parameters. Besides, because it gives rise to chaotic dynamics, their model is not open to the same criticism as models generating limit cycles, since it involves no compulsory periodicity of movement. The model is outlined below.

Given the consumption function, the induced investment function and LM, it is possible to obtain a dynamical equation only involving income. If in addition a Robertson-type lag is introduced, a first difference equation of the following type is obtained: $Y_{t+1} = \theta\,(Y_t;\ \mu;\ M;\ A)$ where M is the equilibrium quantity of money and μ a parameter measuring the intensity of induced investment. When $\mu = 0$, the model only makes room for autonomous spending denoted A; when $\mu > 0$, induced investment differs from zero. Total investment is thus given by: $A + \mu I\,(r,\ Y)$, where Y stands for income and r for the equilibrium interest rate. It is well established that the solution to a difference equation of this non-linear type is very sensitive to the *ad hoc* lag structure introduced. This is one of the main limits to this way of proceeding. Day (1987) argues that this is, however, the normal price to be paid when the just as *ad hoc* assumption, namely that adjustment is instantaneous, inherent in continuous-time models, is dropped. Without going in its detail, let us note that the main idea here is the following: when μ increases and induced investment is raised, the curve representing aggregate demand exhibits a more pronounced hump, which gives rise to a set of endogenous cycles of increasing periods (2, 4, 8,...). This sequence converges towards a value, $\mu*$, where function θ satisfies the conditions, stated by Li and Yorke, required to ensure the existence of a chaotic dynamics.

These results lead to the two following observations. First, the irregular fluctuations that arise are induced by the intrinsic properties of the Keynesian model and do not require the real exogenous shocks that are characteristic of stochastic cycle models. Second, the exploitation of the capacity the model has to generate complex dynamics, simply and for a wide array of parameters, sheds new light on the possibilities models of this kind can offer. In particular, in spite of the virulent critiques the post Keynesian approach has formulated against the IS-LM synthesis, there is a striking similarity between the results we have here and the conception of dynamics developed by the post-Keynesian theory. For Minsky, in particular, the endogenous dynamics of market economies is not 'necessarily nice: monotonic explosive, explosive amplitude cycles and even chaotic cycles are possible paths through time'.[15]

The post-Keynesian authors have, however, been right in noting that this IS-LM formulation does not provide an altogether satisfactory setting for the modelling of fluctuations that display the main features implied by Minsky's financial instability hypothesis. While extremely rich, the dynamics generated by the introduction of non-linearities is not founded on the interconnection between real accumulation and the variation of producers' indebtedness, highlighted in the linear Minsky-type models studied in the previous section.

4   THE FINANCIAL INSTABILITY HYPOTHESIS AND CHAOTIC DYNAMICS

The recent models proposed by Skott provide a tentative synthesis between the linear Minsky-type analyses of financial instability and the formalizations in terms of chaotic dynamics.[16] To a large extent Skott's works overcome the shortcomings of both these approaches. The models he develops describe the main mechanism underlying the financial instability hypothesis whereby, during periods of expansion and financial 'tranquillity', the financial behaviour of decision-makers tends to become increasingly risky, which is precisely what increases the fragility of the system. It is thus assumed that changes in financial behaviour, in fragility, depend on the current level of the system's tranquillity. Accordingly Skott proposes to formalize Minsky's analysis of economic fluctuations by using two indicators: F represents the degree of financial fragility; T denotes the degree of financial tranquillity.

Such hybrid indicators, and their adoption in the place of the more usual financial parameters, reflect Skott's willingness to offer a more faithful account of the multidimensionality of the financial aspects underlying Minsky's theory of financial instability. It is, however, necessary to provide a precise definition of what these complex indicators stand for. Fragility refers to the financial system and to the state it is in. The financial system is fragile if small disruptions – such as an unanticipated drop in income or an unforeseen rise in the interest rate – make it difficult, if not impossible, for a significant percentage of agents to meet their contractual obligations. Thus, an increase in financial commitments in proportion to expected cash flows, by intensifying agents' vulnerability to shocks, is an indicator of greater fragility. Given that an agent's default is likely to have repercussions on the financial situation of his or her creditors, the fragility of the system is affected by the whole network of financial commitments linking businesses, households, financial institutions and the public sector. The form of the network depends on the kinds of relationships that develop between private agents, the regulation that applies to financial institutions as well as the more general influence of economic policy.[17] From this perspective strong levels of indebtedness and the development of Ponzi finance, as well as the laxity of constraints affecting the activities of thrift institutions at the beginning of the 1980s, are typical instances that gave rise to increased fragility.

Development of financial fragility should be distinguished from the effective outbreak of a crisis: a fragile system is not necessarily synonymous with a lack of tranquillity. Financial commitments are entered into on the basis of expectations that can prove to be either well-founded or not. Tranquillity – the capacity of agents to meet their commitments – depends on realized cash flows and on the amounts of contractual repayments. It is thus the result of the interaction between real and financial factors. It is at its minimum level during those financial crises that are the most acute, characterized by debt-deflation and/or the collapse of large financial institutions. Apart from these extreme cases, variations in the degree of tranquillity are also observed during more 'normal' periods: rates of default and of bankruptcy, in particular, clearly appear as indicators of lack of tranquillity.

These interpretations of fragility and financial tranquillity invite two comments. First, even though these hybrid indicators cannot be defined as precisely as the more usual parameters (like the debt ratio or the interest rate), it is possible to provide definitions for them that are operational for the empirical analyses of financial instability.[18] Wolfson, in particular, builds hybrid indicators of variations of tranquillity and fragility for the American economy between 1946 and 1987 that he utilizes in econometric regressions linking tranquillity to various measures of fragility.[19] Second, as stated by Skott, 'the focus on a single well-defined element of the financial system – and the exclusion of other aspects of the system – would need to be justified, and the constant evolution of the financial system makes it especially difficult to provide any such justification' (1992, p. 8). The formalizations of Minsky's theory examined previously, centring on the usual economic variables, therefore appear to be particular cases of the more general model, based on scalar representations of fragility and tranquillity, that Skott proposes. In particular the 'state of confidence' variable that Taylor and O'Connel make use of in their model corresponds to Skott's 'fragility' (as forms of fragile finance are more likely to be set up when forecasts are 'confident'), while the interest rate used by earlier authors can be considered as an indicator of lack of 'tranquillity' in the sense of Skott. Examination, however, of the way these financial variables are related to the rest of Skott's model shows that sharp differences exist between his analysis and the one underlying the Minsky-type linear models considered so far. A study of the main features of the formalizations used by Skott will substantiate this assertion.

Thus Skott proposes a formalization of Minsky's financial instability hypothesis in a first model (1992, pp. 12-17). The analysis is carried out in discrete time; investment and saving functions are linear. A first relation describes the endogenous evolution of fragility and tranquillity:

$$F_{t+1} - F_t = T_t \tag{4.1}$$

In accordance with the way Minsky views financial behaviour, this equality implies that variations of fragility depend on the degree of tranquillity: in the absence of financial difficulties, agents are more sanguine and resort to riskier forms of financing. A second relation defines how tranquillity is determined:

$$T = A\sigma + f(F) \tag{4.2}$$

where σ denotes the actual output to capital ratio, Y/K.[20] This equality accounts for the fact that financial difficulties ensue from lack of correspondence between the optimism that has motivated the adoption of certain forms of financing and actual outcomes. Thus T depends positively on the rate of profit ($A > 0$) as well as on financial fragility. The shape of relation f linking T and F is specified below. As for the savings function, it is simply determined as follows:

$$S/K = s\sigma \tag{4.3}$$

where *s*, representing the (average and marginal) propensity to save, can be interpreted as a weighted average of propensities to save on wages and profits. Finally the investment function allows for the influence of fragility and tranquillity. It is defined by relation:

$$I / K = g(\sigma, F, T) = a\sigma + bF + cT + d \tag{4.4}$$

In this linear specification of the investment function, the rate of utilization, tranquillity and fragility have a positive effect on accumulation: *a*, *b* and *c* are positive. Actually, as Skott shows, in the general case the relation between accumulation and fragility is not linear (1992, pp. 30–34). Indeed, during 'normal' periods, an increase in fragility – relaxation in prudential norms for financial structures – stimulates accumulation. This positive relation may however turn round in periods of crisis: weak levels of utilization rates and/or of the degree of tranquillity may involve a negative response of investment to a rise in fragility. Also to be noted: the linear form of the investment function excludes the possibility of an inversion of the sign of g_F as σ or T varies, a simplification that does not however lead to any significant modification in the dynamics generated by the model. As Skott demonstrates, the non-linearities between accumulation and *F* only reinforce the results obtained (ibid.).

The equilibrium value of σ for which $I/K = S/K$ is given by:[21]

$$\sigma = [bF + cf(F) + d] / (s - a - cA) \tag{4.5}$$

By combining equation (4.1) with equations (4.2) and (4.5), we have:

$$F_{t+1} = F_t + A[bF_t + cf(F_t) + d] / (s - c - a)$$

which can be written more compactly as:

$$F_{t+1} = \alpha_1 F_t + \beta_1 f(F_t) + \gamma_1 \tag{4.6}$$

where $\alpha_1 > 0$, $\beta_1 > 0$, and $\gamma_1 = Ad / (s-c-a)$. Properties of the dynamical system represented by (4.6) depend on the shape of function *f*. Although the nature of the two financial variables makes it difficult to construct a simple functional form describing the relation between *T* and *F*, it is nevertheless, possible to afford a rationale for a concave representation of function *f*. In fact, tranquillity is insensitive, in Minsky's analysis, to variations in financial behaviour, as long as a reasonable margin of safety is maintained. It is therefore relevant to assume that the relaxation of the financial constraint, which has a given impact on accumulation, might have a greater effect on tranquillity in a fragile system than in a robust financial environment. In particular, marginal changes in indebtedness will affect to a lesser extent the risk of bankruptcy of robust businesses (in Minsky's words, of those engaged in hedge finance) than that of firms whose ratios of financial commitments to expected profits are high (of those engaged in speculative or Ponzi finance).

The non-linearity of function f may be specified by way of a quadratic function:

$$f(F) = BF - CF^2 + D, \qquad (4.7)$$
$$C > 0,$$

from which it follows that:

$$F_{t+1} = \alpha_2 Ft + \beta_2 F^2_t + \gamma_2, \qquad (4.8)$$

with $\alpha_2 = \alpha_1 + \beta_1 B$, $\beta_2 = -\beta_1 C < 0$, and $\gamma_2 = \gamma_1 + \beta_1 D$. It is then possible to study the dynamics generated by this non-linear difference equation. If function f in equation (4.7) is concave, and if either:

a) equation (4.8) has two stationary solutions, $F^* < F^{**}$, and

(i) at $F = F^*$ we have $dF_{t+1} / dF_t < -1$, and

(ii) $F_{t+1} (F^{max}) < F^*$ where $F^{max} = max \, F_{t+1} (F_t)^{22}$

or:

b) equation (4.8) has a single solution F* and

(i) at $F_t = F_t^*$ we have $dF_{t+1}/ dF_t < -1$, and

(ii) the function linking F_{t+1} to F_t has a global maximum,

then equation (4.8) gives rise to regular cycles or to chaotic trajectories. Figures 4.2 to 4.4 illustrate some of the dynamics generated by the system, depending on the more or less pronounced hump of the phase curve depicting the quadratic equation.

Figure 4.2 depicts the situation where $dF_{t+1}/dF_t > -1$ for $F_t = F^{**}$: fragility monotonously converges towards stable equilibrium value F^{**}.

When the slope of the curve at F^{**} evolves in such a way that $dF_{t+1}/dF_t < -1$, equilibrium F^{**} becomes locally unstable. When the slope becomes steeper, the diagram of bifurcations exhibits a set of endogenous cycles of increasing periods (2, 4, 8...) up to the point where three-period cycles appear. This, in compliance with the Li and Yorke theorem, induces chaotic dynamics, i.e., aperiodical and bounded trajectories (because $F(F^{max}) > F^*$). This type of oscillation is illustrated in Figure 4.3.

A steeper slope of the curve implies that $F (F^{max}) < F^*$: fluctuations are no longer bounded and the system exhibits a cumulative downward divergence. This situation is illustrated by Figure 4.4.

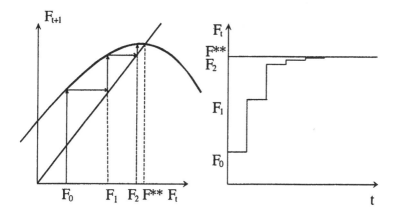

Figure 4.2 Monotonic convergence

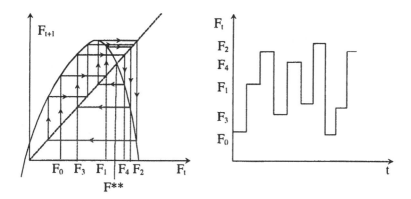

Figure 4.3 Chaotic dynamics

In sum the non-linearities of the relation between fragility and tranquillity imply that in spite of the simplicity of the model, the economy can generate behaviour that is akin to Minsky's conception of economic evolution. In particular trajectories illustrated by Figures 4.3 and 4.4 emulate Minsky's vision according to which 'the endogenous dynamics of market economies [may lead to] monotonic explosive, explosive amplitude cycles and even chaotic cycles'. [23]

Skott recognizes, however, that this model is open to criticism in one essential respect. Even though the assumptions he retains do not appear implausible, the non-linearities focus exclusively on the financial variables.

Now, the complex and multidimensional nature of these variables makes it difficult to provide them with a well-defined functional form.

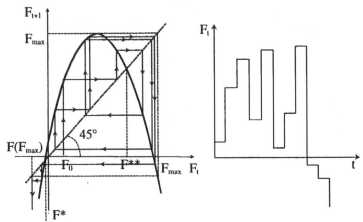

Fig. 4.4 : Cumulative divergence

Therefore, the introduction of non-linearities – crucial to the dynamics of the system – in terms of these variables can be considered as non-satisfactory. This has led Skott to propose a different model (1992, pp. 17–23). Thus in his 'Kaldor-Minsky model' non-linearities no longer apply to rather vague financial indicators but to well-defined variables related to the real sector.

The starting point of this new formalization is Kaldor's 1940 model of business cycles. This model was one of the first attempts made in dynamic economics to study the effects of non-linearities and, for many commentators, it is the first endogenous business cycle model.[24] As we know, Kaldor introduced non-linearities in his savings and investment functions and assumed that both the level of output and the size of the capital stock influenced savings as well as investment. Algebraically, using the same notations as before, the general form of the Kaldor model is given by the following equations:

$$S = S(Y, K) \tag{4.9}$$

$$I = I(Y, K) \tag{4.10}$$

The usual assumption with regard to the adjustment process that takes place in the case of disequilibrium is made, namely that income reacts positively to the excess demand in the goods markets. Thus:

$$\dot{Y} = [I(Y, K) - S(Y, K)], \lambda > 0 \tag{4.11}$$

Finally we have:

$$\dot{K} = I \tag{4.12}$$

The system formed by equations (4.9) to (4.12) can be reduced to a one-dimensional differential equation. For that it is sufficient to reintroduce the output to capital ratio, or rather its evolution over time, in the form of its logarithmic derivative $\hat{\sigma} = \dot{\sigma}/\sigma$, and to assume that the savings and investment functions are homogeneous of degree one in output and capital. Under these assumptions, and after several simple transformations, the system reduces to:

$$\hat{\sigma} = (\lambda/\sigma)[g(\sigma) - h(\sigma)] - g(\sigma) \tag{4.13}$$

where $\sigma = Y/K$, as previously, and g and h are now defined as: $g(\sigma) = I(\sigma,1) = I/K$ and $h(\sigma) = S(\sigma,1) = S/K$.

Thus defined, the system does not generate persistent cycles, as equation (4.13) implies that σ converges asymptotically to some equilibrium value σ^*. This means that the economy converges towards a steady growth path. In itself this result is interesting. As it has been shown in other works, restrictive and often not very convincing hypotheses are necessary in order to obtain persistent fluctuations in Kaldor's model.[25] In the present case merely making the simple assumption that the savings and investment functions are homogenous of degree one, an entirely acceptable hypothesis, one would think, is sufficient to preclude self-sustained fluctuations, of the limit cycle-type, from arising.

Let us see how the introduction within the analysis of the two Minsky-type variables, F and T, can modify this conclusion. For that it is sufficient to rewrite the investment function in the general form adopted previously, that is:

$$I/K = g(\sigma, F, T); \ g_\sigma > 0, \ g_F > < 0, \ g_T > 0 \tag{4.10a}$$

In accordance with the previous discussion on non-linearities, we assume that financial variables F and T are incorporated in a linear fashion into the investment function. A second assumption is that, in line with Kaldor's model, investment is depicted by an S-shaped function, ϕ, of σ, which also depends on F and T. Thus we have $I/K = \phi(\sigma) + bF + cT$. However, contrary to Kaldor, Skott retains a linear savings function of the form $S/K = s\sigma$, as in the previous model. In continuous time (4.1) can be expressed as $\dot{F} = T$ and, rewriting (4.2), we have $T = T(F,r) = T(F,\sigma)$, where T is assumed to be linear in both F and σ. Having made these special assumptions, and using the results already obtained, the dynamical system of our Kaldor-Minsky model can be spelled out as follows:

$$\dot{F} = T = A\sigma - BF \qquad (4.14)$$

$$\dot{\sigma} = (\lambda / \sigma) [\phi(\sigma) + (b - cB) + (cA - s)\sigma] - \phi(\sigma) - (b - cB)F - cA\sigma \qquad (4.15)$$

For 'large' values of the adjustment parameter, λ, the $\hat{\sigma} = 0$ locus takes the form depicted by Figures (4.5a) and (4.5b), respectively for $b - cB > 0$ and $b - cB < 0$.[26]

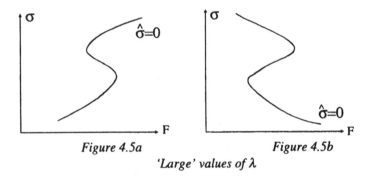

Figure 4.5a   Figure 4.5b

'Large' values of λ

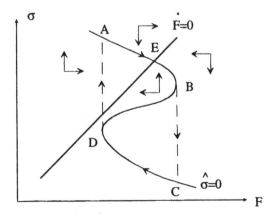

Figure 4.6 A single-rotation cycle

If $b - cB > 0$, graphic analysis of system (4.14)–(4.15) brings to light the possible existence of multiple equilibria (that is, points of intersection between the increasing straight line for which $\dot{F} = 0$ and the $\hat{\sigma} = 0$ locus).

These belong to two categories: locally stable equilibria, on the one hand, and saddlepoints, synonymous with unbounded divergence, on the other. Therefore, this configuration does not allow cyclical dynamics to emerge in this economy.

However, various reasons lead Skott not to retain this first possibility and to insist on the case where $b - cB$ is negative. Indeed, as he explains, the existence of upper limits on the output-to-capital ratio suggests that increasing fragility cannot ultimately be offset by improved utilization: some point exists where an increase in fragility will affect tranquillity adversely. With a linear specification of the functional relation between T and F, this implies that $b - cB$ in equation (4.15) must be negative. In this case two different dynamical forms can emerge. One or the other arises, depending on two factors: the location of the point where curves $\dot{F} = 0$ and $\hat{\sigma} = 0$ intersect, and the level reached by adjustment parameter λ.

Let us now consider the extreme case where λ is very large (where $\lambda \rightarrow \infty$), an assumption whereby σ becomes a very 'fast' variable and F a 'slow' variable. Two main configurations are then to be distinguished. They can be examined quickly by referring to Figures 4.6 and 4.7.

Equilibrium points north-west of B are characterized by a high degree of tranquillity (profitability is great with regard to financial commitments) and agents are induced to resort to more risky financial arrangements: a decreasing movement ensues until critical point B is reached. Similarly equilibria south-east of D are situations of financial turbulence (profitability is relatively weak in proportion to commitments) that urge agents to adopt more prudent financial schemes and to move towards point D. Let us assume first that the long-period equilibrium is locally stable. Figure 4.6 shows that the point where the two curves intersect is located on one of the downward-sloping segments of the $\hat{\sigma} = 0$ locus. A small exogenous disturbance of equilibrium E, if the disturbance is very small, will cause the system to return to E fairly rapidly, as implied by the dynamics of F. However, once F has increased to the point where B is crossed, a 'catastrophe' occurs and profitability σ jumps down to the lower branch of $\hat{\sigma} = 0$.[27] A slow movement is initiated until bifurcation point D is reached where another catastrophe occurs and where σ jumps back to the upper branch. Gradually σ will move back to equilibrium E, at which point the story ends. A 'cycle' thus occurs with only one single rotation initiated by the initial exogenous shock. Another configuration is, however, possible. It appears if the dynamical system is modelled so as to make the long-run stationary equilibrium locally unstable, i.e. located on the upward-sloping portion of the $\hat{\sigma} = 0$ locus. In this case the system generates persistent and entirely endogenous cyclical fluctuations, as illustrated in Figure 4.7.[28]

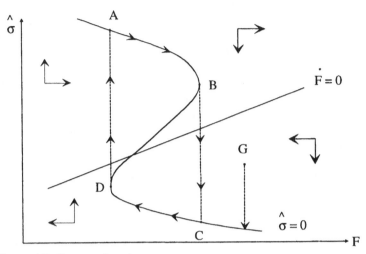

Figure 4.7: Perpetual cycles

As can be seen, starting from some arbitrary point G, the economy jumps (almost) vertically onto the $\hat{\sigma} = 0$ locus. The dynamics of the 'slow' variable F makes the economy move upwards, along the lower segment of the curve until a catastrophe takes place in point D and the economy is projected onto point A. From there onwards, fragility increases and the system evolves downwards along the higher segment of the curve. In point B a new catastrophe happens, characterized by a collapse of the economy and a drop to point C, on the lower segment of the curve. Thus we have perpetual cycles along points A, B, C and D. This final result is interesting, especially if we refer to the previous discussion of the simple non-linear Kaldorian model. When it comes to modelling the Minsky cycle, it appears clearly then that in Skott's, as in Minsky's model, instability – here in the form of potentially persistent endogenous fluctuations – does not result from disturbances arising in the real sphere, but from the interaction between the behaviour of investors and their financial structure.

CONCLUSION

The analysis developed in this chapter has shown that the financial instability hypothesis helps us to understand why market economies do not enjoy steady growth: the interaction between financial factors and long-run investment behaviours intensifies the economy's fragility and breeds irregular and endogenous dynamics. We have examined several macrodynamical models aiming at formalizing this central idea of Minsky's theory. The main characteristic of these models is that they embed simple financial variables (interest rates and indebtedness ratios) or more complex ones (indicators of fragility and of financial tranquillity) into standard macroeconomic frameworks. We have provided evidence that, under certain circumstances, these models produce fluctuations analogous to those imagined, but not modelled, by Minsky. Financial factors are indeed capable, in systems that are otherwise stable, of being at the origin of unstable endogenous dynamics. Exclusively divergent in linear models, such dynamics can be more complex (and therefore closer to what Minsky originally had in mind) in non-linear models and can lead to periodical trajectories (limit cycles) and aperiodic (chaotic) time paths.

Lately, economists have nonetheless produced models of financial instability founded on a methodology differing quite strongly from the one underlying the works examined so far. It is this more recent approach that we study in the next Chapter.

NOTES

1. See, for example, Friedman and Laibson (1989, p. 139) for whom 'Minsky's hypothesis is typically stated with less than explicit grounding in the theory of economic behavior'. Quoted from Taylor and O'Connel (1985 p. 871).
2. The Keynesian synthesis and the real business cycles theory focus exclusively on the role played by money, thereby overlooking all other aspects related to the financial sphere. Moreover the successive versions of monetarism, from Friedman to Lucas, contend that a variation in the quantity of money can only give rise to transitory fluctuations of economic activity.
3. Conversely the assumption of strong substitutability between assets retained in the model, because it appears to be compatible with the interest shown by Minsky (for instance in Minsky 1989b) in the emergence of 'money manager capitalism', does not seemingly need to be questioned.
4. Ferri and Minsky (1989, p. 124).
5. See Samuelson (1971–72).
6. A rigorous textbook presentation of the Poincaré-Bendixon theorem can be found in Hirsh and Smale (1974), Chapter 11, to which the interested reader is referred.
7. Chang and Smyth (1971).
8. Torre (1977); B. Schinasi (1981); Benassy (1984).
9. Feingenbaum (1978); Ruelle and Takens (1971).
10. Gleick (1987) provides a survey of these contributions.
11. Van Der Pol (1927); Lorenz (1963); May (1976).
12. As evidenced by the publication of a great number of recent articles and books. For a complete list of references, see the book by Lorenz (1989), as well as the article by Baumol and Benhabib (1989).
13. The second equilibrium is negative and therefore does not belong to admissible set $\{y_t \in [0,1]\}$.

14. For a more precise statement of this theorem, see Guckenheimer and Holmes (1983, p. 311).
15. Ferri and Minsky (1989, p. 137).
16. Skott (1992). A slightly different version of this model is proposed by Skott (1995).
17. This model thus partly incorporates the 'institutional dynamics' of Minsky's theory (see Chapter 7), generally neglected in non-linear modelling of the financial instability hypothesis.
18. Precise definitions are difficult to work out, mainly because financial innovation and institutional changes imply that these kinds of multidimensional indicators will be undergoing constant change.
19. Wolfson (1990). Wolfson does not use the term 'tranquillity', but his general concept of 'financial instability' is inversely related to Skott's definition of tranquillity.
20. Skott adopts a standard Kaleckian approach. He assumes a constant mark-up. Given the fixed technological coefficient, rate of profit r is proportional to the rate of utilization of capital u: $r = \pi u \; \sigma^* = \pi\sigma$, where π represents the (constant) share of profits and σ^* the maximum, technically determined output-capital ratio.
21. Under the assumption that $s > a + CA$, corresponding to the standard stability assumption made in short-period Keynesian models: $dS/dY > dl/dY$.
22. Condition (i) is associated with the existence of two stationary solutions and the concavity of function f ensures the existence of the global maximum F^{max}
23. Ferri and Minsky (1989, pp. 124 and 137).
24. Gabisch and Lorenz (1989, p. 129).
25. See Skott (1989), Chapter 3. See Flaschel (1985) for a critique of the goods market adjustment process and also Chang and Smyth's reformulation of the Kaldor model. Chang and Smyth show in particular that Kaldor's assumptions as to the signs and relative magnitudes of the different partial derivatives of I and S are not sufficient to ensure exclusively cyclical behaviour.
26. A situation which, as underlined by Skott, corresponds to the implicit assumptions of the standard short-period macroeconomic equilibrium models. If λ does not satisfy this standard condition, the $\hat{\sigma} = 0$ locus is monotonic and there is a single equilibrium which is either a saddle point or a stable node (or a centre). See Skott (1989) Chapter 6, for a more detailed analysis of the implication of the standard approach for the output adjustment speed.
27. The catastrophe theory is one of the branches of the recent developments in dynamical systems. The aim of this theory is the analysis and classification of sudden jumps – or catastrophes – in the behaviour of dynamical systems. Introductions to the theory are to be found for example in Saunders (1980), Arnold (1984). See also Gabisch and Lorenz (1989, pp. 202–15). Also to be noted is that we probably owe Varian (1979) the first application of the mathematical theory of catastrophes to economics and, more specifically, within the framework of the familiar Kaldor model.
28. If a less extreme assumption is made as to the level of λ (i.e. if we simply suppose high values for λ), persistent fluctuations take the form of a limit cycle (a dynamic path without sudden jumps) circling around a locally unstable equilibrium.

5.   New-Keynesian Models

1 INTRODUCTION

The analysis in terms of non-linear aggregate models examined in the previous chapter is not widely accepted today by authors seeking to model economic fluctuations. This relative disregard is mainly due to the devastating effects of the criticism voiced by supporters of the standard theory of business cycles, that is, the theory of equilibrium cycles and the theory of real business cycles. The essential point of this criticism, developed initially by Lucas (1976), is that none of the aggregate approaches of fluctuations comply with the basic premises of microeconomic theory. Accordingly, what is proposed instead is an analysis of fluctuations founded on the three following assumptions: 1) markets are competitive and always clear; 2) agents act according to their individual interests; 3) expectations are rational as asserted by new classical economists. Non-linear aggregate models of financial instability, notwithstanding their interesting findings, cannot on logical grounds provide a fully suitable alternative to the stochastic theories of the cycle worked out on the basis of individual optimizing behaviours. To this objection new-Keynesian economics offers, so it seems, an adequate response insofar as it has the merit, while taking into account Lucas's critique of the Keynesian macroeconomic theory of fluctuations, of describing a world characterized by Keynesian-like outcomes, or rather by those post-Keynesian economists define as such: '1) the creation and persistence of unemployment even though all units are maximizing [and] 2) the possibility that the dynamics are chaos inducing' (Ferri and Minsky, 1989, p. 129).

The present chapter deals with this particular form of Keynesianism and its main purpose is to show how new-Keynesian economists have succeeded, within an analytical and methodological setting that differs strongly from the post-Keynesian framework, in establishing results analogous in many ways to the findings obtained by building on the financial instability hypothesis. The analysis is conducted in two stages. First, we examine the main new-Keynesian models seeking the connection between economic fluctuations and the operation of capital markets. Second, we focus our attention on 'more Minskyan' models. These works, without being developed within a strictly new-Keynesian setting, rely nonetheless on concepts developed within this approach in order to propose models that can account for the financial instability hypothesis.

2 NEW-KEYNESIAN ECONOMICS AND FINANCIAL INSTABILITY

2.1 Introduction

New-Keynesian economics emerged as the result of a merger between isolated contributions. What the authors of these contributions had in common was their denial of the robustness of the conclusions reached by new classical economists, be it the existence of a natural level of unemployment and activity, the non-persistence of shocks or the ineffectiveness of economic policy. Their approach has consisted in adding frictions, asymmetries or other imperfections to the basic new classical models. The unity of new-Keynesian economics has been achieved on the basis of the recognition of a few stylized facts: the existence of unemployment, of rationing and disequilibria, the persistence of cycles. The aim was to develop a form of macroeconomics consistent with these stylized facts.

In contrast to new classical economists, for whom macroeconomics must have Walrasian microeconomic foundations, new-Keynesian economists have sought to adapt microtheory to macrotheory. In fact the microeconomic foundations they refer to have been developed within the economics of information. Uncertainty in the form of imperfect information no longer occurs in the form of exogenous disturbances appearing in the structural equations of the model, but is endogenized instead. It either concerns the characteristics of the commodities traded in the different markets (the capital, goods or labour markets) or relates to the actions undertaken by individual agents.

Accordingly, the most striking feature of new-Keynesian economics is its critical stance towards new classical economics. However, this criticism has less to do with the rational expectations hypothesis *per se* than with the other assumptions also made in most of the rational expectations literature. New-Keynesian economists actually insist that the conclusions reached by new classical economics with regard to the efficiency of markets do not depend fundamentally on the rational expectations hypothesis. In particular, in papers co-authored by Greenwald and Neary, Stiglitz shows that the presence of rational expectations neither entails market equilibrium efficiency, nor rules out unemployment and self-amplification of small disturbances (Greenwald and Stiglitz, 1986). In the words of Greenwald and Stiglitz, 'new Classical economics obtains results similar to old Classical economics, not because it has added a new set of insights, derived from rational expectations, but because it has retained an old set of assumptions, concerning perfect markets and market clearing' (1992, p. 70). Amidst this 'old set of assumptions', one is that individuals' knowledge of the characteristics of the goods and services they trade is perfect. Another assumption is that each agent is able to observe the actions undertaken by the other agents, as in standard microeconomics.

The question raised by new-Keynesian economists is whether, when rational expectations are assumed, it is also necessary to suppose that all agents have access to the same information. In their opinion, that agents form rational expectations is a straight consequence of the axiom that choices are made rationally. In contrast, that all agents have the same information is not. That is why the idea that agents may have asymmetric access to information is frequently seen as the true starting point of new-Keynesian economics and, more specifically, of the whole family of analyses drawing from the works of Stiglitz, sometimes designated as 'informational Keynesianism' (Arena and Torre, 1992, p. 31).

Asymmetric information means either that it is very difficult if not impossible for an individual to ascertain the quality of a good or service he plans to acquire, or that it is very costly if not impracticable to monitor another agent's actions. These are problems that can emerge in many situations: when someone purchases a used car; when an employer hires workers of different skills; when loans are granted to firms of various types; when a company's shareholders entrust managers with the task of making profits.

When information is not uniformly distributed among agents, problems of two sorts might arise: 'adverse selection' and 'moral hazard.' Adverse selection refers to a situation where goods and services of different qualities are being exchanged and where, while the agents on one side of the market can make direct observations, those on the other side have at best a statistical knowledge of those qualities (for instance, a knowledge of their probability distribution). Within this setting the actions undertaken by the better-informed agents are likely to have undesirable effects, as they may have an unfavourable influence on the quality of the goods that are actually delivered. As we shall see, the efforts made by the worse-informed agents to overcome such effects may in turn produce serious allocative distortions.

The problem of moral hazard characterizes two situations. On the one hand, if two agents enter an agreement, but the actions of one of the agents are not observable by the other, the problem that arises is one of moral hazard with hidden action, since the former can derive some benefit from the situation by behaving in a way that improves his own welfare to the detriment of the latter's. On the other hand, if two agents enter an agreement, but a particular state of nature that is perceivable to only one of the two agents occurs only later, what occurs then is a problem of moral hazard with hidden knowledge. The better-informed agent may then decide not to reveal the true outcome of the state of nature and again take advantage of the situation, thereby impairing the other agent's welfare.

Although the problems of moral hazard and adverse selection can both appear in a context of asymmetric information, they are fundamentally different. Adverse selection is a problem that occurs *ex ante*. It concerns a situation where one of two sets of individuals has acquired prior knowledge of the outcome of a state of nature (for instance, the quality of the good that is traded). Consequently, the non-informed individuals can try either to influence the mix of the agents with whom they are negotiating, or to incite them to reveal, through the actions they take, part of their information.

In contrast moral hazard stems from *ex post* asymmetric distribution information between a principal and an agent, in which case neither the principal nor the agent has any prior information on the random state of nature and/or on the behaviour of the agent. In general, a contract which establishes how products and costs of risk-bearing are to be shared will only be acceptable to the principal if she eliminates all incentives for the agent to act in a fashion that is contrary to her own interests. It is then in general impossible to reach a risk-sharing agreement that is Pareto-optimal, and in equilibrium the contract generally affords only a second-best solution.

Asymmetries of information prevent the law of supply and demand and the law of one price from applying and thereby preclude markets from clearing, as underscored by Stiglitz (1985). The labour market in particular is populated by firms whose information regarding the skills and the potential commitment of individual workers is imperfect. Under these conditions it is not in the individual firm's interest to reduce the real wage rate, since productivity (effort or efficiency) of workers is not independent of the wage level. The 'efficiency' wage that maximizes the firm's profits may then not coincide with its market-clearing level (Stiglitz and Weiss, 1983).

With regard to the analysis of financial markets, the main goal of 'informational Keynesianism' has been to show that the financial constraints resulting from information being shared asymmetrically between firms, on the one hand, and external agents (lenders or shareholders), on the other, are likely to lead to disequilibria and to amplify the instability of the economic system.

2.2 Credit Rationing and Economic Fluctuations

Reference to credit rationing is not something new. This theme has appeared from time to time in the works of authors belonging to different schools of thought. Present as early as two hundred years and more ago in Smith's *Wealth of Nations*, credit rationing takes the form in Keynes's *Treatise on Money* of an 'unsatisfied fringe of borrowers':

[A]s loans are concerned, lending does not – in Great Britain at least – take place according to the principles of a perfect market. There is apt to be an unsatisfied fringe of borrowers, the size of which can be expanded or contracted, so that banks can influence the volume of investment by expanding or contracting the volume of their loans, without there being necessarily any change in the level of bank rate, in the demand schedule of borrowers, or in the volume of lending otherwise than through banks' (Keynes, CW V, 1971 p. 190).

As analysed by Schumpeter (1954), credit rationing is an instrument of economic policy. Tobin (1952) considers it as just one of the various forms taken by the distribution of goods and resources, waiting lists being another. In both cases credit rationing results from maladjustment between the supply and the demand for loanable funds. This kind of approach has left scholars dissatisfied for two reasons. First, the lack of supply with regard to the needs expressed by potential borrowers is owed either to credit distribution regulation or to non-competitive organization of banking. Second, this approach proves to be extremely restrictive, since it concerns situations where the fundamental assumptions made by neoclassical theory are not respected.

These limits were first brought to light by authors such as Hodgman (1961), for whom lenders may refuse to finance certain clients despite there being perfect competition. This viewpoint is shared by the founders of informational Keynesianism. Within a framework that does not differ substantially from the standard one except, as was underlined previously, for the assumption of asymmetric information, they have shown that relations of dependency may arise between prices and quality of credit that result in equilibria where demand for credit is rationed. These works consider that the knowledge related to risk of default is not equitably shared: borrowers who take out loans in order to finance investment projects have private information as to their default risk that is not accessible to lenders, even when the latter allocate some of their resources to appraise it.

2.2.1 Credit rationing

Asymmetric information has a fundamental implication insofar as the profit made by banks is not a strictly increasing function of the lending rate. Beyond a certain level, the effects of adverse selection and moral hazard will increase substantially the number of borrowers who fail, thereby considerably reducing the return for the lending institutions. These, in consequence, will not serve all potential borrowers, which will lead directly to credit rationing. In other words supply and demand of loanable funds will not be equal, in contrast to what standard theory predicts.

This behaviour by financial intermediaries is explained by what is the main feature of bank loans. Granted in exchange for a promise of repayment in the distant future, they always involve the risk that the client may default. Because loanable funds are traded within a world of uncertainty, their equilibrium price does not necessarily correspond to the price for which supply equals demand.

In the literature on credit rationing, contracts include two types of provisions: the first refer to the interest rate; the second to guarantees such as collateral. In the case of the simple debt contract, an individual is subject to rationing when she cannot obtain the entire amount of credit she has applied for, even if she agrees to pay a higher rate. One of the seminal contributions in this area is Stiglitz and Weiss's article (1981). The aim of the authors is to show that a credit rationing equilibrium is compatible with the assumption that banks maximize their expected profits. Accordingly, they assume that lenders and borrowers are sensitive to movements in the price of loans. With this assumption, as the lending rate increases, the situation of all market participants is likely to deteriorate. Thus, not only does the rise in the cost of credit generate a risk that borrowers confronted with larger financial costs will default on a larger scale but, because the probability of default is higher, banks' expected incomes will also drop. This phenomenon of greater risk affecting the loans market, resulting from an increased lending rate, finds a rationale in the notions of adverse selection and adverse incentives. Stiglitz and Weiss examine these two effects in succession, highlighting them as the essential factors of credit rationing.

In the adverse selection model they propose, credit rationing results, in much the same way as in the Jaffee and Russell's (1976) model, from changes, harmful to the lender, in the mix of borrowers. The market consists of firms and a large number of competing banks that set the interest rate so as to maximize their profits. Each firm arrives at the loans market with a certain amount of collateral, C, and borrows the same amount, B, from a bank to finance its income-generating activity. For the individual firm income R is a random variable whose distribution function $F(R, \theta)$ is continuously derivable, where θ is a parameter measuring risk, an increase in θ meaning greater risk – of the mean-preserving kind.[1] Depending on outcome R, each firm will either pay back its debt or default. If the difference between income and costs (in the present case, the principal plus interest on the loan), $R - rB$, is greater than $-C$, the firm pays back its debt; if $R - rB < -C$, the firm defaults on the loan.

Let $R' = rB - C$ be the maximum value below which the firm fails. If the firm does not default, its profit is $R - rB$. In the case of failure the firm loses collateral C. Consequently, the expected profit of a firm of type i taking out a loan at interest rate r is:

$$\pi_i(r) = \int_{R'}^{\infty} (R - rB) \, dF(R, \theta_i) - \int_{-\infty}^{R'} C \, dF(R, \theta_i) \qquad (5.1)$$

Firms participate in the market if and only if their expected profits are greater than zero. For each firm it is possible to determine a reservation interest rate r_i^*, that is, the rate below which it will not apply for credit.

Let us consider the profits a bank makes when it lends to firm i. If the firm is successful, the bank's profit comprises both the interest and the principal. If the firm fails, its profit consists of the firm's income plus the value of collateral C. Thus the expected rate of profit achieved by the bank at rate r is defined by:

$$\rho_i(r) = \frac{1}{B} \left[\int_{R'}^{\infty} rB dF(R, \theta_i) + \int_{-\infty}^{R'} (R + C) dF(R, \theta_i) \right] \qquad (5.2)$$

As a means of simplification Stiglitz and Weiss assume that two types of firm participate in the market, low-risk firms indexed by l, and high-risk firms, indexed by h. Assuming that θ is a mean-preserving parameter, the low-risk firms have a lower reservation interest rate than the high-risk ones. Moreover, the authors suppose that the bank cannot discriminate between the two types of firm. If μ_h is the number of high-risk firms in the market and μ_l the number of low-risk firms, the average rate of profit is:

$$\bar{\rho}(r) = \frac{\mu_h \rho_h(r) + \mu_l \rho_l(r)}{\mu_h + \mu_l} \qquad (5.3)$$

An increase in the interest rate begins by improving the rate of profit because loans will provide banks with more earnings. However the low-risk firms will prefer to withdraw from the market when the interest rate exceeds their reservation rate, which will tend to diminish the average rate of profit. If this negative effect dominates the positive effect, the banks' rate of profit decreases. As a result the banks' rate of profit is a non-monotonous function of the interest rate. Under the influence of competition the supply of credit increases in step with the banks' rate of profit. Because beyond a certain point the rate of profit starts to decrease, it becomes optimal for the banks to cease raising the lending rate, and to begin rationing loans, in order for the market to retain the less risky firms.

In addition to this adverse selection effect more stringent lending conditions imposed upon clients may also induce an adverse incentive effect (Stiglitz and Weiss, 1981, p. 401). This phenomenon presents some similarities with those caused by moral hazard, insofar as changes in the decisions of one of two categories of agents may lead to shifts in the behaviour of the other. Thus, should lenders decide to increase the interest rate in order to absorb excess demand in the loans market, they would also provoke a change in the characteristics of borrowers and especially in their risk of default. Indeed, an increase in the cost of the external resources provided by banks may tempt indebted firms into undertaking higher-earning but also riskier projects so as to maintain their profit margin. Consequently, the only clients who will agree to increase their indebtedness, when lending conditions become more stringent, are those ready to face a higher probability of failure, thus lessening the likelihood that such borrowers will really pay back their debts. More generally the adverse incentive effect occurs when there are two investment projects, characterized by identical levels of expected profits but by different degrees of riskiness, the project retained becoming more risky as the interest rate rises. True for the rational individual entrepreneur, this proposition can easily be extended to the case of n borrowers who will deliberately incur large risks when banks apply stringent lending conditions in order to maintain the profit margin they consider sufficient.

In the context of moral hazard, and as in the case of adverse selection, the rate of profit is a non-monotonous function of r. The existence of adverse incentive effects can also rule out the possibility that an equilibrium being reached where supply of and demand for loanable funds are equal. This is because profit maximization leads lenders not to seek to satisfy the largest possible number of customers, but rather to search for borrowers of at least some minimum quality (Santomero, 1984).

Rationing is thus quite inevitable in an environment of adverse selection and adverse incentives. It may, however, strike at random and affect both good and poor borrowers. It is still possible to avoid credit rationing by discriminating among the borrowers. Different discrimination procedures have been contemplated in the literature. A first procedure is the establishment of long-term relationships between lenders and borrowers. The idea developed by Stiglitz and Weiss (1983) is that an effective threat of cutting off credit may have important incentive effects on the behaviour of borrowers, who will thus be induced to undertake less risky projects, thereby reducing their likelihood of default. The main explanation of such behaviour is that the rejected borrower might not find another bank that will grant him a loan. As demonstrated by Jaffee and Stiglitz, 'banks earn profits on their initial loans; they take a loss on the continuation of the loan contract. But they do so because the contractual arrangement with the borrower allows them to cut off credit when the default circumstances occur. As a result, when credit has been terminated by one lender, no other lender would be willing to lend to the individual' (1990, p. 865).

A second procedure is the so-called signalling credit contract whose many forms have been imagined by different authors. The focus of this kind of contract is not the rate of interest, but rather other characteristics, among which are the value of collateralized assets, the size of bank loans or the borrower's net worth.[2] The main purpose of collateral requirements is to reduce the consequences of adverse selection and moral hazard by diminishing the losses incurred by the lender in case of failure. In addition, the introduction of collateral that falls due to the bank in the case of default transforms the debt contract into an incentive or discriminating contract. By offering a set of differentiated contracts, the bank can distinguish between borrowers and the risks they represent by observing the contract they choose. Borrowers with the more risky projects will favour those contracts that cost more but call for the smallest collateral requirements, as the likelihood is strong that such agents might fail and be required to hand over their guarantee. Conversely, those borrowers with the less risky projects will choose contracts stipulating high-valued collateral and the lower lending rates.

In recent years new-Keynesian economists have developed an interest in this kind of credit contract provision. The link between net worth and rationing has become a focal point in their work. A good example is the model proposed by Gertler and Hubbard (1988). These authors suggest that moral hazard induces borrowers to underinvest by diverting a certain fraction of the sums they borrow towards the holding of non-detectable liquid assets which remains theirs if they fail. In doing so they reduce the probability of success for their investment project. To overcome this problem, lenders will allocate funds according to the level of the borrower's net worth. The latter comprises both existing wealth, in the form of internal resources, and prospective earnings, that is, discounted cash flows. A high level of net worth that the bank might entirely recover, whether or not it serves as collateral, worsens the borrower's losses in case he fails and thereby prevents underinvestment. Accordingly, large amounts of net worth make external finance more accessible, which tends to stimulate aggregate investment.

Similarly, according to Bernanke and Gertler, a firm exhibiting sizeable equity, or rather whose 'insiders' stake' is high, avoids the asymmetric information problem (and its cost), because its debt-to-equity ratio is low and its overall situation not very risky.[3] It can thus obtain bigger loans on better conditions. It also has greater capacity to invest and to maintain its 'reputation' (of which its equity value is a good indicator) or to use its borrowings for genuine investment projects rather than for repayment of arrears.

Finally, for Calomiris and Hubbard (1990), large amounts of internal financial resources make it possible to reach equilibrium with complete separation of borrowers according to their type (thus making it identical to equilibrium with complete information). Quite intuitively, large quantities of internal resources involve greater losses when risky projects fail, and thus discourage firms with such projects from borrowing, thereby making them easier to distinguish: if a borrower's internal resources are low, he is detected and rationed.

Large amounts of equity thus apparently make it possible for rationing to be limited or even avoided completely. Their presence creates a situation that closely resembles the one where information is perfect. However this is a conclusion that must be qualified. In reality, net worth is not the only variable which may affect the extent of rationing. Account must also be taken of uncertainty, of the level of the interest rate on riskless assets, of bankruptcy costs, etc. In order to take these aspects into account, Davis (1992) examines the complex nature of the debt contract. He notes that its enforceability is not always certain and differs depending on the borrower's identity. Being a promise of repayment, it requires *ex ante* that the sum to be repaid be specified, as well as the lending rate, the due date, the amount of collateral, the circumstances when the lender is allowed to take title to the failed borrower's assets and the conditions for rescheduling or rolling over the loan. Now, during the running period of the contract, the state of some of these variables may change. Owing to an improper appraisal of the future state of the environment or to opportunistic behaviour, guarantees and assets belonging to the borrower may depreciate and the risks and costs of default may increase. Banks may then exhibit positions that are not totally hedged, which might cause them to ration even those contracts offering strong guarantees.

2.2.2 Credit-induced financial instability

Asymmetries of information between lenders and borrowers do not only prevent the loans market from reaching the equilibrium which would prevail were information perfect. They also play an important part in explaining macroeconomic fluctuations. Many of the recent new-Keynesian contributions consist in highlighting the existence of financial instability due to the information-constrained behaviour of loan market participants. Bernanke and Gertler's (1989) model can be considered as representative of the analysis of credit-induced financial instability developed by new-Keynesian economists. This model is a modified version of Diamond's (1965) overlapping-generations model but, whereas Diamond assumes that output and capital goods are perfectly homogenous, Bernanke and Gertler suppose that the technology used for the production of capital goods involves asymmetric information. The market is such that entrepreneurs have private information about an investment, while lenders face monitoring costs of a fixed amount. This small transformation of Diamond's model creates a radical change in the dynamics exhibited by the system.

The model generates results, before asymmetric information is introduced, that are analogous to the ones usually obtained by real business cycles theory. In particular, financial structure has no impact whatsoever on equilibrium. By contrast, the incorporation of asymmetric information imparts a role to borrowers' net worth that is decisive in affecting the ability of entrepreneurs to obtain external finance. Holding an initially large amount of net assets allows the borrower to benefit from larger resources. Likely to be used either as a means of financing projects directly or as collateral, they facilitate the access to external funds. By diminishing the informational risk supported by her lenders, the amount of net worth permitting the borrower to reduce the cost of her external resources becomes one of the main determinants of her investment.

Another essential aspect of Bernanke and Gertler's model is that it assumes there is a strategy of random monitoring. Since entrepreneurs differ from the viewpoint of efficiency, they can be divided into three categories: 'good', 'poor' and 'fair'.[4] The efficiency of the 'good' entrepreneurs is such that their investment projects exhibit a positive discounted return.[5] This is true even when the worse of the two states of nature is realized, which unavoidably involves costly monitoring (1989, p. 22). Bernanke and Gertler show that, for this group of entrepreneurs, there is always an opportunity to invest (ibid., p. 23). As for the 'fair' entrepreneurs, they are certain to achieve positive net returns only if there is no auditing, that is, if there are no dissipative agency costs. Whether these entrepreneurs decide to invest or not, that is, to increase their inventories, depends on the level of their savings.[6] Finally the 'poor' borrowers have investment projects displaying negative expected net returns, even when agency costs are nil. These entrepreneurs will put all their savings into inventories and undertake no projects.

Within this framework of asymmetric information the optimal financial contract implies that only those entrepreneurs whose net worth is sufficient will invest. This is the only configuration allowing avoidance of monitoring costs. As a result, the stock of capital in the next period is a function of both the borrower's net worth and of his savings and is also influenced by the current stock of capital. As the amount of capital depends on the previous scales of capital accumulation and production, any rise in productivity will be spread over several periods. Therefore the fluctuations of accumulation, and thus of production, will depend on the level of the entrepreneurs' net worth.

This model thus allows conclusions that are extremely interesting about the relationship that exists between the financial structure of firms and macroeconomic fluctuations. Collateral that is pledged by borrowers can both trigger and propagate business cycles. The greater its value, the lower the agency costs involved in financing investment with external resources. A drop in its value during a recession increases such costs, which depresses the demand for investment and amplifies the variations in real output. As Bernanke and Gertler note, 'this rationalizes a sort of accelerator effect of income on investment', since the rise in income relaxes financial constraints (ibid., p. 27). Moreover, their model highlights the fundamental influence of 'countercyclical agency costs' on the evolution of the economy. In contrast, when the fall in value of collateral is due to autonomous factors, namely to independent movements of output, the effect is no longer one of amplification, but rather one of triggering variations of production.[7] Thus Bernanke and Gertler's model offers the formal demonstration that phenomena affecting the financial sphere cannot be considered as the mere consequences of real shocks. On the contrary, they play an active part in the emergence and/or development of these real shocks. This conclusion is reached, it should be noted, thanks to an approach conducted within the standard microeconomic framework, merely modified by the incorporation of asymmetries of information.

However, the assumption of mainly *ex post* asymmetric information on which Bernanke and Gertler base their model is somewhat questionable. On the one hand, the uncertainty of actual project outcomes is evidently not as strong as the uncertainty of their *ex ante* quality, if only because the proceeds generated by projects are deposited in bank accounts and, most often, at the bank that has granted the loan. On the other hand, as the two authors remark (1990, p. 89), to merely identify agency costs with the costs incurred by monitoring borrowers *ex post* is not entirely satisfying, insofar as such costs appear to be empirically quite small. This observation had led Bernanke and Gertler to focus, in a later article, on the destabilizing effects of *ex ante* asymmetries of information (ibid.). These asymmetries concern not only project qualities but also types or actions of borrowers. For the distortions that arise to be related exclusively to the presence of asymmetric information, all the other assumptions the authors make are identical to those of standard theory (all agents are risk-neutral, they maximize their expected utility, a central planning agent exists whose goal is to maximize overall welfare). However, they suppose that the investment process lasts for two periods. At the beginning of the first period the individuals, who form a countable infinite set, are designated as either entrepreneurs or non-entrepreneurs, depending on a given probability distribution. They are then endowed with a certain amount of non-consumable input good, distributed continuously over the population. The endowment may either be stored or invested. Also during the first period, projects are appraised and decisions are taken as to whether to buy capital goods or acquire assets paying the riskless rate r. The resulting incomes – $R > r$ in case of success and zero in case of failure – are available for consumption during the second period.

Only entrepreneurs have the ability to make the appraisal informing them that, if undertaken, the project will succeed with probability P. A prerequisite for the project to succeed, the appraisal is costly in terms of effort. The probability of success, P, denotes the quality of the project. It is a random variable that is distributed independently among an infinity of potential projects, $H(P)$ representing its cumulative distribution function. $P*$ is the reservation probability of success.[8] $H(P*)$ is then the proportion of rejected projects and $[1 - H(P*)]$ the proportion of accepted ones. The world is one of asymmetric information with respect to (1) the probability of success of projects – only $H(P)$ is common knowledge; (2) whether borrowers are entrepreneurs or non-entrepreneurs; (3) whether they undertake appraisal of projects or not. As a result, an agency problem arises when the capital endowment of some borrowers is insufficient.

Entrepreneurs must borrow the resources they are lacking from the non-entrepreneurs who undertake no project and thus either lend out their funds or buy the riskless asset. The optimal loan contract takes the form of a contingent contract entered in the first period. It specifies the repayments the borrower must make in the second period, depending on what becomes of the project. The three possible outcomes are also common knowledge: either the project is undertaken and it succeeds, or it is undertaken and it fails, or else it is not undertaken.

Bernanke and Gertler demonstrate that in this information-constrained context, the optimal contract exhibits three characteristics. First, when the entrepreneur can self-finance his project entirely, he maximizes the expected surplus of the project, which leads to setting P^* at its socially optimal level: $P^* = r/R$. Second, when external finance proves to be necessary, the greater the size of the loan, the higher the entrepreneur's incentive to carry out projects with a low return in proportion to the optimal social return, as the cost due to asymmetric information increases. In fact the agency problem which arises takes the form suggested by Jensen (1988): entrepreneurs are induced to choose projects displaying a negative present value, $P^* < r/R$. Thus, on the one hand, the reservation probability of the projects becomes lower than the one defined for the first-best optimum and, on the other, it proves to be an increasing function of the net worth owned by the entrepreneur. Third, if the borrower's net worth is very low, the agency costs become so overwhelmingly high that they use up too great a fraction of the borrower's surplus for them to be able to borrow and invest. In other words, there exists a minimum threshold for net worth which dictates that any project endowed with an amount of capital that is lower than this threshold will be neither appraised nor undertaken, as no loan contract will be profitable.

The information-constrained general equilibrium achieved is such that all entrepreneurs whose net worth reaches the threshold appraise their projects, while the others become lenders. Both the entrepreneurs whose projects exhibit a probability of success lower than the reservation probability and the non-entrepreneurs lend (or store) their endowments. Thus, the number of appraised projects turns out to be an increasing function of the fraction of entrepreneurs endowed with an amount of net worth greater than the minimum threshold. It also ends up being lower than the number of entrepreneurs making up the economy, as a result of the crowding out of those entrepreneurs who are poorly endowed and have no access to the investment market. This means that, even within the setting retained by the authors where all agents are risk-neutral, the distribution and the amount of net worth owned by borrowers appear to be the main determinants of social surplus (or welfare) and of the level of output.

Moreover their analysis makes it possible to characterize financial fragility with greater precision. It depends on the level reached by the ratio of the net worth agents can invest in the global cost of their projects. A financially fragile economy is then one where entrepreneurs' net worth is small in proportion to the size of their projects. They become dependent on external finance that becomes difficult to obtain on account of their lack of creditworthiness, an effect of the agency costs associated with external finance when its amount is too large. In a financially fragile economy, even if the average fundamental value of the projects is acceptable, the number of investments appraised and the average return on projects undertaken prove to be small.[9] Indeed, a large exogenous shock on the value of net worth increases the agency costs associated with external finance to such an extent that they prevent many projects from being undertaken. The ensuing investment crisis is all the stronger because the shock is transmitted to the many firms that have no funds at their disposal.[10] A complete collapse of investment may occur even if the net worth held by the entrepreneurs taken as a whole is lower than the minimum threshold. In equilibrium, then, no investment project is either appraised or undertaken. What we have is an investment collapse, akin to the one examined by Mankiw (1986) in the case of simple debt contracts.

In sum, the models of credit-induced financial instability provide evidence that, when it comes to financial fragility, new-Keynesian economists basically share the same view. Financial fragility is caused by the diminished effectiveness of the information-generating and risk-of-default-limiting devices which permit a lender to form his opinion externally as to the quality of investment projects whose outcomes are uncertain. When these devices, namely the collateral pledged by borrowers or the net worth invested by entrepreneurs in a project, are small in proportion to the size of their projects, the economy becomes financially fragile. In particular, fragility of this kind implies that a sudden and noticeable increase in agency costs, related to the changes in one or more provisions in the loan contract, is likely to produce strong macroeconomic instability. In this analysis increased instability manifests itself in a sudden worsening of credit rationing, which can go so far as to lead to a collapse in the loans market and to marked effects on the real economy, in particular to an investment crisis.

The aim of the next paragraph will be to examine, on these grounds, whether the financial market allows potential borrowers to escape from the constraints affecting the loans market, or to what extent, on the contrary, asymmetric information in financial markets contributes to amplifying and to prolonging economic fluctuations of informational and financial origin.

2.3 Financial Instability Generated by the Financial Market

The economic fluctuations analysed in the previous paragraph were related to problems of credit rationing. However the analysis of financial instability that was carried out is subject, even according to Stiglitz (1984), to qualifications of two kinds. First, at the aggregate level, the question to be raised is why firms enduring credit rationing do not resort to the equity market. The answer generally provided by new-Keynesian economists is, as we shall see, that rationing also affects the equity market. Second, credit rationing alone cannot explain the extent of the downturns of aggregate demand for investment. Although not all firms are rationed during an economic setback, a decrease in their demand for investment does take place. It is thus necessary to investigate the possible link between the malfunctioning of equity markets and macroeconomic fluctuations. For that we examine a model representative of the new-Keynesian position we owe to Greenwald and Stiglitz, in order to highlight the important role played by constraints on net worth in the emergence and development of persistent macroeconomic instability.

2.3.1 Rationing in the market for net worth

In the above-examined models the focus was on the way equilibrium was reached in the market for loans. Bank credit was therefore assumed to form the producers' single source of external finance. As a consequence, choosing a certain amount of indebtedness was a residual decision, made once the level of wealth and the optimal scale of investment had been determined. However, in a large number of cases, firms can also finance their investment by issuing shares. Then, besides deciding on the amount of their investments, firms must also choose how to finance them.

The standard theory of corporate finance, on the basis of the conclusions reached by Modigliani and Miller, states that in an efficient capital market, where there are no transactions costs or taxation, the kind of finance that is relied upon is irrelevant. As stated by Proposition 1 of the Modigliani-Miller theorem: 'the market value of any firm is independent of its capital structure and is given by capitalizing its expected return at the rate ρ appropriate to its risk class' (1958, p. 268). Consequently, debt and equity are perfect substitutes. Accordingly, firms will undertake any investment project whose net present value is positive and do not have to worry about how to finance it.

Notwithstanding the many restrictive assumptions on which it is founded, the Modigliani and Miller irrelevancy proposition has been very influential: the neoclassical theory of investment, as developed in particular in the works of Jorgenson (1963), ignores the financial structure of the firm entirely and relates investment to real variables alone. However we shall see that, when informational asymmetries are taken into account, issues relating to finance become essential determinants in the decision-making process that leads to real investment. In the same way that firms forgo some of their profitable investment opportunities because their demand for credit is not satisfied, firms might very well not undertake projects whose net present value is positive because of the large costs associated with raising equity.

Let us consider a situation frequently observed, where a firm's managers have access to inside information they do not share with outside investors, information concerning the profitability of investment projects and/or of assets. A typical adverse selection problem arises in this situation because the potential buyers of the shares the managers may want to issue cannot verify the quality of the firm's underlying assets. As a result they will try to capture whatever signals they can, by observing the managers' behaviour. In particular, if the actions carried out by the managers are perceived as a signal that the firm's situation is too risky, the outside investors might react accordingly (possibly by selling the shares they already own), which may affect the firm's market value adversely. This kind of situation has led new-Keynesian economists to account for the rationing that might occur in the equity market, as well as in the loans market. The analyses of Myers and Majluf, of Greenwald, Stiglitz and Weiss and of Leland and Pyle are the main contributions in this particular area.[11]

Myers and Majluf propose a signalling model where 'old' shareholders have the ability to assess the true future value of a firm, as well as the value of the projects it might undertake, because they know whether the 'state of nature' that is unfolding is a 'good' one or a 'poor' one. In contrast, potential 'new' shareholders can only assign probabilities to possible states of nature. Let us suppose that a firm owns cash L_i and tangible assets T_i, whose value depends on the prevailing state of nature (good or poor), as shown in Table 5.1.

Table 5.1 Values of the firm

	Do Nothing		Issue and Invest	
States of nature	Good	Poor	Good	Poor
L_i	50	50	50	50
T_i	280	100	380	200
R_i	0	0	20	10
V_i	330	150	450	260

Its value also depends on whether or not the firm decides to carry out an investment project that requires an initial outlay of 100. Conditional on the state of nature, good or poor, the project – if undertaken – generates outcome R_i, the net present value of the project, with probability 0.4 and 0.6, respectively. Moreover, the old shareholders are assumed to maintain their ability to keep full control over the cash and the net present value of the new project. T'_i is thus equal to $T_i - E$ where E is the amount of newly issued shares.

The unconditional mean value of the equity held by old shareholders would be, if they decided to do nothing:

$$V_0 = \sum_i p_i(L_i + T_i) = 0.4(330) + 0.6(150) = 222$$

and, otherwise, if they decided to issue new shares and invest,

$$V'_0 = \sum_i p_i(L_i + T'_i + R_i) = 0.4(350) + 0.6(160) = 236$$

Taking the information available to outsiders as given, let us consider the insiders' wealth, contingent now on the state of nature and the strategy they adopt. Then:

$- (V_0 \mid good\ state,\ issue\ and\ invest)$ $\qquad = \dfrac{V'_0}{V'_0 + E}(L_1 + T'_1 + R_1 + E)$

$\qquad\qquad = \dfrac{236}{236 + 100}(450) = 316{,}07$

$- (V_0 \mid poor\ state,\ issue\ and\ invest)$ $\qquad = \dfrac{V'_0}{V'_0 + E}(L_2 + T'_2 + R_2 + E)$

$\qquad\qquad = \dfrac{236}{236 + 100}(260) = 182{,}62$

$- (V_0 \mid good\ state,\ do\ nothing)$ $\qquad = 330^*$

$- (V_0 \mid poor\ state,\ do\ nothing)$ $\qquad = 150$

It is assumed, however, that not only do outsiders know the probability distribution of the states of nature, they also know all the other relevant parameters. In addition they form rational expectations. As a result they anticipate that insiders will not issue shares and invest when the state of nature is good, since it would not be in their interest to do so, as evidenced by the values taken by V_0. Issuing shares thus signals to outsiders that the state of nature is the poor one, which reduces the insiders' worth to $L_2 + T_2 + R_2 = 50 + (200 - 100) + 10 = 160 > 150$.

The rational expectations equilibrium so reached leads to a paradoxical situation. On the basis of our numerical example, we see that insiders will not issue new shares. Should they do so, they would signal that the prevailing state of nature is the poor one. Thus there may be cases (as here) where it would be in their interest not to undertake an investment project, even if it exhibited a positive net present value, should it require issuing shares.

Another important implication of the model is that a firm will invest more easily if it holds large amounts of cash and marketable securities. In an environment with asymmetric information, holding 'financial slack' is a signal of sound management: cash enables firms to undertake profitable investment projects that would otherwise be forgone for the reasons we have just seen. This means that firms will always prefer self-finance to issuing new shares. The amount of liquid assets a firm holds is then likely to become a fundamental determinant of investment.

The model may also be adapted to account for the decision that managers make when choosing between issuing more debt and new equity (Myers and Majluf 1984, p. 207). Myers and Majluf show that issuing debt has a lower impact on the value of the firm than selling new shares.[12] Therefore, if an investment project requires external finance, firms will prefer to issue more debt rather than more shares. The model is in fact an illustration of the 'pecking order' principle, according to which entrepreneurs who wish to invest rely first on retained earnings, next on debt, and, only in the last resort, on external equity finance.[13]

Greenwald, Stiglitz, and Weiss (1984) obtain very similar results. In their model, firms are identical except for the net cash flow θ they earn from current activities and their new investment opportunities. Parameter θ describes the 'quality' or the 'value' of a particular firm. Managers' intention to issue shares is announced at the beginning of the period, which sets their market value. Managers then decide on the level of their investments, choose whether or not to issue shares and finance any residual balance with debt. The outcomes of new investment are known at the end of the period, at what point some firms go bankrupt, while the values of the remaining ones become common knowledge. If a firm does not default, its managers receive a compensation that depends both on current market value θ and on the share of terminal market value held by original shareholders. In the event of default, managers support a given fixed cost. It turns out that only firms with a low net cash flow and thus a high risk of default, issue shares: the difference between the compensation managers receive when they only issue debt and their remuneration when they sell shares is an increasing function of θ. Therefore 'firms entering the equity market will be adversely selected . . . and any firm that issues equity obtains a "bad" label' (1984, pp. 197–8). Market reaction leads then to a reduced market value for the shares of such firms, which increases their financial costs to a level that might become prohibitive.

The model proposed by Leland and Pyle (1977) is also based upon the idea that issuing shares is likely to convey a negative signal to the market. As a result many investment opportunities will not be matched by adequate funding. However the authors also assume that entrepreneurs' information as to the expected value of their projects is more accurate than outsiders'. In addition the entrepreneurs' inside information can be transmitted to investors simply because it is in an owner's interest to invest a greater fraction of her wealth in successful projects. Thus her willingness to invest in her own projects can serve as a signal of project quality. The value of a firm increases accordingly with the size of her equity position. As a result the equilibrium that arises under asymmetric information differs from the one reached under full information. Hence a firm's financial structure becomes an important determinant of investment. First, entrepreneurs hold larger portions of firms' equity than they would under different conditions. Second, if a firm's value is positively related to the percentage of the equity held by its owner, then the firm will have greater debt capacity and will issue greater amounts of debt. Even though debt plays no signalling role in this model, the amount of indebtedness is positively correlated with the value of the firm.

In sum, when asymmetric information prevails, a firm's liability structure influences the amount of investment it can undertake. The previous models have shown that, in general, external equity finance can prove to be extremely costly, as it is most often perceived as a negative signal. Either it is interpreted by the market as an indicator that the firm issuing new shares holds low-valued assets (Myers and Majluf), or it signals a high risk of default (Greenwald and Stiglitz). Because such problems exist, firms comply with the pecking order principle and/or forgo profitable investment projects that would otherwise have been carried out. As was the case for the loans market, liquidity – and more generally a firm's net worth – also proves to be essential determinant of investment and therefore of the level of aggregate output, as we shall see.

Thus, the influence these financial variables are likely to have on investment decisions reinforces the results obtained previously when analysing the market for credit. As one might expect, firms that are rationed on the market for loans will find it difficult if not impossible to solve their financial problems by issuing equity. Investment and production can therefore be constrained both by wealth owners' perception of the average risk firms represent and by the extent of information imperfections.

2.3.2 Financial market imperfections and economic fluctuations
New-Keynesians, Greenwald and Stiglitz in particular, have tried in recent years to develop a theory of economic fluctuations based on the analyses outlined above and thus strongly differing from those proposed by the theorists of real business cycles. Their most representative model (Greenwald and Stiglitz, 1993) aims to show explicitly that economic fluctuations are caused by information imperfections whose main effect is to reduce firms' ability to issue new shares in order to finance their activity. The authors add that empirical facts confirm the theoretical analyses in terms of adverse

selection, moral hazard, and signalling, insofar as share issues actually represent only a small fraction of the financial resources collected by firms (ibid., p. 78). A direct consequence of this form of rationing is that the risks these firms represent are not entirely diversifiable, that is, divided among a large number of equity-holders. Consequently, the behaviour of firms is in general one of great risk aversion. It is, however, recognized at large that all firms' economic decisions are risky – whether they concern production, investment or the setting of prices. Moreover, as underscored by Greenwald and Stiglitz, the effects of a risky decision depend both on the level of total net worth and on the amount of liquid assets easily convertible into cash. These assets play to some extent the role of buffer stocks allowing shock absorption (ibid., p. 77).

For simplicity, then, the authors assume the enterprises cannot issue new shares, and that the level of dividends for existing shares is fixed. In addition, decisions regarding production are made by managers who, it is assumed, behave so as to avoid failure. Finally, there are no forward markets and inputs must be paid for long before output is sold. Thus, any decision to produce is inherently a risky investment decision. Building on these assumptions, Greenwald and Stiglitz develop their model in two stages. They begin by determining the global supply that obtains from the aggregation of the supplies of the individual firms. Individual supply curves are constructed by making room for an aspect that is neglected by traditional microeconomic analysis, namely that bankruptcy is costly and that the firms take this into account when deciding how much to produce. This has several important implications. First, because it is difficult to diversify risk, the risk of bankruptcy rises in step with production. Second, when the bankruptcy risk is considered, the marginal cost, which now includes bankruptcy costs, is higher than within the more standard framework. The authors show then that the level of output is weaker than in a riskless environment (ibid. p. 91). Finally, and above all, output is strongly influenced by the amount of net worth a firm owns. Indeed, the higher the level of net worth, the weaker the marginal bankruptcy cost and the higher the level of production (ibid. p. 92). Confrontation between aggregated individual supplies and the demand of a representative consumer, presenting the usual neoclassical characteristics, allows determining aggregate output that only depends on the average level of net worth in the economy. The relation obtained is a concave function of the form $q_t = H(a_t)$, where q_t denotes aggregate supply and a_t the level of net worth. Thus, the fluctuations of output over time are determined by the dynamics of net worth.

The study of the dynamics of net worth thus forms the second stage of the model. The net worth in each period is the net worth of the previous period, incremented by the issues of new securities, and diminished by the amount of

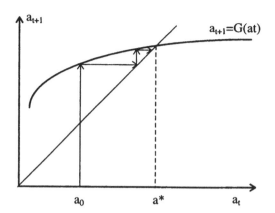

Figure 5.1 Convergence towards stationary state

dividends that are paid out. At the aggregate level, and in real terms, this gives:

$$a_{t+1} = q_t - (P^e_{t+1}/P_{t+1})(1+\sigma)[w_t\phi(q_t) - a_t] - m_{t+1}(a_t) \equiv G(a_t) \quad (5.4)$$

where P_{t+1} is the general price level in period $t+1$, P^e_{t+1} the expected price level, σ the individuals' (constant) discount rate, $\phi(q_t)$ the demand for labour and m_{t+1} the level of net worth outflows – equal to the real value of dividends less the issues of new share. The authors assume that m_{t+1} is an increasing function of a_t and that this influence is particularly marked when high levels are reached for a_t. This assumption prevents net worth from increasing indefinitely, and the curve representing the relation $a_{t+1} = G(a_t)$ can then cut the 45° ray from above (Figure 5.1).

The interest of the model is that it allows two kinds of analyses of cycles, or rather of 'persistent fluctuations'. The first consists in assuming that expectations regarding the general price level are perfect, i.e. $P = P^e$ in each period. This hypothesis allows the study of the strictly endogenous dynamical properties of the model. In this configuration, relation (5.4) reads as a non-linear deterministic difference equation. Two cases can then be distinguished, depending on whether G is monotonously increasing or not.

When G increases monotonously, as in the Figure 5.1, stationary state a^*, the unique solution to $G(a^*) = a^*$, is stable. This means that the economy converges regularly towards level of net worth a^* and thus towards associated aggregate output level q^*. In this case the economy does not generate

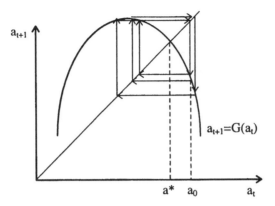

Figure 5.2 Endogenous cycles

endogenous cycles. These can only arise when function G loses its strictly increasing character and presents a sufficiently negative slope in the neighbourhood of a*, as in Figure 5.2.

Here function G has the form that is required to generate endogenous persistent cycles if two conditions are met. First, paid-out dividends, net of new issues, must vary quite strongly when the amount of net worth changes. Second, real wages must be strongly procyclical. If these two conditions hold, the economy yields alternating endogenous phases of prosperity and depression. Even multi-periodical cycles might appear if the slope of G is sufficiently negative. Such cycles can be interpreted economically in the following way. During a period of prosperity, both output and the level of net worth rise. Therefore real wages rise, which reduces profits and internal resources. In addition dividends increase. The outcome of these evolutions is that the levels of net worth and of output diminish. Both reductions allow a restoration of profits, as an effect of reduced wages and lower dividends. A new cycle can then begin.

The second way of analysing the dynamics of the model is to consider the general price level as a random variable. Here equation (5.4) becomes stochastic. The random shocks on the price level can lead to unexpected variations in the real value of debts and thus of real net worth levels. The main idea here is that even small variations of this kind can develop into large and persistent fluctuations of economic activity. This is obviously due to the difficulties firms encounter in restoring the level of their net worth rapidly enough (when an unexpected reduction of the general price level is what is assumed). Indeed, any large increase in the scale of production is hindered by the development of risk, the level of which is considered unacceptable. Moreover, these firms cannot issue new shares for the informational reasons examined above.

Let us consider then an economy in a stationary state, such that $a = a*$. Should a price shock occur, so that $P_{t+1} < P^e_{t+1}$, relation (5.4) entails that this unanticipated decrease in the general price level will cause the equity level to drop below $a*$, leading to a decrease of output. Relation (5.4) also implies endogenous dynamics that might result in a gradual return to the stationary state. Two configurations are in fact possible: either G takes the form represented in Figure 5.1 and the economy slowly returns to $a*$, in step with the successive increments of a_t; or G takes the form depicted by Figure 5.2 and the economy does not revert to the initial stationary state but is subject instead to persistent cycles.

At first glance this type of reasoning involving random price shocks (and rational expectations) is reminiscent of the new classical construct. Yet the two approaches are very different. To begin with, for Greenwald and Stiglitz, price flexibility does not ensure that the economy will converge towards a stationary state. On the contrary, flexibility is likely to cause a deeper economic recession inasmuch as it has negative effects on the real value of debt and of equity instruments. More important, the nature of the shocks does not really matter insofar as the non-anticipated change of prices can be caused either by a change in the money supply or by an unanticipated shift in the demand curve or even by an oil price shock (Greenwald and Stiglitz, 1993, p. 107). What matters instead are the kind of effects the shock creates. First, even small disruptions have important macrodynamic consequences: there is an amplification – rather than a reduction – of the initial shock (as shown in Figure 5.2). Second, the effects of the shock are lasting: persistence is the direct consequence of the informational problems with which businesses are confronted. A quick recovery by the firms of their initial equity level would require then that they either take major risks, which they cannot do on account of the incomplete and imperfect nature of the markets they participate in, or issue new shares, which is impossible because of the problems of asymmetric information affecting the capital market.

This rapid survey of the most representative financial instability models developed by new-Keynesian economists points to two essential aspects, which are related to the analysis of disequilibrium and macroeconomic instability. First, new-Keynesian economists develop an endogenous vision of the disequilibria that appear in the loans and equity markets in particular. Such disequilibria result from the rational behaviour of agents in an economy where information is asymmetric and problems of adverse selection and moral hazard widespread. Their origin therefore merely lies in the way market economies operate and not in rigidities, as in the neoclassical synthesis, or in exogenous shocks, as in the theory of equilibrium cycles.

As for the analysis of economic fluctuations, the new-Keynesian authors develop a view that differs sharply both from the conception of the new classical economists and the position defended by the Keynesians of the neoclassical synthesis. First, in many of their works, new-Keynesian economists emphasize that the flexibility of prices and wages does not diminish the phenomena of economic instability. Second, they show that small disruptions affecting the variables describing the economy's financial structure are likely to generate deep and lasting changes in economic activity. In sum, informational Keynesianism clearly belongs to the tradition of approaches, like Minsky's, that propose an endogenous and financial explanation of the phenomena of self-amplification and persistence of economic instability. It is this observation that has led to the recent reinterpretations of Minsky's theory of cycles, using the tools developed by the new-Keynesian school.

3   TOWARDS 'MORE MINSKYAN' NEW-KEYNESIAN MODELS

The authors of the new-Keynesian models studied previously, although they deal with the problem of financial instability, rarely mention the works of Minsky. The reference to Minsky is, however, explicit in the models that we are going to examine now.

3.1 Non-Linearity, Asymmetric Information and Minsky Cycles

Since the beginning of the 1990s Delli Gatti, Gallegati and Gardini have built several business cycle models with the more or less explicit intention of formalizing the assumptions, the behaviours and the results present in Minsky's approach. The originality of their works has consisted, on the one hand, in reinterpreting the financial instability hypothesis, relying on the tools derived from the mathematical analysis of non-linear dynamical systems and, on the other, in incorporating into these models some of the results of the new-Keynesian analysis of financial markets. In sum, their models offer a synthesis between the two approaches with a view to formalizing the endogenous and financial conception of macroeconomic fluctuations found in the works of both Minsky and some of the new-Keynesians.

The analysis of a recent model by Delli Gatti *et al.* (1993a) will allow us to highlight the main aspects of their contribution. First, we shall examine the structure of the model and in particular the non-linearities contained in the functions depicting agents' behaviour in the goods, credit and equity markets. As we shall show, these functions are built on the basis both of Minsky's financial theory of investment and of the new-Keynesian theory of rationing (point 3.1.1). Second, we shall analyse the dynamical properties of the model and highlight its capacity to account in a formalized mode for the dynamical behaviours associated with the financial instability hypothesis (point 3.1.2).

3.1.1 The structure of the model

The authors consider a closed economy consisting of three groups of agents: households, firms and banks. Households supply labour and demand consumption goods, money (deposits) and equities. Firms sell goods, issue bank assets (loans) and equities, and demand labour and investment goods. Banks supply liabilities (deposits) and demand assets (loans and reserves). The economy is composed of five markets: the goods, labour, money (deposits), credit (bank loans) and equities markets. In accordance with the Keynesian tradition, the labour market is considered as residual and its analysis is not formally developed in the model.[14] Besides Walras's law allowing them to disregard one of the four remaining markets, the authors choose to neglect the money market.[15] Therefore, the analysis considers the goods, equities and credit markets. We shall study in succession the equilibrium conditions for these three markets and distinguish for each one the Minsky-type ingredients from the aspects that result from the analytic foundations stemming from new-Keynesian economics.

3.1.1.1 Equilibrium in the goods market   The determination of equilibrium in this market requires an analysis of consumption and investment. The consumption function is of Kaldorian inspiration and is a linear function of current and lagged income:

$$C_t = c_0 + c_1 Y_t + c_2 Y_{t-1} \qquad (5.5)$$

where c_0 is autonomous consumption and c_1 and c_2 are the propensities to consume out of current and lagged income. Propensity c_1 is defined as follows: $c_1 = c_w (1 - \pi)$, where c_w represents the propensity to consume of wage-earners $(0 < c_w < 1)$ and π the share of profits in national income $(0 < \pi < 1)$. Propensity c_2 is such that: $c_2 = c_d (1 - \theta)\pi$, where c_d is the propensity to consume out of dividends, θ is the retention ratio and $(1 - \theta)$ is the dividend payout ratio, with $0 < c_d < 1$ and $0 < \theta < 1$.

The investment equation is written as:

$$I_t = aV_t + bIF_t \qquad (5.6)$$

where V is the price of capital assets and IF represents internal finance. It is defined as retained profits net of debt service (lagged one period):

$$IF_t = \theta \pi Y_{t-1} - r_{t-1} L_{t-1} \tag{5.7}$$

where r denotes the interest rate on the market for credit and L the firms' outstanding debt. The investment equation is the cornerstone of the model. On the one hand, as we shall see, it is crucial to the determination of the global dynamics of the system. On the other hand, it allows certain results associated with the analysis of both Minsky and the new-Keynesians.

Let us first consider aV, the first component of equation (5.6). Here we recognize Tobin's 'q' theory of investment, as well as the two-prices approach Minsky develops in his financial theory of investment. The second component of the investment function (bIF) has a specific Minsky flavour: it summarizes Minsky's interpretation of the Keynesian theory of the lender's risk and of the borrower's risk. It brings to light two essential aspects: (1) the key effect of the self-financing constraint on investment decisions, and (2) the procyclical character of the elasticity of investment with respect to internal finance.

The influence of firms' financial structure on decisions to invest is affirmed by the new-Keynesian school as well as by Minsky. Both reject the Modigliani-Miller theorem and the assumptions made by the standard neoclassical theory of investment. In the first place, the proportionality of investment to internal finance – Minsky's self-financing constraint – captured by component bIF in relation (5.6) finds both a theoretical and empirical foundation in the works developed by new-Keynesian economists. From a theoretical standpoint we have seen that cash flows, profits, net worth, equity or collateral brought in by potential borrowers influence investment decisions positively. The general idea that appears notably in models by Bernanke and Gertler (1989 and 1990) is that informational asymmetries between lenders and borrowers impart a crucial role to the latter's net worth by enabling them to obtain external finance. As we saw earlier, holding a large amount of net worth provides the borrower with resources that can be used as a means of financing projects directly and/or as collateral facilitating access to external funds. The amount of equity a borrower owns, which makes it possible to reduce the cost of his external financing by diminishing the informational risk incurred by lenders, is therefore considered by new-Keynesian economists as a fundamental determinant of investment. Moreover, the second component of investment equation (5.6) clearly reflects the pecking order which prevails, according to new-Keynesians, in the presence of moral hazard and adverse selection in capital markets. In other words, internal financing, IF, is preferred to other possible sources of investment finance (loans and new share issues).

Furthermore, several empirical studies, examining the effects of asymmetric information in capital markets, have confirmed the existence of the relationship between internal funds and investment suggested at the theoretical level. The main reference here is the study by Fazzari, Hubbard and Petersen (1988) that shows, on the basis of the analysis of time series, that investment proves to be more sensitive to the level of cash flows than is predicted by standard neoclassical theory. In addition, drawing from a cross-section analysis borrowed from Srini Vasan (1986) covering the period 1960-1980, they show that this phenomenon appears more sharply still for new or small and medium-sized firms. According to Vasan such firms have very restricted access to external finance, and almost exclusively in the form of bank loans.[16] Likewise Gertler and Hubbard (1988) observe that the more firms retain profits and rely on self-finance, the higher their liquidity constraint. For example, there exists a strong correlation between investment and cash flows for the small and medium-sized firms, a correlation that is more pronounced in periods of recession because of the worsening of agency problems. Conversely, large businesses are subject to a weaker liquidity constraint. This is explained by phenomena of reputation linked to size, know-how and business relations.[17]

In the second place, this type of analysis in terms of asymmetric information and financial constraints affords a rationale for the fundamental feature of the present model, also highlighted by Minsky, the procyclical nature of b, the propensity to invest. Referring to the results obtained by Fazzari, Hubbard and Petersen, it is possible to show that in an asymmetric information environment the procyclicity of b is due to a 'composition effect'. Bringing it to light requires making a distinction between small-payout firms, indexed by s, and high-payout firms, indexed by h. Small-payout firms are characterized by a small capital stock, high real sales and capital growth rates, a high retention ratio and a high propensity to invest out of their cash flows. Such behaviours are those adopted by relatively young businesses whose financial needs are greater than their cash flows: small distributions of dividends enable them to preserve the inexpensive source of financing that their internal funds provide. High-payout firms own a large capital stock, exhibit low real sales and capital growth rates, a low retention ratio and a low propensity to invest out of their cash flows. They are generally relatively large and mature businesses that face less stringent financial constraints than small-payout businesses.[18]

The aggregate propensity to invest can be considered as a weighted average of s-firms and h-firms' propensities to invest (b_s and b_h respectively), where weights are represented by the share of cash flows of every class in the global cash flow: $b = b_s if_s + b_h if_h$. Magnitudes b_s and b_h are known and given constants, and verify the inequality $b_s > b_h$. Besides, $if_s = IF_s / IF$ and $IF = IF_s + IF_h$. Therefore, $if_h = IF_h / IF = 1 - if_s$. It follows that $b = b_s if_s + b_h (1 - if_s)$. Thus $b = (b_s - b_h) if_s + b_h$. Under these conditions, we have: $db/dif_s = b_s - b_h > 0$. In other words the aggregate propensity to invest depends positively on the share of the total cash flow produced by s-firms. Analogously, let g_s

and g_h be the known and given growth rates of cash flows of s-firms and h-firms, respectively. The aggregate cash flow growth rate g is provided by:

$$g = g_s if_s + g_h(1 - if_s) = (g_s - g_h)if_s + g_h$$

where $g_s > g_h$. As a result:

$$\frac{dg}{dif_s} = g_s - g_h > 0$$

Thus g depends positively on the share of the total cash flows produced by the s-firms. Finally, we obtain:

$$\frac{db}{dg} = \frac{db}{dif_s}\frac{dif_s}{dg} = \frac{b_s - b_h}{g_s - g_h} > 0$$

This expression means that the aggregate propensity to invest is positively correlated with the aggregate rate of growth of cash flows and therefore with income Y, as indicated by equation (5.7). The above inequality therefore permits us to reach Minsky's conclusion that b is procyclical. It is possible to justify this conclusion economically by considering that recovery is brought about by young businesses paying low dividends and financing their investments mainly thanks to internal funds. During the ascending phase of the cycle the mature h-firms develop rather less quickly, implying that their weight in the global profit composition will decline. Thus, on average, the propensity to invest out of internal finance increases. In a more straightforward way, it is also possible to consider b as an adverse selection parameter: the weaker the risk of adverse selection deemed by banks, the higher the quality they assign to borrowers (businesses), the greater the value of parameter b and, therefore, the more investment there is. The economic interpretation of the procyclicity of b is then the following: during a phase of economic expansion (recession), the increasing (decreasing) flow of profits augments (reduces) the amount of internal finance that becomes available. A drop (rise) in riskiness of the average investment project ensues, as well as a decrease (increase) in the degree of adverse selection as appraised by banks, which stimulates (depresses) investment.

The propensity to invest can therefore be modelled as a positive function of the (one-period lagged) profit flow, Y_{t-1}. The authors opt for the following linear specification:[19]

$$b = b_0 + b_1 Y_{t-1} \tag{5.8}$$

where $b_0 > 0$, $b_1 = b_2\pi$, and $b_2 > 0$. The equilibrium condition on the market for goods is: $Y_t = C_t + I_t$, which can be rewritten by replacing C_t and I_t by their respective expressions in (5.5) and (5.6), and by replacing b and IF_t by their values:

$$Y_t = \left(\frac{1}{c-1}\right)\left[c_0 + (c_2 + b_0\theta\pi - b_1 r_{t-1}L_{t-1})Y_{t-1}\right]$$
$$+ b_1\theta\pi Y_{t-1}^2 + aV_t - b_0 r_{t-1}L_{t-1} \tag{GG}$$

which depicts a relation between Y_t, Y_{t-1}, V_t, r_{t-1} and L_{t-1}, forming the (GG) locus.

3.1.1.2 Equilibrium in the equities market The demand for equities of households is assumed to be a linear function of the dividend rate of return, that is, of the flow of dividends to the current stock price ratio. It can be written as:

$$E^d = d\left[\frac{(1-\theta)\pi Y_{t-1}}{V_t}\right] \tag{5.9}$$

where $d > 0$. From equation (5.9) it follows that demand for equities increases with the dividend rate of return, that is, it increases with income and decreases with the stock price. Since the portfolios of households are assumed to be composed solely of money and equities, this implies that the share of money in total wealth ($1 - e$) is affected negatively by income and positively by the stock price.

In accordance with the results provided by 'informational Keynesianism', it is assumed that businesses are subject to rationing in the equities market. In order to show the effects of such rationing, the model assumes complete rationing: businesses cannot issue new shares in order to finance their investments. Consequently the supply of equities (E^S) may be considered as given and constant:

$$E^S = E \tag{5.10}$$

By replacing equations (5.9) and (5.10) in the equilibrium condition:

$$E^d = E^S \tag{5.11}$$

we obtain:

$$V = \frac{d(1-\theta)\pi Y_{t-1}}{E} \tag{EE}$$

(EE) is the locus of equilibrium pairs (Y_{t-1}, V_t) generated by the stock market. For equilibrium to be maintained, lagged income and the price of capital assets are positively correlated: an increase in the current stock price leads to an excess supply of equities and must thus be associated with a rise of income that stimulates demand.

3.1.1.3 Equilibrium in the credit market   Demand for bank loans (L^d) is the sum of the outstanding debt inherited from the previous period (L_{t-1}) and the need for external finance (EF_t) defined as the difference between planned investment spending and internal finance, since rationing in the equities market prevents businesses from issuing new shares to finance their investments. Given the definitions of these variables, the demand for bank loans can be written as follows:

$$L^d = L_{t-1} + aV_t + \left[(b_0 - 1)\theta\pi - b_1 r_{t-1} L_{t-1}\right]Y_{t-1} \\ + b_1\theta\pi Y_{t-1}^2 + (1 - b_0)r_{t-1}L_{t-1} \tag{5.12}$$

It is a function of the stock price, of (lagged) income and of the interest rate. A positive correlation clearly appears between the price of capital assets and the demand for bank loans $(dL^d / dV = a > 0)$. However the sign of the partial derivatives of the demand for loans with respect to income and to the interest rate can be positive or negative. Let us also note that the partial derivative of the demand for loans with respect to internal finance is: $dL^d / dIF = b - 1$.

Thus if $b > 1$, then $dL^d / dIF > 0$, and businesses, encouraged by the growth of profits and more confident in their capacity to face their financial commitments, tend to increase their indebtedness in proportion to their internal resources. Such behaviour is quite consistent with Minsky's hypothesis of financial instability whereby financial fragility increases during periods of economic prosperity. But when $b < 1$, $dL^d / dIF < 0$, and businesses become cautious borrowers who reduce their demand for loans when internal finance increases. This situation corresponds to the behaviour of businesses engaged in hedge finance in the period occurring in the wake of a depression. This more conservative behaviour on the part of firms implies a reduction of financial fragility – a decrease of the relative weight of the speculative and Ponzi agents as compared with that of hedge agents – during periods of prosperity.

As for the supply of bank loans, it is an increasing function of the interest rate:

$$L^s = H\mu r_t \tag{5.13}$$

where H is the amount of reserves supplied by the central bank and μr is the credit multiplier. Rewriting (5.13) in the form that gives us the interest rate, we have:

$$r_t = \frac{L^s}{H\mu} \tag{5.13'}$$

The credit multiplier is limited by the reserve requirements imposed by the central bank. Thus there exists a threshold level for the interest rate, $\hat{r}$. If $r < \hat{r}$, the multiplier is μr and the supply of bank loans is represented by (5.13); if $r > \hat{r}$, the multiplier is μ_{max} and the supply of bank loans is $L = H\mu_{max}$. By integrating relations (5.12) and (5.13) into the equilibrium condition for the credit market $L^d = L^s$, we obtain:

$$\begin{aligned} H\mu r_t &= L_{t-1} + aV_t + \left[(b_0 - 1)\theta\pi - b_1 r_{t-1} L_{t-1}\right]Y_{t-1} \\ &+ b_1\theta\pi Y_{t-1}^2 + (1 - b_0)r_{t-1}L_{t-1} \end{aligned} \tag{LL}$$

which is a relation between r_t, Y_{t-1}, V_t, r_{t-1}, and L_{t-1}, forming the LL locus. When the system is in equilibrium, we have $L_t = L^s = H\mu r_t$: the feasible indebtedness of businesses is equal to the supply of credit.

3.1.2 The dynamical properties of the model: endogenous and financial cycles

By integrating relation (EE) and equation (5.13') into relations (GG) and (LL) we obtain a system, (F), of two non-linear difference equations. The first describes the dynamics of the real sphere, while the second characterizes changes in the financial sphere.

$$\begin{aligned} Y_t &= \left(\frac{1}{1-c_1}\right)\left\{c_0 + (c_2 + \Gamma)Y_{t-1} + b\left[\pi(1-\theta)Y_{t-1} - \frac{L_{t-1}^2}{H\mu}\right]\right\} \\ L_t &= L_{t-1} + \Gamma Y_{t-1} + (b-1)\left[\pi(1-\theta)Y_{t-1} - \frac{L_{t-1}^2}{H\mu}\right] \end{aligned} \tag{F}$$

This system defines current income and indebtedness in terms of the level of production and of outstanding debt reached in the previous period. It exhibits two types of non-linearities The first results from interests payments being determined as the product of the interest rate – as established by equation (5.13') – lagged one period, times the outstanding debt inherited from the past. The second non-linearity appears because the propensity to invest, which multiplies the flow of internally generated funds, is procyclical.

Analytic resolution of such a model is tedious and generally the analysis of the dynamical properties simply takes the form of a numerical simulation. It can nevertheless be useful to examine the way the economy behaves when parameter b takes a particular value. The case where $b = 0$ is of particular interest since it corresponds theoretically to a situation where financial structure is assumed to be without influence on the real variables. In other words the Modigliani and Miller proposition applies. The availability of internal funds exerts no constraint on investment activity and may therefore be ignored. The investment function may then be written as: $I = aV$. Under this assumption (F) takes the form of a system of two linear difference equations. The analysis of the system shows that equilibrium in the two (real and financial) markets is more stable, the weaker the propensity to consume, the more restrictive the dividend policy (the lower the dividend payout rates), the more inelastic the demand for equities in terms of dividends and the greater the supply of shares. As noted by Delli Gatti *et al.*, a regime of 'debt neutrality' sets in, since the dynamics of the market for credit does not affect the equilibrium determination of the system in any way.

The outcome is quite different when we make room for the effects of the dynamics of the markets for goods, equities and money on the market for bank loans. Indeed, in order to solve the second difference equation determining the evolution of corporate debt (and therefore of the interest rate through equation (5.13')), we need to know what the dynamics of income is. It is then easy to show that when the retention ratio is sufficiently weak, an increase of income exerts a positive effect on the accumulation of the firms' debt. In this case a cumulative process of debt accumulation begins and continues as long as banks have the capacity and the will to satisfy the demand for loans.

Thus, two interesting theoretical findings emerge from the analysis of the case of debt neutrality ($b = 0$). First the second equation of system (F) is not at all redundant: taking it into account allows us to bring to light the existence of an unstable dynamics of indebtedness, which is ignored by traditional macroeconomic models. Second, the evolution of indebtedness is likely eventually to disturb the real economy, owing to the way the credit market is characterized. In fact, when the demand for bank loans on the part of firms exceeds maximum supply ($L_{max} = H\mu_{max}$), credit rationing occurs, which forces businesses to reconsider their investment projects, since the total amount of funds (the sum of internal resources and the fixed amount of loans supplied) is now limited. The paradoxical outcome is thus that in an environment of debt neutrality, variations of indebtedness end up determining the evolution of investment activity.

The analysis of the system in its general form (for all values of *b*) is carried out by way of a numerical simulation. The study of the results obtained from this simulation shows there is a series of critical values of parameter *b* for which a bifurcation occurs, which affects the nature of the attractors of the dynamics. Interestingly the successive trajectories followed by the economic system, as a result of variations of parameter *b*, account very faithfully for the different phases of the economy – from recovery to financial crisis – which Minsky describes.

Simulating the model for sufficiently small values of *b* shows that the system converges towards a steady state. This means that, when investment is mainly financed from internal resources, the growth rate of the economy diminishes but the system is more stable than in any other situation. A careful examination of the model's equations shows that the economy behaves the way Minsky describes it when it is recovering. At the very start of a recovery, income as well as propensity to invest are weak. As recovery unfolds, income increases under the influence of the Keynesian multiplier, which improves profits and hence investment. Accordingly, the values retained for the parameters are such that the propensity to save and the retention ratio are assumed to be greater than the propensity to invest, which implies that retained earnings and households' savings increase more than investment expenditure. This leads to a smaller need for external finance, a lower interest rate and lower interest payments. In the market for equities greater dividends increase the shareholders' demand for, and the price of, capital assets. Growth in investment, in income, in cash flows and in the price of capital assets is accompanied by a reduction in the interest rate, outstanding debt and financial commitments. These are the main features of what Minsky calls a 'financially robust' economy, one dominated by agents engaged in hedge finance.

When *b* increases (when agents raise their debt to equity ratio) a cascade of period-doubling bifurcations occurs (generating stable limit cycles of order 2, 4, 8,... 2n). When *b* reaches a certain threshold, chaotic dynamics emerges (leading graphically to the appearance of a strange attractor). Finally, when *b* attains a certain critical value, attractors of all forms disappear and the dynamics takes the shape of divergent trajectories. The increasingly unstable dynamics that arises as *b* increases is the mathematical expression of the economy entering a phase of augmenting indebtedness and financial fragility, a situation, in Minsky's words, where speculative and Ponzi finance become increasingly prevalent, announcing the financial crisis that finally breaks out.

To see this, we examine the repercussions of the increase of *b* on the different variables of the model. It is clear that when the propensity to invest becomes greater than both the propensity to save and the retention ratio, conditions develop that lead to a cumulative boom of investment and profits. A greater need for external finance and an increase of the interest rate ensue. Moreover, the substantial rise in the price of capital assets during the boom encourages investment and the demand for bank loans. However, as soon as retained earnings no longer allow firms to face the continuous growth in their financial commitments, a turning point in the business cycle is reached. The recession that sets in is then characterized by a reduction in investment, income and the price of capital assets. In addition, profits decrease more quickly than investment so that more external finance is needed, implying that firms' outstanding debt, the interest rate and financial commitments increase. Finally, as b is procyclical, its value diminishes during the recession. However, as long as b remains greater than both the propensity to save and the retention ratio, such behaviour only makes things worse. Indeed, as shown initially by Fisher and restated many times by Minsky, the more prudent strategy of entrepreneurs associated with the decrease of b has a paradoxical consequence, as it helps to accelerate the deterioration of the firms' financial structure.

However, the financial crisis and the economic depression that follows do not last indefinitely. Here again the essential feature of the propensity to invest, its procyclical nature, comes into play. It results in an entirely endogenous change in direction affecting the cycle.[20] This change takes place when, income having fallen sufficiently, the propensity to invest becomes lower than the propensity to save and the retention ratio. A situation eventually arises where investment falls more quickly than profits. Consequently the need for external finance and for corporate debt declines, as well as the interest rate. A 'robust recession' pattern of this kind is then likely to lead to a trough. As the system thus becomes ready to enter a robust expansion phase, the entire process described earlier begins all over again.

To a large extent the strict endogeneity of the different phases of the cycle stems from behavioural relations borrowed from the theoretical models of the new-Keynesian school. Thus we have seen that financial variables, such as retained profits and financial commitments, play a predominant role in the determination of investment. This role is an effect of the asymmetric distribution of information with regard to the reliability of borrowers and the behaviour of managers respectively, in the markets for credit and for equities. Because of the crucial part played by investment in the evolution of the model's dynamics, financial constraints associated with asymmetries of information exert a considerable influence on the emergence and the development of economic fluctuations.

More important, in contrast to many models of cycles developed by new-Keynesian economists, the triggering of the crisis is not attributable here to an exogenous nominal shock affecting real production through its impact on the net worth of businesses. In the present model the environment of asymmetric information affecting the credit and equity markets contributes to generating chaotic and unstable dynamics in a completely endogenous fashion, dynamics characterized by the appearance of closed orbits of irregular and unpredictable periodicity. Thus the evolution of the system emulates a time series generated by stochastic disruptions to the steady state.

Finally, it is necessary to underscore two interesting aspects, related to the nature of the non-linearities exhibited by the model. On the one hand, these non-linearities, at the origin of the self-sustained fluctuations of the system, are not assumed in any *ad hoc* manner, but result instead from the behaviour of agents subject to a decision-making environment where fundamental uncertainty and asymmetry of information coexist. On the other hand, these non-linearities affect mainly the financial (rather than the technological) variables of the model and, more particularly, parameter *b* which represents the propensity to invest and whose procyclical character determines the entire pattern of the system's dynamics. Thus, this dynamical non-linear model of the financial instability hypothesis faithfully reproduces one of the essential ideas contained in Minsky's approach: the succession of phases of comparative stability and instability to which contemporary market economies are prone is, contrary to what is asserted by new classical economists, induced by endogenous processes and financial phenomena.

3.2 Sunspots, Financial Constraints and Macroeconomic Instability

In spite of the genuine merits of the formalization proposed by Delli Gatti *et al.*, this interpretation of the financial instability hypothesis ignores an important aspect of Minsky's theory of cycles: the role played by changes in long-term expectations in the emergence and the development of economic fluctuations. These variations induce permanent changes in the equilibrium position of the system. This position is then, to use a phrase coined by Minsky, a 'moving target' towards which the economy is always tending without ever having reached it:

> Each state, whether it be boom, crisis, debt-deflation, stagnation, or expansion, is transitory. During each short-period equilibrium, ... processes are at work which will 'disequilibrate' the system. Not only is stability an unattainable goal; whenever something approaching stability is achieved, destabilizing processes are set off (1975, p. 61).

From this point of view, Minsky's analysis is in line with Keynes's analysis of 'shifting equilibrium'. By inducing variations in long-run expectations, animal spirits cause instability simply because 'a mere change in [long-run] expectation is capable of producing an oscillation of the same kind of shape as a cyclical movement, in the course of working itself out' (Keynes, CW VII, 1973, p. 49). This point is of utmost importance according to many post Keynesian authors. Kregel, for instance, considers that the invariability of long-term expectations would be contrary to the very idea of dynamic analysis.[21] In other words the assumption, implicit in the models of cycles examined so far, that long-period expectations are given, as though the agents' appraisal of the extent of uncertainty were constant, needs to be reconsidered.[22]

Paradoxically, the rehabilitation in recent years of 'expectational' instability in economic analysis was first accomplished thanks to the models with rational expectations developed by a particular strand of new-Keynesian economics, one that seemingly resulted from a synthesis between new classical economics and Keynesianism, namely 'strong' new-Keynesianism, to use the phrase coined by Rosser (1990). In fact, even if this approach retains the standard assumptions as to the rationality of expectations, the flexibility of prices and the competitiveness of general equilibrium, it also makes room for Keynesian animal spirits, by explaining the volatility of investment with the help of the notion of 'sunspot equilibrium'. One of its variants even accounts for economic fluctuations by considering the role financial constraints play in conjunction with expectational instability. Accordingly to a certain extent it may be regarded as an attempt to synthesize the contributions of the new-Keynesians and of Minsky.

In many respects strong new-Keynesian sunspot models appear to be more akin to the analysis of Minsky and, more generally, to Keynesian theory than the traditional new-Keynesian models developed by Bernanke and Gertler or Greenwald and Stiglitz. On the one hand, the latter place more emphasis on the endogenous character of propagation and amplification of fluctuations than on the endogenous way economic crises arose. As noted by Woodford, one of the prominent theorists of sunspot analysis, 'Greenwald and Stiglitz suggest that [financial] constraints play an important role in the propagation of aggregate fluctuations, although they do not consider the possibility of endogenous fluctuations' (1988, p. 243). On the other hand, by considering the changes in 'the state of opinion' and in long-run expectations, Keynes and the post-Keynesians account for cycles by assigning a pivotal role to the variations in the degree of uncertainty. This aspect is not taken into account by the new-Keynesian models examined so far. To a large extent the recent emergence and development of strong new-Keynesianism, its reliance on sunspot models and sometimes on financial constraints, within an analytical framework that is akin to the one adopted by the first new-Keynesians, have helped to overcome these two shortcomings.

It is interesting to note beforehand that this approach belongs an already old tradition including authors such as John Stuart Mill, Lavington and Hawtrey. Like these old authors it aims to explain persistent cyclical fluctuations of economic activity by alterations in economic agents' level of optimism or confidence, in other words by changes in expectations that do not relate to any objective modification in economic circumstances. The apex of the traditional literature was Keynes's *General Theory* where fluctuations in the demand for investment were explained by long-run expectations.

Variations in expectations did not, however, play an important role in the formalized literature on cycles that immediately followed Keynes's contribution. The reasons for this neglect are twofold. To begin with, the old tradition came up against the positivism that prevailed in social sciences, at its apogee in the post-war period, and that rejected subjective factors as a means of explaining cycles. For the authors of the post-war period, and in particular for Hansen, 'in the end it is cold objective facts that control, not simply psychological moods of optimism and pessimism' (1964, p. 288). In addition it was argued that ignoring subjective expectational instability was justified, inasmuch as assuming it would instead have resulted in a simplistic and unsatisfactory explanation of economic phenomena. The emergence of any economic event could have been accounted for *ex post* by supposing the existence of some arbitrary modification of expectations, while the possible occurrence of such variations in expectations would have precluded predicting the evolution of economic variables.

A careful examination of the first works devoted to expectational instability would show that this criticism is to a large extent unfounded. In this literature we actually find authors endeavouring to measure how changes in expectations produce effects that confirm and reinforce them. Thus, although like Keynes he attributes business cycles to 'the inherent instability of business confidence', Lavington asserts that an initial improvement in the confidence of some producers, 'whether or not this confidence is justified', induces actions that are themselves 'a real cause of increased confidence on the part of many producers', which leads to a boom (1921, pp. 171–2). In the same spirit Hawtrey relates the cycle to 'the inherent instability of credit' that is induced by self-fulfilling expectations of two kinds. On the one hand, fluctuations in traders' expectations as to the state of demand may be self-fulfilling, owing to the comparatively passive adaptation of banks to the variations in the demand for credit (1926, p. 344). On the other hand, changes in each bank's beliefs concerning the amount of credit it can grant without provoking a dangerous deterioration of its reserves depends on the rhythm at which other banks increase their own supplies of credit (ibid., pp. 342–3). Consequently, as in Keynes's famous beauty contest (CW VII, 1973, p. 156), it is indeed the self-fulfilling character of expectations that is the essential feature of the old analyses of expectational instability. In these contributions emphasis is placed on the role of the economic structures that create the conditions under which revisions of expectations may become self-fulfilling. The aim is, then, to explain the particular sequence of events that unfolds once the economy departs from its initial stationary state. As Woodford puts it, 'while little attempt is made to predict why the initial triggering event occurs or even what sort of event it must be, there are many predictions about the typical course of a "business cycle" and about the kind of economies that should be subject to instability of that sort' (1991, p. 78).

Yet, little room is made even in recent models of cycles for self-fulfilling expectational changes. The main reason is that the expectational instability approach seems at odds with the mere idea of rational expectations. For the new classical school, if expectations vary in the absence of any change in economic fundamentals, it is because they are biased. In the theoretical framework defined by new classical economists, the emergence of spontaneous variations in the state of confidence can only be the result of irrational behaviours on the part of entrepreneurs. The expectational instability approach thus hardly seems compatible with the general objective of these authors, which is to explain macroeconomic outcomes as being the result of rational individual choices.

Ironically, though, it is the development of models with rational expectations that has generated renewed interest in the modelling of cycles embodying self-fulfilling expectations. In fact, one of the most significant recent developments in dynamic modelling of rational expectations has been the emergence of sunspot models of cycles.[23] At the end of the 1970s and at the beginning of the 1980s several contributions appeared, aiming to show that, in models with rational expectations – which also featured complete flexibility of prices, market clearing, intertemporal optimization, and constant over time private sector real fundamentals – prices and quantities might 'fluctuate persistently under laissez-faire, if private economic units predicted that they [would] do so'.[24] Thus, the notion of sunspots allowed the introduction of 'market psychology' or animal spirits into the analysis, thereby showing that business cycles need not be associated with any market imperfection. This contrast with the usual conclusions drawn from more standard rational expectations models is even more striking when we consider that sunspots theorists have demonstrated, in addition to the existence of sunspot equilibria, that there may be a multiplicity of such equilibria. An expectational coordination problem arises then that cannot be solved efficiently by the market's invisible hand (Grandmont and Malgrange, 1987, p. 10).

On these grounds several rational expectations analysts have claimed there is some resemblance between their models and Keynes's theory. They claim there are similarities concerning methodology as well as conclusions. For Grandmont and Lagrange 'it is amusing to note, incidentally, in an era where some pretend to have learned little from Keynesian theorizing, that by using the methodology of self-fulfilling expectations, one reaches a conclusion – the intrinsic unpredictability of the future in a free market – that is fundamentally Keynesian' (ibid.). More generally the utilization by sunspot theorists of the Keynesian notion of animal spirits – a concept that refers to the volatility of expectations, or 'extrinsic uncertainty', resulting from factors that are in no way related to the economic system itself – in order to explain business cycles is an indication that the methodologies applied in these theories are similar.

Sunspots thus appear to be a case where the notion of extrinsic uncertainty applies. A sunspot is more precisely defined as a random variable, the distribution of which is constant and the expected value of which is zero.[25] Its other particularity is that, although it conveys no information about the economy's fundamentals (preferences, technology, public policy and endowments), agents take it into account when they form their expectations. In other words, it is a variable that does not appear in any of the model's equations, except as part of the information set agents use to form their conditional expectations. The extrinsic uncertainty associated with the notion of sunspots is, thus, to be opposed to the 'intrinsic uncertainty' of the new classical models. It is, therefore, important to distinguish between the introduction of a random variable of the sunspot kind and the monetary or real shocks that characterize stochastic theories of the cycle. Sunspot equilibrium has indeed nothing to do with errors made by agents, whose expectations prove instead to be right, although they are subject to correction when the value of the sunspot changes. It is in this sense that it is possible to revive analyses of fluctuations that attribute importance to alternations in the level of entrepreneurs' optimism and pessimism throughout the cycle and to reversals in the state of opinion that are not grounded on any objective conditions.

The preferred setting for the study of fluctuations connected with sunspots still remains the overlapping-generations model such as the simple one imagined by Samuelson.[26] A recurrent theme in most contributions has been the need to explain how small departures from a perfectly competitive structure à la Arrow-Debreu may generate sunspot equilibria. It is for this kind of structure and for a pure exchange economy that the formal analysis of the properties of sunspot equilibria has been carried out most often. Thus extrinsic uncertainty mainly concerns the price level – or the expected rate of inflation – that is determined when market equilibrium is attained in the following period. In this sense the aim in these works has been more to explore the sunspot equilibrium concept as such and to provide some of the generic conditions for sunspots to arise, than to develop a positive model of the fluctuations of activity centred on the volatility of entrepreneurs' forecasts.

The willingness to take explicit account of the role sunspots play when entrepreneurs must decide how much to produce or to invest lies at the heart of Woodford's concerns. This author's aim has been to analyse from a Keynesian viewpoint how, in a world with imperfect financial markets, entrepreneurs' self-fulfilling expectations are revised as the result of a sunspot. His starting point is the observation that the interpretation usually put forward by sunspot theorists, in particular by Azariadis, Guesnerie and Grandmont, is too specific to be proposed as a general formulation of the business cycle. He has thus cast doubts on the relevance of the overlapping-generations model in which agents only live two periods. Fluctuations generated by these models actually unfold over long periods of time (periods that last the lifetime of an agent or more) as compared to an agent's lifespan. Instead he proposes a model in which agents live infinitely (Woodford, 1985, 1986, 1988). This specification allows his construct to generate business cycles that not only persist in a lasting manner, comparatively to the length of the discrete period, but also overlap only a small part of the agents' lifespan.

In order to achieve such a result, the deviation from the Arrow-Debreu structure chosen by Woodford consists in introducing a financial constraint (in addition to the budget constraint to which each agent is subject) that makes it possible to obtain a dynamic equilibrium similar to the one generated by overlapping-generations models. Accordingly Woodford (1985) proposes an economy composed of two types of agents, capitalists and workers. They differ, on the one hand, in the origin of their incomes and, on the other, in their access to credit. Workers supply their labour and finance their consumption entirely from their wages; capitalists do not provide their own labour and finance their consumption and their demand for investment with profits procured from the ownership of productive capital.

In accordance with the tradition initiated by Clower (1967), Woodford introduces a cash-in-advance constraint. In Woodford's model, workers must settle their consumption expenses with the cash they have in hand at the beginning the period during which spending takes place. Therefore, the wages earned during a particular period cannot be spent before the following period ('periods' are considered as short and last no more than a month or so). It is also assumed that wage earners cannot borrow money against future wages. In contrast, capitalists have the ability to buy on credit, inasmuch as they can actually spend their profits during the period they are created and not only in the following period. For Woodford this difference in the access to credit, though voluntarily exaggerated in the model, is based on the fact that financial institutions do not treat all agents alike. They lend only to borrowers with certain kinds of collateral. Capital goods are obviously much more transferable than labour power, for which reason the latter sort of 'wealth' makes poor collateral. Moreover, in the traditional Keynesian consumption function the constraint to which the workers are subject is implicit, as consumption depends on current rather than permanent income, as is confirmed by econometric studies on aggregate consumption.[27]

Both the dependence of businesses on their profit streams and the asymmetry between workers and capitalists as to the availability of credit contribute to the emergence of unstable macroeconomic dynamics, attributable in particular, in this financially constrained decisional environment, to the appearance of stationary sunspot equilibria. Indeed Woodford (1985, p. 26) shows that, in the economy displaying the financial constraints depicted above, the perfect foresight equilibrium is determined by a relation of the following type:

$$mk_{t-1}v'(mk_{t-1}) = \gamma(ak_t - \beta^{-1}k_{t+1})u'(ak_t - \beta^{-1}k_{t+1}) \tag{5.14}$$

where m is a positive constant characterizing the single-sector-production-technology with fixed coefficients assumed in the model: m units of period-t labour are employed with each unit of capital to produce one unit of output which may either be consumed or used in the following period's production process. The capital stock, k_t, is purchased in period t, u and v are C^2 functions that represent the utility and the supply of labour by workers (they verify the usual monotonocity and concavity assumptions), γ and β ($0<\gamma<1$ and $0<\beta<1$) are respectively the discount factors applied by the workers and the capitalists. It is noteworthy that β also represents the share of profits devoted to investment. If then we write $V(n) = nv'(n)$ et $U(c) = cu'(c)$, (5.14) can be written more compactly as:

$$V(mk_t) = \gamma U(ak_{t+1} - \beta^{-1}k_{t+2}) \tag{5.15}$$

This non-linear difference equation is an equilibrium condition involving the evolution of the capital stock only. Any sequence of values for k_t, t = 2, 3,..., that satisfies (5.15) for given initial level of capital stock, k_1, is a perfect foresight equilibrium. For a given k_t sequence, it is possible to construct unique sequences for the price level, wages, etc., that satisfy all the equilibrium conditions of the model.

Analysis of the stability of the stationary equilibrium and of the existence of endogenous equilibrium cycles involves studying the solutions of equation (5.15). Given the above assumptions as to preferences and technology, it is easy to establish the existence of a single steady-state capital stock k^*. The perfect foresight equilibrium dynamics in the neighbourhood of the steady state may be characterized by examining the linearization of (5.15) in this neighbourhood, i.e.

$$\begin{bmatrix} k_{t+2} - k^* \\ k_{t+1} - k^* \end{bmatrix} = \begin{bmatrix} a\beta & -\beta E \\ 1 & 0 \end{bmatrix} \begin{bmatrix} k_{t+1} - k^* \\ k_t - k^* \end{bmatrix} \tag{5.16}$$

where

$$A = \begin{bmatrix} a\beta & -\beta E \\ 1 & 0 \end{bmatrix}$$

is the Jacobian matrix, with

$$E = (a - \beta^{-1})(e^{-1} + 1) \tag{5.17}$$

In (5.17) e denotes the elasticity of labour supply with respect to the real value of wages. The characteristic equation of the model is the following:

$$\lambda^2 - trA\lambda + detA = \lambda^2 - a\beta\lambda + \beta E = 0$$

and the discriminant is expressed as:

$$\Delta = (trA)^2 - 4detA = (a\beta)^2 - 4\beta E$$

Focusing on the case where $a\beta > 1$ and $e > 0$, it may be shown that the Jacobian matrix admits two real eigenvalues whose moduli are smaller than one if $(a\beta/2)^2 > \beta E$ (i.e., $\Delta > 0$) and $\beta E < 1$, i.e. $detA < 1$, and two complex eigenvalues whose moduli are smaller than one if $(a\beta/2)^2 < \beta E < 1$ (i.e., $\Delta < 0$) and $detA < 1$.[28] For the present analysis these two cases are especially interesting. As established by Azariadis and Guesnerie, there exists a narrow link between the deterministic dynamics studied above and the existence of stationary sunspot equilibria within a neighbourhood of steady state $k*$ (Azariadis and Guesnerie, 1986; Guesnerie 1987). In particular the indeterminacy of perfect foresight equilibria is a sufficient condition for the existence of stationary sunspot equilibrium. In other words all that is needed is that there be a continuum of perfect foresight equilibria all converging asymptotically to the steady state. Indeterminacy obtains when the Jacobian matrix admits two eigenvalues with moduli lower than one. This configuration amounts to having $detA < 1$, that is in the present case, $\beta E < 1$. Considering the expression of E given by relation (5.17), the inequality becomes:

$$\beta(a - \beta^{-1})(e^{-1} + 1) < 1$$

and, eventually, indeterminacy obtains when:

$$e > \frac{a\beta - 1}{2 - \beta} \tag{5.18}$$

Thus, when the elasticity of the labour supply with respect to the real value of wages is greater than $(a\beta - 1) / (2 - \beta)$, fluctuations of small amplitude and of expectational origin occur in the neighbourhood of $k*$.[29] They result from capitalists basing their decisions in each period on a sunspot, denoted x_t, an independently and identically distributed random variable of t, belonging to compact set $X \subset IR$, whose distribution function is F(x). While x_t conveys no information about preferences, endowments or technology, capitalists believe in the existence of a functional link between realizations of x_t and current investment k_t. Hence relation $k_t = \phi(x_t, x_{t-1},...)$ where $\phi : X^\infty \to IR^+$ is continuous and defines a stochastic process for k_t that satisfies equilibrium condition (5.15).

It is possible to interpret sunspot realization x_t as an unpredictable change in the producers' expectations regarding the income they will receive from their activity in period t. In response to the sunspot they will decide to change their desired level of investment expenditures. Prices (P_t) are however given in the model by equation:

$$P_t = M(ak_{t-1} - \beta^{-1}k_t)^{-1} \qquad (5.19)$$

where M represents the money holdings of workers, and real return on each unit of capital purchased in period t is given by:

$$r_t = k_t / \beta k_{t-1} \qquad (5.20)$$

Thus each producer's budget in period t depends on the level of expenditure of producers as a group. Let us suppose a realization of sunspot x_t leads producers to anticipate a higher return r_t from which each will wish to spend more. Greater desired aggregate expenditure on the part of producers as a whole gives rise to a larger volume of the credit they are granted. Prices then increase up to the point where the sum of consumption expenditures of wage earners (whose money expenditures are limited by the cash-in-advance constraint) and desired expenses of producers do not exceed total output. Given that the labour market clears for a wage rate $w_t = M/n_t = M/mk_{t-1}$, the rise of the price level results entirely in increased returns on capital, in the amount given by relation (5.20).[30] Therefore, the income from capital that each producer receives corresponds precisely to the average spending of producers as a group – in Kaleckian terms 'capitalists get what they spend'. Thus every producer, when deciding how much to spend on credit in a given period, must try to determine the level of expenses of others, and so on. In this context fluctuations are explained by the feedback effects of the self-fulfilling expectational kind associated with the sunspot. The feedback effect results in the existence within the period of the following sequence: favourable (unfavourable) value of $x_t \to$ expectations of a rise (drop) of $r_t \to$ increase (decrease) of $k_t \to$ rise (drop) of r_t. In other words a change in expectations about future return on capital induces a change in current magnitudes. From this point of view, the author's position is akin to the one defended by Keynes for whom 'today's employment can be correctly described as being governed by today's expectations in conjunction with today's capital equipment' (Keynes, CW VII, 1973, p. 50).

On the other hand, if $\tilde{r}_t$ and $\tilde{k}_t$ denote respectively the discrepancies between the rate of profit and the demand for investment goods with respect to their stationary value in t, the model highlights still more the self-fulfilling character of expectations. As we know, a positive interrelationship exists between x_t and $\tilde{r}_t$. If the same rule still prevails in t + 1 for the formation of predictions, the realization of a favourable value of x_t in t increases the likelihood of the same state replicating itself. The following sequence ensues: favourable (unfavourable) value in x_t → expected rise (drop) of $\tilde{r}_{t+1}$ → increase (decrease) of $\tilde{k}_{t+1}$ → greater (smaller) $\tilde{r}_{t+1}$. In other words the realization of x_t entering the forecasting of $\tilde{r}_{t+1}$ implies a corresponding realization of $\tilde{r}_{t+1}$.

It is now possible to summarize the outcomes of the dynamics associated with the configuration where $e > (a\beta - 1)/(2 - \beta)$. As we have seen, in this case the perfect foresight stationary equilibrium is not unstable but indeterminate. Thus, for given values of the initial conditions, there exists a continuum of equilibria in the neighbourhood of the steady state. Such indeterminacy – which does not take place in optimal growth models with perfect financial markets – gives birth to a kind of 'intrinsic instability' in the competitive process, based on the imperfection of the financial system in conjunction with the revision of self-fulfilling expectations on the part of producers.[31] Woodford's analysis thus provides formal results that correspond to insights suggested in particular by Leijonhufvud. For the latter, serious macroeconomic instability occurs when the exhaustion of liquid 'buffer stocks' causes liquidity constraints to become binding and, in such a case, instability arises because revisions of expectations about future incomes become self-fulfilling.

In spite of these important theoretical steps forwards, the 'indeterminate-stable-equilibrium-self-fulfilling-expectations' configuration does not appear to be completely satisfactory from the viewpoint supported in this book where an endogenous approach to macroeconomic instability is preferred, in accordance with Minsky's financial instability hypothesis. The configuration is indeed one where the existence of fluctuations is exclusively linked to revisions of expectations. In fact, the persistence of fluctuations is explained here by the feedback effects and by the self-fulfilling character of expectations, in connection with the sunspot, and not by the non-linearity of the initial model. This aspect is noted by Woodford when he observes that the structure of this type of sunspot model 'is similar to that found in other recent exercises in equilibrium business cycle theory (such as those of Kydland and Prescott).... The method of analysis used here characterizes equilibrium fluctuations in terms of linear stochastic difference equations' (1988, p. 232). Thus Woodford develops a conception where the main source of instability is 'expectational instability' to which real shocks are appended. As was emphasized in Part One, if expectational instability is present in Minsky's model, as in the analyses of Keynes and the post Keynesians, it does not act separately. It is conceived as complementary to the 'natural' evolution of the economy's financial structure, to the endogenous factors of macroeconomic instability.

It is nevertheless possible partly to overcome this shortcoming by no longer considering the configuration of indeterminate stable stationary equilibrium, but rather the configuration where equilibrium is unstable, where inequality (5.18) is inverted. It is then possible to show that, under certain conditions, the model gives rise to a Hopf bifurcation and therefore to endogenous cyclical dynamics. First let us examine the condition allowing complex roots to be obtained, that is:

$$\Delta = (ab/2)^2 - bE < 0$$

Using the expression of E given by (5.17), the condition becomes:

$$0 < e < \frac{a\beta - 1}{(a\beta/2)^2 - (a\beta - 1)}$$

In other words a necessary and sufficient condition for complex roots to be obtained is that the labour supply should not be too elastic with regard to the real wage. A Hopf bifurcation will occur when these roots reach the unit circle and, at the point of bifurcation, we have:

$$detA = \beta E = 1$$

By choosing for example β, the share of profits that are reinvested, as the parameter of bifurcation, a Hopf bifurcation appears for value $\tilde{\beta}$ such that:

$$\tilde{\beta}\left(a - \tilde{\beta}^{-1}\right)\left(e^{-1} + 1\right) = 1$$

which solves for:

$$\beta = \tilde{\beta} = \frac{2e + 1}{a(1 + e)}$$

It is possible to show then that for $\beta > \tilde{\beta}$ the model has two eigenvalues whose moduli are greater than one. Steady state k^* is then unstable (reciprocally for $\beta < \tilde{\beta}$ the system converges towards this steady state)

(Woodford, 1989, p. 34). For critical value $\beta = \tilde{\beta}$, the economy exhibits closed trajectories around k^*, that is, endogenous cycles.

It is then possible to extend the notion of indeterminacy and thereby that of stationary sunspot equilibrium to the existence of stable orbits. Such solutions mean that for all initial conditions k_0 in the neighbourhood of k^*, there exists a sequence of perfect foresight equilibria that converges towards the stable orbit. In this case a condition may be found for stationary sunspot equilibria to exist that may be associated with the presence of endogenous cyclical dynamics. Thus when $\beta = \tilde{\beta}$ gives rise to a stable orbit and when producers' expectations change under the effect of a sunspot, a richer dynamics emerges, combining both the properties of endogenous cycles resulting from the model's non-linearity and the stochastic character of the linear system.

This kind of strong new-Keynesian model has the merit of placing, as Minsky does, expectations and financing constraints at the centre of the analysis of fluctuations. Like the financial instability hypothesis, Woodford's modelling of fluctuations, by showing that self-fulfilling prophecies in equilibrium models may generate endogenous cyclical dynamics, stands quite distinctly apart from the usual new classical approach where business cycles derive from monetary or real exogenous shocks.

CONCLUSION TO PART TWO

The recent new-Keynesian models of financial instability offer a vision of business cycles that differs sharply from the one suggested earlier by the new classical economists. In fact when we compare the results of these more recent models with those obtained by Minsky, and examined in Part One, we are struck by the similarity between the two approaches.

Three important ideas underpin new-Keynesian models. First, changes in real economic fundamentals (technology, preferences or initial endowments) are not the only – nor the main – factors inducing instability in economic activity. Variables characterizing the financial structure of the economy play a central role in the emergence and/or amplification of economic fluctuations. Second, these models reflect an endogenous – or in any case a not entirely exogenous – vision of economic fluctuations. Cycles appear very often in the absence of any exogenous shock, as the result of the rational behaviour of agents participating in the market for financial assets where information is far from perfect and where relations between the different economic variables are non-linear. Third, the merit of these models, in particular those building on the notion of sunspots, is that of focusing on expectations and on their variations (and not on actual changes in the fundamentals of the economy), thereby reviving one of the key insights contained in Keynes's theory of business cycles.

Notwithstanding this, as in all formalized macroeconomic works, the authors of these models in their eagerness to achieve rigorous mathematical treatment, have omitted some of the institutional and behavioural features inherent in financially sophisticated market economies. By contrast, these features are clearly taken into consideration in Minsky's contributions. The question to be raised, then, is whether these omissions and simplifications are likely to underestimate the originality of Minsky's approach, if not actually to misrepresent the way in which he considers the financial instability that characterizes today's complex market economies. Our aim in the third part of this book is to provide some insights into this issue. The arguments we develop are founded on a closer examination of fundamental aspects of Minsky's analysis that were merely outlined in the previous chapters.

NOTES

1. According to the definition of the mean-preserving spread, the more heavily weighted the tails of distribution of its expected income, the riskier the firm. This implies that the probability of earning a very high or a very low income is proportionately greater for a riskier firm. However, since low income always entails failure and loss of collateral, greater probability of making a higher income means greater expected profits for the riskier firm. Since the higher the risk, the higher its expected profits, the higher the interest rate for which these profits are zero.
2. Besanko and Thakor (1987); Chan and Thakor, (1987); Bester (1985); Riley (1979); Milde and Riley (1989).
3. See Bernanke and Gertler (1990 p. 111, footnote 23) for the definition of the 'insiders' stake'.
4. The most 'efficient' projects are those exhibiting the lowest investment costs. See Bernanke and Gertler (1989, p. 16).
5. Defined as the expected value of output, minus the opportunity cost of inputs and minus the expected monitoring costs.
6. In Bernanke and Gertler the alternative to investment is stock-building, but like the usual alternative to investment, the purchase of the riskless asset, it earns the riskless return and is not subject to the indivisibility constraint. As for the 'fair' entrepreneurs, other more complex parameters also come into play, influence the decision to invest and mitigate somewhat the weight of this assertion, as shown by the authors (Bernanke and Gertler 1989, p. 24).
7. Bernanke and Gertler refer to the situations of debt-deflation analysed by Fisher (1933) and, more generally, to the drop in relative prices of collateral. They allude, in particular, to the price of farm land.
8. This probability is such that only projects whose probabilities of success are greater or equal to P^* are undertaken.
9. The fundamental value simply assumes the form here of the probability of success and is part of the borrower's private information.
10. Let it be noted that, in this setting, economic policy is quite difficult to apply since the equilibrium that is reached is a second-best optimum, exhibiting the property of efficiency

in the sense of Pareto: improving the satisfaction of some agents is impossible without diminishing that of others.

11. Leland and Pyle (1977); Myers and Majluf (1984); Greenwald, Stiglitz and Weiss, (1984).

12. Ibid. pp. 207–8. For an empirical confirmation of this result, see for example Dann and Mikkelson (1984). In a recent article, Slovin, Johnson and Glascor (1992) even observe that announcements of banks' commitments increase the price of shares of large firms. The explanation of why bank loans have a positive effect on the value of firms generally put forward is that financial markets interpret a bank's commitment as a guarantee of the quality of an investment project. The key idea, as already stressed, is in fact that financial intermediaries have better information than market lenders. In addition, problems related to free riding (i.e. where the individual shareholder stops monitoring because he thinks other shareholders are doing it in his place) suggest in particular that it will not be in the interest of any shareholder of a company that is largely equity financed to try to obtain information regarding the firm (See Stiglitz, 1985).

13. See also Myers (1984).

14. Taking it into consideration does not modify the conclusions drawn from the model, as shown in Delli Gatti, Gallegati, and Gardini (1993b).

15. Delli Gatti and Gallegati (1990). For models integrating the money market, see Delli Gatti, Gallegati, and Gardini (1992) and Delli Gatti et al. (1993b).

16. To which we shall return later.

17. We could state countless references to this 'financial' approach to investment in empirical works by new-Keynesian economists. See for instance Calomiris, Hubbard, and Stock (1986), Calomiris and Hubbard (1989); Hubbard and Kashyap (1990).

18. In the paper by Fazzari et al., the s-firms, characterized by a dividend payout ratio that is lower than 0.1, display on average \$320 million in capital stock in 1984, a real sales growth rate of 13.7% over period 1970–84, a retention ratio of 94 per cent and a propensity to invest of 0.461. As for h-firms, those whose dividend payout ratio is greater than 0.2 own a capital stock of \$2,190.6 million, exhibit a growth rate of 4.6 per cent, a retention ratio of 58 per cent and a propensity to invest of 0.23.

19. Other non-linear specifications of b do not modify the model's conclusions fundamentally. See Delli Gatti, Gallegati and Gardini (1993b) who use functions: $b = barctg(Y)$ and $b = b_0 + b_1Y - b_2Y^2$.

20. Conversely, as we shall see, in Minsky's analysis the presence of an 'institutional stabilizing mechanism' (due to the central bank's interventions as lender of last resort, to the fiscal deficit...) appears fundamental in avoiding the emergence and/or the development of an economic depression. Delli Gatti et al. who contemplate the possibility of an intervention by the monetary authorities, in the form of an injection of liquidity, do not rule out this possibility in their model. The direct (in the market for loans) and indirect (through portfolio arbitrage) effects contribute to preventing or putting an end to a financial crisis.

21. For Kregel (1976) considering long-period expectations as given is synonymous with reasoning in terms of a static and not a dynamic equilibrium.

22. An exception being the Taylor and O'Connel model.

23. The idea of associating self-fulfilling expectations with the concept of sunspots was first suggested by Shell (1977), even if Jevons (1884) was the first author to refer to the role of sunspots in his own theory of business cycles.

24. Among the most significant contributions we find: Blanchard (1979); Tirole (1982); Cass and Shell (1983). Cited from Grandmont and Malgrange, 'Introduction', in Grandmont and Malgrange (1987).

25. Independence is often assumed but is not an indispensable condition: the realised value in t of the sunspot can very well influence its realization in t + 1.

26. See in particular the models by Azariadis (1981), Guesnerie (1987) and Grandmont (1986).

27. See in particular Hall and Mishkin (1982) and Flavin (1984).

28. Condition $a\beta > 1$ is necessary in order that capitalists in a stationary equilibrium should be willing to maintain a positive quantity of capital.
29. See proof in Woodford (1986).
30. In the model the equilibrium labour demand is always $n_t = mk_{t-1}$.
31. See Woodford (1985, pp. 22–6) and Woodford (1989, p. 19).

PART THREE

Rationality, Institutions and Financial Instability

6. Modelling Minsky's Theory with New-Keynesian Concepts

1 INTRODUCTION

As we saw in Part Two, recent models of the financial instability hypothesis provide interesting results. In these models non-linearities, combined with relations depicting financial arrangements, are not assumed in some *ad hoc* fashion. To a large extent non-linearities provide an adequate description of the investment behaviour Minsky analyses in his theory. More important, these models quite accurately account for one of the essential aspects contained in Minsky's approach, namely that the economy is subject to 'financial dynamics', insofar as its evolution is depicted as a succession of phases of comparative stability and instability. Moreover, in contrast to what is asserted by new classical economists, this succession of phases is induced by endogenous processes and financial phenomena.

However, a closer examination of Minsky's analysis suggests the need for substantial enrichment of the assumptions made by the authors of non-linear and new-Keynesian models. In fact these authors neglect two key aspects of the financial instability hypothesis. The first refers to the way Minsky analyses the rationality of agents and the formation of their expectations in situations of uncertainty. The analytical tools developed by the new-Keynesian economists have been used, quite successfully, to reach conclusions akin to some of Minsky's own deductions. It seems nonetheless legitimate to question the way these authors proceed. By referring to concepts such as sunspots and to assumptions such as asymmetric information the new-Keynesian school cannot entirely account for Minsky's analysis of economic behaviour and instability.

2 THE MODELLING OF EXPECTATIONS

Sunspot analysis omits some of the key ingredients of Minsky's (and Keynes's) conceptions of the instability of expectations. It is, therefore, necessary to turn to other models of financial instability where expectations are formed in a way that is more in accordance with Minsky's view.

2.1 Sunspot Models and Expectations: An Impoverished Interpretation of Keynes and Minsky

In spite of the standard analytical framework in which are embedded 'strong' new-Keynesian sunspot models, both the study of indeterminacy properties of equilibria with rational expectations and the focus on self-fulfilling sunspot equilibria have shed new light on Keynes's notion of expectations instability. In particular, the concept of sunspots has allowed emphasis to be placed on two important aspects of the Keynesian theory of cycles: the nature of investment fluctuations, namely their exogenous – or rather their not entirely endogenous – character (insofar as they are not necessarily related to variations in the economy's fundamentals); the self-fulfilling character of long-period expectations, actually at the root of investment fluctuations.

In addition, sunspot equilibrium is a concept that has allowed the introduction of uncertainty within a deterministic approach of endogenous instability.[1] However, in contrast to new classical models where external shocks affecting agents constitute the single cause of instability, randomness in the form of sunspots, representing changes in 'the state of opinion', is an additional feature of an intrinsically unstable economy. It has to do exclusively with the beliefs of agents with regard to their environment, beliefs that prove to be self-fulfilling.

Thus, substantial progress has been made and sunspot analysis does afford an interesting representation of the Keynesian conception of unstable expectations. However, because certain crucial factors are ignored, sunspot analysis cannot claim to replace Keynes's theory of expectations to any large extent. Similar reasons as well as more specific ones also lead to raise doubts as to whether the analysis in terms of sunspots can offer a suitable model for describing the process by which, according to Minsky, expectations are formed.

An important analytical difference, pertaining to the way the volatility of expectations in market economies is conceptualized, distinguishes the approach developed by Keynes and Minsky, on the one hand, from the one underlying sunspot models, on the other. In these models sunspots are characteristic of the way individuals form their expectations. More important, they are considered as extrinsic to the economic system. As a result, whatever the factors responsible for the existence of sunspots, no attempt is made to relate sunspots to the institutional or financial features of the modern market economy. Hence, analyses in terms of sunspots provide only a subjectivist foundation to the volatility of expectations. In other words, the main origin of the instability of expectations is to be sought in individual subjectivity, in 'whim or sentiment or chance' (Keynes, CW VII, 1973, p. 163).

Conceiving expectations in this fashion differs substantially from Minsky's. When he sets out to explain how expectations are formed, Minsky places constant emphasis on the role played by institutions and their evolution over time. As will be seen later, for Minsky, various institutional mechanisms (in particular the budget deficit and interventions by the central bank as lender-of-last-resort) which are characteristic of contemporary market economies are central to explaining agents' expectations and thus economic fluctuations. It is interesting to note here that, in showing this, Minsky revives Keynes's methodology. In *The General Theory* Keynes warns his readers, indeed, against the hasty conclusion that expectations would merely depend on 'waves of irrational psychology'.[2] Even though he considers, like the authors of sunspot models, that individuals' expectations have a psychological basis, he also points out the objective and institutional foundations of individual psychology. In other words a strong idea in Keynes's analysis is that the psychological behaviour of individuals is generated by their institutional environment and, more particularly, by the way financial markets are organized in market economies.

This institutional foundation of the instability of expectations appears distinctly in Keynes's Chapter 12 of *The General Theory*, dedicated to 'The State of Long-Term Expectation'. The analysis of the instability of investment that Keynes develops in this chapter may appear somewhat contradictory, since he attributes shifts in the marginal efficiency of capital curve – as imagined by the entrepreneurs – to changes in share prices – determined by the market: 'a high quotation for existing equities involves an increase in the marginal efficiency of the corresponding capital' (Keynes, CW VII, 1973, fn. p. 151). However this apparent contradiction soon disappears with Keynes's assertion that the levels reached by the two indicators might differ and that it is then the opinion of the financial market that prevails: Speculators dominate over entrepreneurs. In other words appraisal of expected profitability contained in the value of a business's equity dominates over evaluation of marginal efficiency of capital when the two diverge.[3] Accordingly 'certain classes of investment are governed by the average expectation of those who deal on the Stock Exchange as revealed by the price of shares rather than by the genuine expectations of the professional entrepreneur' (Keynes, CW VII, 1973, p. 151).

Correct interpretation of the dependence of the marginal efficiency of capital on financial market prices requires us to refer to the institutional foundations of Keynes's analysis of investment. As shown by Crotty (1990b), *The General Theory* can be considered as a two-level analysis: the first 'abstract' level contains the general analytical structure needed to build the various macroeconomic functions represented by the orthodox Keynesians of the neoclassical synthesis; the second 'institutionally concrete' level includes an analysis of the institutions, the classes of agents and the aspirations specific to each particular period of economic development, and refers to the theoretical and behavioural implications of this institutional setting. Moreover, also according to Crotty, Keynes's writings contain analyses that concern two historical stages: nineteenth-century capitalism and modern twentieth-century capitalism. Each stage is characterized by institutions and practices that are qualitatively distinct: at the first stage, accumulation of capital by firms administered by their owners is mainly self-financed; at the second stage, investment is dependent upon the 'whims' of a unstable class of speculative rentiers.

On the basis of this classification it is possible to reinterpret the analysis of investment developed by Keynes in Chapter 12 of *The General Theory*. First, careful reading clearly indicates that aspirations and behaviours of agents, as determined by the level-two analysis, do not apply at the first stage. The heroic entrepreneurs of this stage were not exposed to the unstable behaviours of their shareholders and did not act according to the fluctuations of the financial market. However, a number of factors contributed to the disappearance of the institutional arrangements typical of this stage. Among these arrangements, Keynes insists upon the separation between ownership and management, the change in behaviour of the class of rentiers and their gradual domination over the class of entrepreneurs. Therefore, the institutions and practices that Keynes describes in his level-two analysis actually emerged to replace those of the first stage. It is thus not surprising to find that the transition took place along with an important qualitative change in the macrodynamic properties of Keynes's model since: 'With the separation between ownership and management which prevails to-day and with the development of organised financial markets, a new factor of great importance has entered in, which sometimes facilitates investment but sometimes adds greatly to the instability of the system' (Keynes, CW VII, 1973, pp. 150–1). Indeed, it is true that the capacity that businesses have to increase their equity by issuing shares on the primary market enables them to loosen their liquidity constraints with an undoubtedly positive effect on investment. As a result the volume of investment no longer depends on the marginal efficiency of capital alone, as computed by managers, but also on how it is reckoned by the potential buyers of shares. Besides, Keynes recognizes that the liquidity provided by organized financial markets sets a limit to the uncertainty investors incur when they commit their funds to investing in durable assets. When claims bearing future income become marketable, investors need not be exceedingly trustful of their capacity to foresee the events that will take place five or ten years later and therefore 'there is an inducement to spend on a new project what may seem an extravagant sum, if it can floated off on the Stock Exchange at an immediate profit' (Keynes, CW VII, 1973, p. 151).

This also means that the uncertainty incurred by rentiers, who are agents not actively involved in the management of capital goods, would be so great in the absence of liquidity that their incentive to finance the acquisition of such goods would be extremely weak.

Keynes underlines nonetheless the ambivalent character of the liquidity provided by organized financial markets. It encourages destabilizing speculative investment, one that is based on agents' expectations of short-run security price movements, rather than on entrepreneurial long-run-return-pursuing investment activity. In *The General Theory*, the propensity to adopt speculative behaviour is in no case related to individuals' preferences, such as their level of risk aversion. As noted by Orléan, 'speculation appears as the agents' suitable response to the social constraints imposed upon them by the development of liquidity' (1988, p. 233). The predominance of speculation over enterprise is therefore the logical consequence of the operation of financial markets organized with a view to rendering investments as liquid as possible. Keynes is himself actually quite explicit in *The General Theory* as to his conception of speculation: 'Thus the professional investor is forced to concern himself with the anticipation of impending changes, in the news or in the atmosphere, of the kind by which experience shows that the mass psychology of the market is most influenced. This is the inevitable result of investment markets organised with a view to so-called " liquidity"' (Keynes, CW VII, 1973, p. 155).

Keynes is thus led to contrast 'enterprise' with 'speculation'.[4] This allows him to analyse how the development of organized markets gradually destroys the logic of enterprise. An important theoretical and practical by-product of this process is the following: to assert that, in modern financial markets, speculation inevitably dominates over enterprise amounts to saying that market valuations will ineluctably move away from fundamental values. Accordingly, the logic of finance cannot provide the rest of the economy with signals permitting an efficient selection of investors. These signals do not reflect information relative to long-term growth conditions. They merely express the short-term state of the psychology of market participants. In addition, for Keynes, it is seemingly more rational, in other words more profitable and less risky, to decide on what market position to take by referring to average prevailing opinion, rather than on the basis of your own long-term forecasts, however uncertain you might feel about how well-founded this opinion is. In other words, it 'is not sensible to pay 25 for an investment of which you believe the prospective yield to justify a value of 30, if you think that the market will value it at 20 three months hence' (Keynes, CW VII, 1973, p. 155). The short-term state of expectations embodied in market psychology must therefore be taken into account, which forces a binding constraint upon everyone. Operators cannot make decisions and in the meantime overlook daily quotations. They are compelled to incorporate them into their own strategies, whatever their own long-term predictions. Speculation is consequently the only rational attitude that is left, since it is the one that integrates this constraint most thoroughly. Speculation will thus develop to the detriment of enterprise, gradually, as the logic of the market becomes more intense. ¹

As underlined by Orléan: 'In introversion-like speculation, financial arbitrage gives us to see its real nature, its rationality. The only profitable information is the one that concerns the market itself. Speculation thus causes the market to enter a self-centered, self-referential logic' (1988, p. 234). If speculation has such an effect, it is because it establishes average opinion as the legitimate evaluation, the benchmark. Indeed, '[speculators] are concerned, not with what an investment is really worth to a man who buys it "for keeps", but with what the market will value it at, under the influence of mass psychology, three months or a year hence' (Keynes, CW VII, 1973, p. 155). For Keynes the highly paradoxical character of self-reference arises from the fact that what one expects is simultaneously a product of one's expectations. However the process that consists in 'discovering what average opinion believes average opinion to be' goes on and on, like 'an infinite interplay of abyss-deep mirrors, until infinite reflexivity finally obtains'.⁵

Thus, Keynes develops an analysis that explicitly takes into account the institutional features of contemporary market economies (separation between ownership and management, rational prevalence of speculation, ambivalence of liquidity, etc.), which leads him to conclusions as to the formation of expectations similar to those obtained by the sunspot models examined earlier. For instance, the states toward which self-referential processes converge are self-fulfilling insofar as *ex ante* predictions are realized *ex post*. Moreover, the purely internal constraint imposed by self-reference means that self-fulfilment implies the complete autonomy of the market and of speculation with respect to fundamental values. Another interesting property is that, as a general rule, there are multiple points of convergence. The realization of one point rather than another is random. Such properties appear in the passages of *The General Theory* where Keynes explains interest rate determination:

> It might be more accurate, perhaps, to say that the rate of interest is a highly conventional, rather than a highly psychological, phenomenon. For its actual value is largely governed by the prevailing view as to what its value is expected to be. *Any* level of interest which is accepted with sufficient conviction as *likely* to be durable *will* be durable... (I)t may fluctuate for decades about a level which is chronically too high for full employment; – particularly if it is the prevailing opinion that the rate of interest is self-adjusting, so that the level established by convention is thought to be rooted in objective grounds much stronger than convention .... (Keynes, CW VII, 1973, p. 203–4).

This is why, according to Keynes, arbitrage causes the interest rate to converge towards an undetermined level. Convergence is defined as the self-fulfilment of opinions. It obtains, not by virtue of compliance of the interest rate with actual constraints – quite the contrary, since this rate does not allow full employment – but because everyone agrees on some arbitrary value.

Thus, for both Keynes and Minsky, the institutional traits of 'financially sophisticated' economies play a central role in the self-fulfilment of expectations and the indeterminacy of equilibria. The absence in sunspot models of any reference to some relationship between institutions and expectations is therefore a first way in which such models and Keynesian analysis of the instability of expectations differ.

A still greater difference appears when sunspot models are more explicitly compared to Minsky's analysis of the formation of expectations. Minsky insists on the interdependence between long-term predictions (the state of confidence) and various objective factors arising from the financial structure of the economy, among which are: '(1) the actual cash-flows from economic activities, (2) the internal finance cash-flows provide, and (3) the success or failure of actual cash-flows to validate, first prior commitments to pay that are embodied in the complex structure of financial interrelations and instruments and, secondly, the prices that were paid for capital assets and investment output'.[6] As the author argues, these fundamental financial variables 'are inputs to the determination of current expectations of future profits: i.e. current long-term expectations'.[7] The evolution of these financial variables affects the formation of expectations by influencing the conventional-type individual rationality of economic agents.

Thus, when investment and past decisions to invest are on the whole validated, the confidence lenders and borrowers have in the model of the economy that guides their decisions is reinforced. In Minsky's model, this leads to an increase in the maximum level of indebtedness that agents deem prudent, to a rise of investment and to a boom. Conversely, when actual profits are, on the whole, insufficient in proportion to financial commitments, confidence in the merits of the system used for determining expectations and prevailing hitherto declines: indebtedness ratios formerly judged prudent are henceforth considered dangerous. Adoption by businesses and by financial institutions of various defensive measures then contributes to diminishing the level of investment, thereby causing a recession and, possibly, economic depression.

Therefore, although their results and their analysis of the instability of expectations display certain similarities with those developed by Keynes and Minsky, models with sunspots of the strong new-Keynesian kind do not consider the influence of financial and institutional factors on the formation of expectations. As a result they do not establish any link between agents' predictions and their financial structure and they can offer only a barren view of the complex interaction mechanism underlying the financial instability hypothesis.

2.2 Moving Closer to Minsky's Analysis of Expectations

The previous developments have shown that, in order to formalize the financial instability hypothesis, models of financial instability must include three ingredients of Minsky's analysis. These concern the way: 1) variations of the liability structure influence the evolution of economic activity; 2) changes in expectations affect economic change; 3) expectations are formed. In particular, for these models to be consonant with Minsky's construct, expectations must be determined both by real and financial objective factors (the rate of interest, the rate of profit and the level of indebtedness of the economy) and by subjective or conventional factors (the state of confidence and acceptable leverage ratios).

Obviously, the need to incorporate these various elements into a model entails discarding the intertemporal equilibrium and rational expectations approaches that underpin new classical and new-Keynesian models, and notably new-Keynesian sunspot models. The main characteristic of intertemporal equilibrium is that it eliminates all uncertainty with regard to the future. Models built on this notion ignore the role of expectations in the explanation of economic fluctuations: any period can serve as a reference, as long as agents' calculations concern only the discounted values of the streams of outlays and incomes occurring during the entire life span of the economy.

Temporary equilibrium models provide a more relevant representation of Minsky's analysis. Whereas transactions are decided upon once and for all in the first period, in an intertemporal equilibrium model temporary equilibrium is conceived within a sequential economy, where new transactions (including those occurring in the securities and credit markets) take place in each and every period. In a sequential economy, agents' expectations thus play a decisive role. As agents make mistakes, they will be required to correct them over time, on the basis of what their realized observations are.

However, from a formal standpoint, building temporary equilibrium models raises at least two delicate problems: expectations prove to be difficult to model; equilibrium may not exist. That is why the temporary equilibrium approach is rarely adopted and why the intertemporal equilibrium – or, what is not basically very different, the rational expectations – approach is preferred. The recent model of financial cycles proposed by Franke and Semmler (1992), because it is explicitly embedded in the temporary equilibrium framework, and because it portrays expectations that have a sufficiently Minsky-like flavour, deserves particular attention. Its dynamical analysis is developed in two main stages. The first consists in defining the conditions for temporary equilibrium to be reached in the goods and financial markets, the level of indebtedness and the state of long-run expectations being given. The second involves the determination of long-period equilibrium, that is, when indebtedness and expectations are subject to change.

Let us consider first the characteristics of temporary equilibrium. The equilibrium in the market for goods is given by an IS-type relation:

$$(1 + \phi)h(r + \rho - i) = s_f r + s_h(r^g - s_f r) = s_0 r + s_h i \lambda \qquad (6.1)$$

where $s_0 = s_F + s_h - s_h s_f$.

In this relation, ϕ is a constant characterizing the monetary policy of the central bank, r the net rate of profit, r^g the gross rate of profit, the two rates being related by the equality, $r^g = r + i\lambda$, where i denotes the rate of interest and λ the level of indebtedness (the debt to assets ratio) of the economy. Function $h(r + \rho - i)$ represents firms' investments. It depends negatively on the rate of interest and positively on the expected net profit rate. The latter is measured by $r + \rho$, where ρ represents the state of confidence or the state of long-run expectations. As for savings, account is taken of both the behaviour of rentiers, whose propensity to save is s_h ($0 < s_h < 1$), and of firms that save fraction s_F ($0 < s_F < 1$) of their net profits in order to finance their investments, the rest being distributed to shareholders in the form of dividends. Finally, equilibrium on the market for goods is reached through the variations of the net rate of profit r.

Equilibrium in the financial market is given by a LM-type relation:

$$e(r + \rho, i) - (r + \rho)/[r + \rho + i(\lambda + \phi)] = 0 \qquad (6.2)$$

where e denotes the fraction of wealth held in the form of shares by rentiers, the remaining proportion being held in form of bank deposits. This fraction is an increasing function of the expected net profit rate and a decreasing function of the rate of interest. Equilibrium in the financial market is achieved by the variation of rate of interest i.

Under these assumptions, it is possible to show that, for all given pairs (λ, ρ), with $0 < \lambda < 1$, there exists a unique temporary equilibrium, $r = R(\lambda, \rho)$, $i = J(\lambda, \rho)$. It is such that $r > i$ and is stable in the short run.

The determination of the long-period equilibrium entails rejecting the assumption that λ and ρ are constant and examining the way these two variables evolve over time. The level of indebtedness varies as follows:

$$\dot{\lambda} = (1 - \alpha - \lambda)h(r + \rho - i) - s_f r \qquad (6.3)$$

where α is a constant representing the policy of firms with regard to new share issues. Firms only finance fraction α of their investments by issuing new shares. This means that they will also need to rely on borrowings (which thus form a residual term) to bridge the gap between the level of their investments, on the one hand, and the amount of self-finance ($s_f r$) plus new share issues, on the other.

The other main variable of the model, the state of the confidence ρ, evolves as follows:

$$\dot{\rho} = v(r\text{-}i, \lambda, \rho) \tag{6.4}$$

First of all, we can see that the state of confidence is, as in the Taylor and O'Connel model studied earlier, a function of the discrepancy between the rate of net profits and the rate of interest. Obviously, the wider this discrepancy, the greater is ρ. The analysis of Taylor and O'Connel is, however, substantially enriched by Franke and Semmler who take into consideration the effect of leverage and of the state of the confidence. Indeed λ measures the risk that firms might default. As a result, in the model any increase in λ induces a deterioration of ρ. Finally the last argument of the function, v, links change in opinion ($\dot{\rho}$) to its present state (ρ). As in Minsky's analysis – where expectations improve and acceptable leverage ratios rise along a cumulative process during investment booms, and where a deteriorating cumulative process unfolds in times of depression – ρ and $\dot{\rho}$ are positively related. In sum, greater or smaller instability in the dynamics of expectations depends entirely on the trade-off between, on the one hand, the stabilizing ingredients of the dynamics – the evolution of r - i and of λ – and, on the other, the destabilizing effect of changes that concern the state of confidence, which tends to amplify instability.

It is now possible to analyse the long-period dynamics of the model. It is determined by system (S), formed by differential equations (6.3) and (6.4), non-linear in λ and ρ. This system can be compactly rewritten the following way:

$$\begin{aligned}\dot{\lambda} &= U(\lambda, \rho)\\ \dot{\rho} &= V(\lambda, \rho)\end{aligned} \tag{S}$$

where

$$U(\lambda, \rho) = (1 - \alpha - \lambda)h(\rho) - s_f R(\lambda, \rho)$$
$$V(\lambda, \rho) = v[\lambda, R(\lambda, \rho) - J(\lambda, \rho), \rho]$$

System (S) admits a stationary (or long-period) equilibrium solution (λ^*, ρ^*), $0 < \lambda^* < 1$, $\rho^* = 0$. It is such that: $U(\lambda^*, \rho^*) = V(\lambda^*, \rho^*) = 0$. The stability of system (S) can be studied by examining the Jacobian matrix, valued for stationary equilibrium point (λ^*, ρ^*). This matrix is written as:

$$J = \begin{bmatrix} U_\lambda & U\rho \\ V_\lambda & V_\rho \end{bmatrix}$$

The analysis of the partial derivatives of the matrix allows to show that: $U_\rho > 0$, $U_\lambda < 0$ and that $V_\lambda < 0$. As for the sign of V_ρ, it varies according to the different phases of the economic cycle. It is positive if the influence of ρ predominates over that of $(r - i)$ in the determination of $\dot{\rho}$.

Let us first consider the configuration where V_ρ is negative or weakly positive. Then the trace of the Jacobian matrix is negative, while its determinant is positive. This means that the two eigenvalues of J have negative real parts and that the long-run equilibrium is locally and asymptotically stable. Conversely, the state of stationary equilibrium becomes asymptotically unstable if V_ρ is sufficiently large. An interesting case is when the trace of the Jacobian becomes positive, while its determinant remains positive (which excludes the possibility of a saddle point), as persistent cycles can then arise. The existence of cyclical dynamics is owed to the fact that, starting from a certain distance from the stationary state, the time-path is subjected to destabilizing effects due to the subjective conventional argument in function v, which are offset by the countervailing forces generated by the reactions of agents facing the unfavourable evolution of objective arguments $(r - i)$ and λ.

In practice a typical cycle will unfold. During its ascending phase the state of confidence will improve regularly, which will invigorate investment (since $h(\rho)$ augments) and stimulate indebtedness ($U_\rho > 0$). However, for the sake of the argument, the authors assume that the increase of leverage will be less pronounced than the rise of ρ. As long as conventional-type behaviour exerts a positive influence, ρ, the state of the confidence, will continue to ameliorate. However, the higher ρ, the greater agents' expectations will become that a reversal in trend is about to take place. Then more prudent behaviour will emerge and result in a reduction of the weight of ρ in v (which, as we have seen, depicts the evolution of the state of the confidence) to the benefit of objective factors $(r - i)$ and λ.

Meanwhile, however, the objective factors will have increased during the cycle's ascending phase. This means that the augmentation of ρ will gradually slow down before it finally begins to diminish (the drop being accentuated by the negative sign of V_λ). The deterioration of the state of confidence, caused by conventional factors, now playing in the opposite direction, will quickly accelerate. This will result in a reduction of investment and cause a recession. However the latter will be checked, as the increase in leverage will come to a halt and be transformed into a decline (as $U_\rho > 0$). Confidence will eventually pick up, thereby ushering in a new cycle.

Thus, the countervailing forces that arise in the neighbourhood of the long-run equilibrium prevent the economy from converging towards its stationary value. Yet, as the contracting forces only come into play within a certain distance from the equilibrium point, fluctuations remain within a bounded interval. As a result persistent cyclical dynamics appears in the form of a limit-cycle.

The main merit of the Franke and Semmler model is to show how rationality of a conventional type can generate instability in expectations and macroeconomic activity. In this model the emergence of new fears or of new hopes will, 'without warning, take charge of human conduct. The forces of disillusion may suddenly impose a new conventional basis of valuation' (Keynes, CW XIV, 1973, p. 115). Each movement of this kind thus induces a change in the equilibrium position towards which the economy tends, although without ever reaching it. What we have here is the idea of a 'moving target' suggested earlier by Minsky.

By assigning a central role to the fluctuations of opinion, Franke and Semmler's model is in keeping with the financial instability models of the post-Keynesian (Taylor and O'Connel 1985) and of the strong new-Keynesian (Woodford) type. However, in these works, changes of opinion are introduced in an *ad hoc* way and are disconnected from the evolution of the economy. This is no longer the case in Franke and Semmler's contribution, where expectations and confidence change in much the same manner as they do in Minsky's analysis. Expectations and confidence vary in an entirely endogenous fashion. They are the outcome of the reactions of agents faced with the evolution of objective factors, such as leverage, and of subjective or conventional aspects, such as the state of confidence, the evolutionary law of which is itself determined within the model.

Notwithstanding this, the Franke and Semmler model, like the Delli Gatti *et al.* one examined earlier, has a basic aim: to a large extent it refers to the new-Keynesian literature on credit and financial constraints aimed at explaining how real and financial sectors are integrated and why financial instability tends to develop. The question to be raised is whether this is a suitable method for obtaining results that are similar enough to those reached by Minsky.

3   MINSKYAN AND NEW-KEYNESIAN BEHAVIOURS IN FINANCIAL MARKETS

The models of financial instability studied in Part Two dealt mainly with the problems of asymmetric information that arise in capital markets. The question is whether this kind of approach – and the methodology which is generally associated with it – can adequately account for Minsky's analysis of financial relations and instability. Before answering this question, it seems necessary to reconsider the more general debate between Keynesians and neoclassicals on the rationality of agents in situations of uncertainty.

3.1 Uncertainty and Rationality: A Comparison between the Neoclassical and Keynesian Approaches

In *The General Theory* Keynes insists on the difference between an economy 'subject to change, but where all things are foreseen from the beginning' and 'the problems of the real world in which our previous expectations are liable to disappointment and expectations concerning the future affect what we do to-day' (Keynes, CW VII, 1973, pp. 293–4). He emphasizes in the Preface to the book that his aim is to study a 'monetary economy, ... one in which changing views about the future are capable of influencing the quantity of employment and not merely its direction'. This, he argues, requires a 'method of analysing the economic behaviour of the present under the influence of changing ideas about the future' which is more general than the method employed by traditional theory (ibid., p. xxii). He thus seeks to replace the hypotheses of traditional theory that 'all things are foreseen from the beginning' with a theory of behaviour based on the assumption that 'previous expectations are liable to disappointment and expectations concerning the future affect what we do to-day' (ibid., pp. 293–4.). The traditional view of Keynes's theory as 'macroeconomics', rather than the theory of a 'monetary economy', has thus quite naturally overlooked what it did not expect to be there, but which Keynes considered to be the very heart of his approach - a theory of individual behaviour.

In what follows, we examine Keynes's ideas on the subject in more detail, showing the decisive influence of the *Treatise on Probability* on his views. Economists who had written before Keynes had not ignored the analysis of the behaviour of economic agents. He felt however that they had not analysed the implications of a changing, unknown future, although most economists who have written after Keynes have ignored his suggestions for a more general approach. Section 3.1.1 provides an analysis of the essential differences, by referring to the recent contributions of post-Keynesian economists. Section 3.1.2 shows how these extensions of Keynes's approach provide the basis for both a criticism of the traditional definition of economic rationality and for an alternative approach to economic rationality.

3.1.1 Keynesian uncertainty, probabilistic risk and non-ergodicity

As noted above, Keynes drew a sharp distinction between the analysis of decision-making in traditional theory and the conditions faced by decision-makers in the real world. But Keynes was not alone in noting this shortcoming of traditional theory. One of the first economists to draw attention to the difficulty of analysing uncertainty was Frank Knight. Knight considered that uncertainty existed when an agent faced what he called a unique situation: since statistics of past experience could not provide the agent with any guide, the distribution of the outcome in a group of instances cannot be known because in general it is impossible to form this group of instances. This means that any formulation of a numerical probability could only be based on a pure 'exercise of judgement' (1921, p. 233). Knight was interested in such cases because he considered they described the conditions that entrepreneurs actually face when they take business decisions. It was therefore essential to analyse them in order to be able to understand the evolution of the real economy. For example a situation of this kind would occur whenever it was necessary to draw out a plan of action based on a proposition like 'investing in technology y is profitable'. In the absence of any prior quantitative knowledge or experience related to operating technology y, the entrepreneur's evaluation of the returns he could earn by adopting it could only be based on his personal intuition. Knight contrasted such a case with what he called 'risk', a situation for which there was 'measurable uncertainty' (ibid., p. 20). Here it was possible to formulate 'a priori probabilities' (determined mathematically) or 'statistical probabilities' (determined by empirical observation of frequency of occurrence) (ibid., pp. 224–5).

By drawing this sharp distinction between risk and uncertainty, Knight sought to highlight the key features of uncertainty that he believed standard theory had neglected. Thus Knight's concerns were very similar to the position Keynes developed in the Preface of *The General Theory*, where he attempts to outline a more 'general' approach to decision-making in the face of uncertainty, one applying to cases in which the future was not perfectly known and probabilities could not be defined over the whole set of possible outcomes.[8] For Keynes events that were uncertain differed from those that were only probable. This appears clearly in the 1937 *Quarterly Journal of Economics* article:

> By 'uncertain' knowledge, let me explain, I do not mean merely to distinguish what is known for certain from what is only probable. The game of roulette is not subject, in this sense, to uncertainty.... The sense in which I am using the term is that in which the prospect of a European war is uncertain, or the price of copper and the rate of interest twenty years hence, or the obsolescence of a new invention.... About these

matters, there is no scientific basis on which to form any calculable probability whatever. We simply do not know. (Keynes, CW XIV, 1973, pp. 113–4)

The crucial point for Keynes – as for Knight – was that statistical quantification in the form of probability was inadequate for analysing uncertainty: 'human decisions affecting the future, whether personal or political or economic, cannot depend on strict mathematical expectation, since the basis for making such calculations does not exist' (Keynes, CW VII, 1973, pp. 162–3). According to Keynes orthodox economists had neglected this 'embarrassing fact' by supposing that simple extrapolation of past events were a suitable guide for the future, that *'natura non facit saltum'*, as Alfred Marshall wrote on the title page of the *Principles of Economics* (1890). Thus Keynes accused 'the classical economic theory of being itself one of these pretty, polite techniques which tries to deal with the present by abstracting from the fact that we know very little about the future' (Keynes, CW XIV, 1973, p. 115).

However strongly they voiced their concern for the importance of uncertainty, both Knight and Keynes seem to have failed in convincing economists that the vast majority of the theorems in economics dealing with uncertainty in fact analysed what the two authors defined as risk. To highlight the difference with the traditional analysis of uncertainty, which uses methods that are basically the same as those applied to the analysis of risk, many post-Keynesian economists have adopted the terms 'true' or 'fundamental' uncertainty to identify the original, but now often overlooked, definition of uncertainty originally formulated by Knight and Keynes. In doing so they hope to distinguish their extensions of the Knight-Keynes analysis from the traditional neoclassical approach in which agents are presumed to know the future outcomes of their actions and are thus able to choose the optimal set of future outcomes. Their aim is therefore to establish a clear distinction between two diametrically opposed traditions in the analysis of the impact of the future on the present.

Post-Keynesians have also attempted to elaborate the explanations of uncertainty given by Knight and Keynes and to distinguish them even more from the traditional analysis of risk. They have tried to develop Keynes's analysis by using methods that do not rely on the existence and/or the knowledge of the probability distributions of future events. Thus, in addition to their insistence on fundamental uncertainty, they have sought to characterize the conditions of its existence by referring to notions such as 'historical time' and 'crucial decision-making'. Thus 'Post-Keynesian theory ... is concerned primarily with the depiction of an economic system expanding over *time* in the context of *history*' (Eichner and Kregel, 1975, p. 1294, emphasis in the original) so that time is 'a real-world device which prevents everything from happening at once' (Davidson, 1980b, p. 158). In fact, since the basic economic decisions concerning production and investment are processes that take time and are essentially irreversible, they are said to take place in historical or calendar time. Decisions that lead to actions that cannot be reversed or repeated to produce more desirable outcomes are called 'crucial' decisions. In the neoclassical approach, in contrast, either time takes the form of a logical and thus a reversible process, or agents are simply discovering an already known future; their actions cannot determine the future. Consequently, when these issues are treated in the neoclassical perspective, it is in terms of probabilistic risk, since true uncertainty as defined by Knight is not considered.[9]

Shackle was the first to note that historical time implied what he called crucial decisions: an agent faces a crucial decision when he 'cannot exclude from his mind the possibility that the very act of performing the experiment may destroy forever the circumstances in which it is performed... Crucialness is the real and important source of uniqueness in any occasion of choosing' (1955, pp. 6 and 63). Thus, as Davidson has shown, 'when agents make crucial decisions they necessarily destroy any stochastic processes that may have existed at the point of time of the decision' (1982–83, p. 192). In other words crucial decisions describe situations in which the act of taking a decision destroys the existing distribution functions.

The identification of cruciality as an important element in economic decision-making under uncertainty produces a clear line of demarcation between post-Keynesian authors and modern neoclassical theory. The latter assumes there is sufficient information available in the present concerning the probability functions of future events so that, whatever decision is actually taken, it is not considered crucial. As Shackle emphasizes, the existence of the distribution functions implies that the future 'is already existent and merely waiting to appear. If this is so, if the world is determinist, then it seems idle to speak of choice. Choice ... is originative, it is the start of a new train of influences' (1972, pp. 122–3).[10]

Among post-Keynesians, Davidson has argued that the two key features aspects related to uncertainty – historical time and crucial decisions – imply that the stochastic process that generates events in the real world is 'non-ergodic'. He has used this observation as the basis for a modern reinterpretation of Keynes's distinction between probable and uncertain events. However such a reinterpretation of the real world in terms of a stochastic process, more usually associated with the frequency-based theory of probability, seems to contradict Keynes's statement that it is impossible to calculate probabilities for some events.[11] Indeed Davidson himself has pointed out that in conditions of true uncertainty 'objective probability structures do not even fleetingly exist, and a distribution function of probabilities cannot be defined' (1991, p. 132). Further, in order to apply the traditional frequency approach, it is desirable to be able to repeat experiments in identical conditions so that the moments of the random functions can be measured on the basis of a large number of realizations. This would be difficult, if not impossible, in the environment to which Keynes referred. All this seems to exclude any application of the mathematical theory of stochastic processes.

However a less extreme interpretation of Keynes's position is possible. For example, even if probabilities are assumed to exist for all outcomes, agents may not possess sufficient information to construct satisfactory probability estimates for some future events. For these agents the objective distribution functions would be, to use Keynes's terms, 'subject to sudden changes' over time, implying that the economic environment could not be assumed to be in a state of statistical control (Keynes, CW XIV, 1973, p. 119). Alternatively agents may recognize that exogenous changes may require radical reconsideration of the subjective distribution functions that they have formulated. In both cases, the psychological functions would not converge on the objective functions, and this would be true even if the objective functions remained unchanged over short periods of calendar time. Such an interpretation would allow Keynes's analysis of uncertainty to be recast in terms of non-ergodic stochastic processes. This interpretation would explicitly make it possible for both the objective and the psychological functions, defined though they may be for every point in time, to be subject to sudden and violent fluctuations. Expectations formed on the basis of the calculation of probabilities and actual future events might then be completely independent.

Nor is the reformulation of Keynes's analysis in terms of non-ergodic stochastic processes incompatible with rejecting the traditional theory of choice under uncertainty, based either on objective or subjective probability distributions. It is in fact consistent with the post-Keynesian criticism of objective probability analysis, since the traditional theory's validity is confined to an ergodic world. However, the criticism of subjective probability analysis appears to be less straightforward, at least when probability is interpreted either in terms of 'degrees of conviction' (Savage, 1954, p. 30) or in terms of 'relative frequencies' (Von Neumann and Morgenstern, 1953), because the assumptions made then are less strict. In particular the model proposed by Savage does not even rely on a theory of stochastic processes.

The approach in terms of expected utility developed by Savage is hardly compatible with Keynes's conception of uncertainty and with the reformulation in terms of non-ergodic processes. Savage defines an event as 'having every state of the world as an element' and insists on an order axiom implying that 'in deciding on an act, account must be taken of all possible states of the world, and the consequence implicit in each act for each possible state of the world' (1954, pp. 10 and 13). Moreover Savage notes that his approach 'makes no formal references to time' (ibid.). Thus the decision-maker seeking to maximize his utility is presumed to have a preferences ordering which is both atemporal and complete over the set of all possible realizations. Clearly, in a situation of true uncertainty, these two conditions are not satisfied. Accordingly, Savage himself recognizes that his approach cannot be considered as a general theory, because it does not cover true uncertainty. The theory of expected utility appears to be a code of coherent conduct for the individual rather than a system describing the actual formation of expectations regarding future events. In other words its aim is not to predict observable behaviour. Rather it is to depict the behaviour that economic agents, entrepreneurs in particular, should adopt in order to be rational and to act in accordance with the basic axioms of expected utility theory.

In sum, the contraposition of analytical structures (certainty/uncertainty, logical time/historical time and ergodic/non-ergodic processes) is superimposed upon a divergence of objectives. In fact, the goal of neoclassical theory is explicitly to derive the optimal state or behaviour from its postulates, while Keynesian theory adopts the opposite path, seeking above all to characterize the decision-making environment and economic decision-making on the basis of empirical observations taken from the real world. Thus the post-Keynesian presentation of the real world in terms of historical time and crucial decisions leads us to reinterpret Keynesian uncertainty as a non-ergodic stochastic process that is clearly incompatible with the decision-making environment assumed in the approaches belonging to the neoclassical tradition, those based on probabilistic risk and analysed in terms of either objective or subjective probability. More important, not only do both the identification of the conditions of non-ergodicity and the rejection of the traditional probability-based analysis point to the deficiencies of the neoclassical definition of uncertainty, they also call into question the traditional analysis of economic rationality in a truly uncertain environment.

3.1.2 Rationality and uncertainty

Around the beginning of the 1970s a new approach to uncertainty emerged in the guise of the 'rational expectations hypothesis'. This hypothesis was a key ingredient in the analysis proposed by new classical economists of equilibrium business cycles. Its purpose was to satisfy the need for a theory of rational choices that would embrace situations of uncertainty, while remaining in harmony with the neoclassical definition of rationality. The idea central to this approach was that, if individuals are presumed to be rational, they will also be rational when seeking information and forming expectations. Their rational expectations are then formed on the basis of the set of available information. A second hypothesis is derived from the Walrasian and 'classical' theoretical framework: the assumption that markets always clear (Lucas and Sargent 1981, p. 304). A third hypothesis concerns the movement of economic systems, considered as stationary and stochastic processes (Lucas, 1985, p. 44). This assumption allows the economic process to be regular and to take the form of a succession of cycles. Taken together, these assumptions define an analytical structure that affords an extremely simplified representation of the economic process. It is an abstraction in which 'nature' makes 'independent drawings from a fixed cumulative probability distribution function' (Lucas and Sargent, 1981, p. xii). Agents are then seen as maximizing their income by making mathematical forecasts, by relying on the distribution of the conditional probabilities associated with the stochastic process that describes the movement of the economy. In acting so, 'on average', agents make optimal forecasts, given the current and future states of the world (ibid., p. xiv). In other words, following the approach indicated by Muth (1961), the formation of expectations is modelled by identifying subjective probabilities with the observed frequency of predictions.

The rational expectations approach can be referred to in order to interpret Keynes's conception of uncertainty as a stochastic process, as suggested earlier. However, as Davidson has argued, the most important feature of the stochastic process assumed by the new classical economists is not that it is stationary, but that it is ergodic:

> for the REH to provide a theory of expectations formation which provides forecasts which are efficient, unbiased, and without persistent errors, not only must the subjective and objective functions be equal at any given point of time, but these functions must be derived from an ergodic process. In other words, the average expectation of future outcomes determined at any point in time will not be persistently different than the time average of future outcomes only if the stochastic process is ergodic (1982–3, p. 185).

As has been emphasized, post-Keynesians define real world evolution as a non-ergodic process. Consequently, the forecasts derived from existing distribution functions can diverge consistently from the averages measured over time on the basis of the actually observed frequencies. That is why post-Keynesians consider the assumptions that expectations are rational and that processes are stationary as incompatible with real world observations.

Despite the attempts made to develop the tradition initiated by Knight and Keynes and to ascribe more importance to uncertainty, mainstream evaluation of the question remains well represented by the position expressed by Walliser. This author writes that Keynes's ideas on uncertainty have: 'remained at the preformal stage, they do not seem to have had any general "cultural" influence on economic thinking except as complications or useless subtleties' (1985, p. 17). Indeed for most economists better-known Keynesian concepts such as 'animal spirits' are considered as purely subjective and thus irrational and unscientific. Consequently in the contemporary literature, Keynes's analysis is either criticized or credited as an approach to macroeconomics that is incompatible with the traditional notion of individual behaviour based on the assumption of economic rationality.[12] This situation is in part linked to the identification of Keynesian uncertainty with radical subjectivism, and the associated scientific and theoretical nihilism. This is clearly the interpretation of Keynes adopted by Lucas who writes that 'in cases of uncertainty, economic reasoning will be of no value' (1977, p. 224). Undoubtedly some post-Keynesian authors have given support to such an interpretation. For example Shackle has claimed to be a 'nihilist' and applied the same term to Keynes (Shackle, 1984, p. 391). In addition, as we have mentioned, the definition of uncertainty associated with Keynes and Knight implies that it is impossible to provide *ex ante* an exhaustive list of all possible future realizations. Thus, the representation of uncertainty by means of probability is problematic, not so much because of it may be difficult to estimate the probability of some given realization, but rather because it may not be feasible to portray the set of future possible realizations. Relying on the assumption that the agent can then specify a 'residual realization' only appears to be a completely arbitrary solution to the problem. As Shackle has pointed out:

> if the list of hypotheses in answer to some question is acknowledged to be endless and incapable of completion ... the language of subjective probability may seem unsuitable. That language distributes a total, representing the certainty of inclusiveness, over a finite number of specified rival answers. Or if not, then instead it includes a Black Box, a residual hypothesis of unknown content (1972, p. 23).

While this criticism clearly indicates why the subjective probability approach cannot be used to describe Keynesian uncertainty and non-ergodic processes, its significance is weakened by the fact that it appears to be based on radical subjectivism and theoretical nihilism. In other words, Keynes' analysis rules out any reliance on the calculus of probability and hence any possibility of building a well-defined theory of expectations in a situation of fundamental uncertainty. This weakness is nonetheless only apparent. To be convinced of this, one only need examine more closely Keynes's explicit references linking the concept of animal spirits to his *Treatise on Probability*. It is in this context that the relation between the tools of probability and the analysis of uncertainty is of importance. A number of post-Keynesian authors have dealt with this question and we can rely on this work to supplement the *Treatise on Probability* (Kregel, 1987 and Davidson, 1987) Their starting point is Keynes's very conception of probability. We have already noted that Keynes did not embrace the frequency theory of probability. First, Keynes's approach to subjective probability was more subtle.[13] Second, it was critical:

> In the sense important to logic, probability is not subjective. It is not, that is to say, subject to human caprice. A proposition is not probable because we think it so. When once the facts are given which determine our knowledge, what is probable or improbable in these circumstances has been fixed objectively, and is independent of our opinion. The theory of probability is logical, therefore, because it is concerned with the degree of belief which is rational to entertain in given conditions, and not merely with the actual beliefs of particular individuals, which may or may not be rational (Keynes, CW VIII, 1973, p. 4).

In contrast to the usual frequency theory of probability, Keynes viewed probability as a logical relationship between propositions, rather than between states of the world. Keynes was concerned with 'logical probability' or the 'degree of confirmation' or the 'degree of rational belief' defined as follows: 'Let our premises consist of any set of propositions h, and our conclusion consist of any set of propositions a, then, if a knowledge of h justifies a rational belief in a of degree α, we say that there is a probability-relation of degree α between a and h' (ibid.).[14]

This vision of the theory of probabilitiy led Keynes to make a distinction between two kinds of propositions: 'primary' and 'secondary' propositions. He defines them in the following fashion:

> if the evidence upon which we base our belief is h, then what we *know*, namely q, is that the proposition p bears the probability-relation of degree α to the set of propositions h; and this knowledge of ours justifies us in a rational belief of degree α in the proposition p. It will be convenient to call propositions such as p, which do not contain assertions about probability-relations, 'primary propositions'; and propositions such as q, which assert the existence of a probability-relation, 'secondary propositions' (Keynes, CW VIII, 1973, p. 11).

The problem that Keynes sets out to solve then is how individuals determine their rational beliefs when their knowledge of a proposition is not certain. [15]

For Keynes, individuals can behave in two different ways in a situation of uncertainty. The first is founded on the formulation of a probability obtained on the basis of uncertain information or of 'doubtful arguments' (ibid., p. 3). In the second case it is impossible to determine a rational belief, so that it is rational to allow animal spirits to determine actions. It is precisely these two types of uncertainty that traditional theory excludes by assuming that individuals have full or certain knowledge of the primary propositions.

Criticism of any use of the frequency theory of probability has tended to confuse these two separate forms of uncertainty. For example, as noted above, Shackle considers the decision to invest as a crucial decision that cannot be repeated. Thus, the facts of experience (or the 'premises' in h, as defined in the *Treatise on Probability*) will not include any repetitions of the event. Moreover, it was pointed out that there is no reason for the sum of the probabilities to be equal to one. It is in this context that Shackle's rejection of the applicability of statistical probabilities should be understood. It is undeniable that the majority of investment decisions refer to situations in which the degree of rational belief, or the secondary propositions, exhibit uncertainty in the first sense defined by Keynes, that is, when the probability associated with the secondary proposition is less than one.

However, even in this case, it is possible to calculate a probability by formulating a secondary proposition concerning the primary proposition that, say, an investment in a particular project will produce a particular return, given the information contained in *h*. In situations related to this first type of uncertainty, the approach suggested by Keynes does not imply that the behaviour adopted will be irrational. In fact every entrepreneur confronting the same situation (and with the same mental capacity) would have the same degree of rational belief and would act in exactly the same way.

The way Keynes interprets rationality clearly differs from the one Shackle refers to. The situation examined above in which it is impossible to calculate a statistical probability that would be based on a frequency distribution. However, in contrast to Shackle who considers that this impossibility implies that the decisions of economic agents must be irrational, Keynes considers that the agents can only form a degree of rational belief that is less than perfectly certain, not as one involving subjective 'caprice' or some kind of irrationality.

This highlights the importance of distinguishing between risk and Keynes-Knight uncertainty and of discriminating between Keynes's notion of rationality and the traditional concept underlying rational expectations. It should first be noted that rational expectations theorists share Keynes's opinion that the theory of probability should refer not to the occurrence of events but to the assertions of individuals concerning the occurrence of events. As Kregel points out, 'rational expectations might thus be described as a theory concerning the formulation of secondary propositions containing primary propositions that are statistical probabilities of events generated on the basis of an economic model and which have probability approaching certainty as the observations of the events occurring over time included in *h* become large' (1987, p. 524). In the analysis underpinning the theory of rational expectations, the certainty of rational belief is linked to the assumption that the subjective probability distribution of the variable under consideration in *h* of the secondary proposition can be assimilated into the objective distribution which actually produces the current values of the variable. However, as underlined before, this is only possible if the process that leads to the events about which expectations are formed is ergodic. Kregel's analysis thus completes the post-Keynesian critique of the theory of rational expectations initiated by Davidson (in particular, Davidson, 1982–3). According to Kregel (1987, p. 524) the term 'rational', as used by traditional theory, can only apply to situations of certainty of rational belief in a world governed by ergodic stochastic processes; making decisions or choices in conditions of uncertainty is thus either ruled out or classified as non-rational. In contrast post-Keynesian analysis develops a theory of the formation of expectations applicable to situations in which the degree of rational belief is less than certain.

It should not be overlooked, however, that Keynes identifies a second type of uncertainty, which precludes the determination of any kind of rational belief. This second form of uncertainty in fact covers two types of uncertainty that it is necessary to keep analytically separate. In the first case it is not possible to compare the probabilities associated with the secondary propositions, which happens when the facts of experience, those incorporated in *h*, are extremely heterogeneous when not non-existent. This provides the basis for Keynes's affirmation that 'our knowledge of the factors which will govern the yield of an investment some years hence is usually very slight and often negligible. If we speak frankly, we have to admit that our basis of knowledge for estimating the yield ten years hence [of an investment] amounts to little and sometimes to nothing' (Keynes, CW VII, 1973, pp. 149–50). In other words, it will often be the case that it will be impossible to place an ordinal measure on the probability in question. In these conditions the principle of 'insufficient reason' or the principle of indifference (that states that, if there is no reason to prefer one possible solution to another, each should have equal probability) must be rejected (Keynes, CW VIII, 1973, p. 45).

It is then necessary, following Hicks, to reformulate the axiom of the comparability of probabilities in the following fashion: starting from a certain information set, it is possible to say of two propositions, *A* and *B*, either that *A* is more probable that *B*, or that *B* is more probable than *A*, or that they are equally probable or that they are not comparable.[16] It is should also be noted that, contrary to certain interpretations of Keynes's analysis that limit uncertainty to those cases where the determination of probability is impossible, the author of the *Treatise on Probability* considered non-calculability and non-comparability to be equivalent as expressions of uncertainty.[17] However, if the non-comparability of probability implies uncertainty, it will be impossible for agents to formulate rational beliefs. To deal with this question, Keynes introduces another ingredient into his theory of logical probability: the 'weight of the argument'. It is this factor which comes to dominate the decision to act:

> It seems that there may be another aspect in which some kind of quantitative comparison between arguments is possible. This comparison turns upon a balance, not between the favourable and the unfavourable evidence, but between the absolute amounts of relevant knowledge and of relevant ignorance respectively... As the relevant evidence at our disposal increases, the magnitude of the probability of the argument may either decrease or increase, according as the new knowledge strengthens the unfavourable or the unfavourable evidence; but something seems to have increased in either case, – we have a more substantial base upon which to rest our conclusion. I express this by saying that an accession of new evidence increases the weight of the argument (Keynes, CW VIII, 1973, p. 77).

Actually when Keynes refers in Chapter 12 of *The General Theory* to the role of confidence in the decision to undertake an investment, it is precisely the weight of the argument that he has in mind (Keynes, CW VII, 1973, pp. 148–9). Thus, when probabilities cannot be compared and it is impossible to formulate a rational belief, it is the weight of the argument that becomes the determinant factor, by allowing the evaluation of investment alternatives that produces a final decision to act. The subjectivity that is inherent in the evaluation of different individuals may then become dominant, since it is individual experience that will determine the weight assigned to new information. As underlined by Kregel (1987, p. 526), it is only at this point that the idea of animal spirits enters into the decision-making framework of *The General Theory*. Animal spirits will determine the moment at which the weight of the argument attached to a proposition is sufficient to make it dominant over all other possible propositions. Animal spirits thus represent, in Keynes's words, the 'spontaneous urge to action rather than inaction'.[18] It is important to note here that Keynes insists that this spontaneous urge to action does not depend on 'waves of irrational psychology' (Keynes, CW VII, p. 162), but rather that this type of decision is securely founded on 'rational spirits' (Kregel, 1987), on 'our rational selves choosing between the alternative as best we are able, calculating where we can, but often falling back for our motive on whim or sentiment or chance' (Keynes, ibid., p. 163).

However, when the weight of the argument is very weak or non-existent, no calculation or use of the concepts of logical probability is possible. At this point, and only in these conditions, is it possible to say that probability is 'non-measurable'. Far from being rare, this case is considered by Keynes as the most likely whenever expectations are formed over the long period.[19] This point of view appears very clearly in the *Treatise on Probability*, which contains repeated warnings against what Keynes calls 'numerical expression' (Keynes, CW VIII, 1973, pp. 21–2). In particular, he points out that:

> It has been assumed hitherto as a matter of course that probability is, in the full and literal sense of the word, measurable. I shall have to limit, not extend, the popular doctrine.... The calculus of probability has received far more attention than its logic, and mathematicians, under no compulsion to deal with the whole of the subject, have naturally confined their attention to those special cases ... where algebraical representation is possible (ibid.).

Keynes thus considered that the possibility of obtaining a numerical (cardinal) measure of the degree of probability as only occasionally possible: 'A rule can be given for numerical measurement when the conclusion is one of a number of equiprobable, exclusive, and exhaustive alternatives, but not otherwise' (ibid., p. 122). In the majority of situations involving decisions with long-term consequences, this is far from realized. It then becomes very difficult to endogenize the process in the course of which expectations are formed and, as Keynes notes, 'the state of long-term expectation ... cannot be inferred from the given factors' (Keynes, CW XIII, 1973, p. 480) so that these decisions must be considered as being taken outside the 'realm of the formally exact' (Keynes, CW XIV, 1973, p. 2). In such conditions Keynes suggests that the optimal behaviour for decision-makers is to fall back on their common sense, as reflected in 'the actual observation of markets and business psychology'

(Keynes, CW VII, 1973, p. 149), rather than on the calculus of probability. Thus entrepreneurs will first consider their past experience and may assume that 'the existing state of affairs will continue indefinitely, except in so far as we have specific reasons to expect a change' (ibid., p. 52). This initial response amounts to adopting an extrapolative attitude and to ascribing to the present and the recent past a role equivalent to that which they play in the short period. At a second stage, conscious of their lack of information and of the unreliability of their individual judgements, entrepreneurs will 'fall back on the judgement of the rest of the world which is perhaps better informed' in such a way that behaviour permanently conforms to that of the majority and 'the psychology of a society of individuals each of whom is endeavouring to copy the others leads to what we may strictly term a conventional judgement' (Keynes, CW XIV, 1973, p. 114). It is against this background that Keynes's remark that 'in practice we have tacitly agreed, as a rule, to fall back on what is, in truth, a convention' (Keynes, CW VII, 1973, p. 152) should be interpreted. Finally entrepreneurs may admit that the 'existing state of opinion', as expressed by the evaluation of the market, is the only one that should be considered the 'correct summing up of future prospects' for investment (Keynes, CW XIV, 1973, p. 114). Included, however, in this market evaluation will be 'all sorts of considerations ... which are in no way relevant to the prospective yield' (Keynes, CW VII, 1973, p. 152). In fact, in these conditions, the calculations of agents count for less than their 'nerves and hysteria, and even digestions and reactions to the weather' (ibid., p. 162).

It thus becomes easier to understand why long-run expectations, and thus the marginal efficiency of capital, can be considered as being subject to sudden, sometimes violent, changes, and marked by waves of optimism and pessimism. In this perspective the conventional methods of calculation are 'compatible with a considerable measure of continuity and stability in our affairs, so long as we can rely on the maintenance of the convention' (ibid., p. 152). Long-period expectations are as a result volatile, but not violently unstable. However the appearance of new fears and new hopes 'will, without warning, take charge of human conduct. The forces of disillusion may suddenly impose a new conventional basis of evaluation' (Keynes, CW XIV, 1973, p. 115). Thus, , even in the most extreme conditions of uncertainty, Keynes rejects purely random decision-making. That his approach to decision-making in the long period has been termed 'irrational' is due to the failure to recognize that the traditional definition of rationality does not apply in such conditions and must be reformulated.

The examination of Keynes's analysis of agents' behaviour under conditions of uncertainty has shown its originality. It differs strongly from the traditional approach, which fails to distinguish between risk and uncertainty. The first point of difference is in the characterization of the informational environment facing decision-makers. In opposition to the standard approach which follows classical physics in assuming that realizations are independent of their dates, Keynesian theory is underpinned by the idea that economics has to deal with actions in historical time where random functions are not in a state of statistical control. This difference in the assumptions that are made concerning the analytic framework applicable to probability has led to a divergence of objectives between the two approaches. The axiomatic construction of neoclassical theory seeks to derive optimal states and behaviours. On the other hand, the Keynesian approach takes the opposite tack and seeks to determine the informational environment for decision-making on the basis of observations taken from the evolution of the real world. Two references within this approach – to historical time and to crucial decisions – is what allows Keynesian economists to explain the persistent inability of standard theory to deal with fundamental uncertainty, which they define in a way that distinguishes it radically from the familiar notion of risk.

The fact that post-Keynesian economists reason within a changing non-ergodic environment has enabled us to highlight a second point of difference with neoclassical approaches, and more particularly with new classical economics. It is linked to the elaboration by Keynesian economists of a conception of rationality that differs fundamentally from the robot-like mental attitude depicted by the theory of rational expectations. This different form of rationality, capable of creating expectational instability, has little to do with irrational psychological fluctuations. It is not based on the idea that, once uncertainty is taken into account, it is no longer possible to make theoretical statements about initial conditions and outcomes. Rather it leads to certain specific rational responses to uncertainty that may be identified and formalized. If in fact the notion of uncertainty calls into question the traditional approach to rationality, the latter can be expressed nonetheless in the form of codified rules of behaviour. It is thus possible to submit it to scientific analysis and debate. Thus, the Keynesian analysis of behaviour in conditions of uncertainty founded upon the notion of 'rational spirits' cannot be interpreted as the result of some irrationality of agents. Rather it is based on the notion of logical probability developed by Keynes in his *Treatise on Probability* and on the 'conventional individual rationality' described in *The General Theory* and to which he refers in his 1937 *Quarterly Journal of Economics* article.

3.2 Minsky and New-Keynesian Economics

The previous discussion has allowed us to distinguish clearly between the Keynesian theory of behaviour in situations of uncertainty and the analysis proposed by the new classical authors. Comparison between the post-Keynesian analysis and the works of new-Keynesian economists leads to similar conclusions (3.2.1). In contrast, when we confront new-Keynesian analysis with Minsky's theory, our conclusions are less clear-cut, inasmuch as the two approaches exhibit some similarities (3.2.2). Nonetheless, the existence of these similarities does not impair the specificity and the originality of Minsky's analysis (3.2.3).

3.2.1 New and post-Keynesians: are they reconcilable?

For many post-Keynesian authors analytical differences exist between new-Keynesian theory and theirs, differences that are as important as those separating the Keynesian approach from new classical economics. Therefore, post-Keynesians (often categorized as 'fundamentalists') exclude the very idea of reinterpreting one theory in terms of the other. Several arguments can be used in support of their point of view. A first obstacle to such a reinterpretation lies in the specification of the decision-making environment retained by each approach. Post-Keynesian writers find it unavailing to try to replace the non-ergodic world, characterized as they see it by fundamental uncertainty, with the probabilistic-risk environment considered by new-Keynesian economists. In particular they insist that the rational expectations hypothesis, a key feature of the new-Keynesian framework, is incompatible with their own view of the way in which individuals make their decisions when uncertainty prevails. A second point concerns the existence of asymmetric information within the new-Keynesian setting. It implies that not all the agents participating in a particular market have perfect knowledge of future market conditions. Besides, some agents know that others are better informed than they are. Nonetheless, those other agents are actually assumed to have complete knowledge of future market conditions, inasmuch as they are capable of associating a probability distribution with the whole set of market outcomes, and insofar as they know that present and future market conditions are determined by this distribution. Such knowledge is irreconcilable with the post-Keynesian notion of fundamental uncertainty. On the one hand, the assumption that all agents act in a fashion that is consistent with the rational expectations hypothesis 'presumes not only that probability distributions regarding historical phenomena have existed, but also that the same probabilities which determined past outcomes will continue to govern future events' (Davidson, 1991, p. 132). On the other hand, some post-Keynesians have criticized the approach consisting in ascribing to asymmetric information and to the financial markets imperfections it involves a role that is equivalent to the one played by uncertainty in Keynes's theory. If one considers the analysis of the credit market, for example, it is undeniable, as Van Ees and Garretsen argue, that in an asymmetric information environment 'a theory of financial intermediation is rationalized from the ability to reduce what may be called transactions costs in financial markets' (1993, p. 42). As a result, the analysis of financial intermediation developed by new-Keynesian economists seems completely at odds with the proposition, central to the post-Keynesian view, that in a world of Keynesian uncertainty institutions and monetary contractual relations derive from the liquidity preference of economic agents.

Another important difficulty encountered when seeking compatibility between the two approaches is linked to the role assigned to price rigidities. In particular, we have seen that in the markets for loans and shares described by new-Keynesian economists rigidities of this sort can cause real values to depart from their optimum level. Such rigidities are required because perfect information, the situation where real values are assumed to reach their optimum levels, remains the reference point. However, in a post-Keynesian perspective, this is a statement that needs to be proven, namely that a first best optimum obtains when the price mechanism is unfettered. Besides, post-Keynesian analysis considers that total flexibility of prices is not necessarily preferable in a world where agents must act despite fundamental uncertainty. On the contrary, the works of Kregel and Davidson related to this issue show that constraints restricting nominal price flexibility (in nominal wage contracts and in debt contracts) can be an important means of reducing radical uncertainty. Therefore, the role price rigidity/flexibility plays in post-Keynesian economics appears to be clearly and analytically very different from the one attributed by most new-Keynesian economists.[20]

Moreover, as Dymski notes, most models developed by new-Keynesian economists are embedded in partial equilibrium settings (1992, p. 315). As a result focus is essentially on the supply side of the economy and aggregate demand is usually exogenous. For example, changes affecting the amount of rationing that occurs in the markets for credit or for new share issues are what induce variations in aggregate supply and, therefore, in output and employment.[21] In contrast, it is undeniable that in post-Keynesian macroeconomic analysis aggregate demand is not 'passive'. Its fluctuations (due, for instance, to the sudden changes in expectations and in liquidity preference) appear on the contrary to be the fundamental factor causing instability of economic activity.

Finally, it is necessary to restate that in most new-Keynesian models the emergence of instability requires at the outset some exogenous shock, whatever its origin: an aggregate shock, such as 'an unexpected decrease in the price level, resulting from a monetary shock' or a shock affecting a particular sector, such as 'an unexpected shift in demand, or the unexpected formation of an oil cartel'.[22] Greenwald and Stiglitz themselves see this as a possible shortcoming of their analysis. They observe that their theory 'does not provide an entirely endogenous business cycle; it only explains how the economy responds to certain shocks' (1987, p. 126). In other words new-Keynesian economics 'has yet to furnish a complete explanation for the business cycle. It shows how shocks can induce protracted, major changes in investment and unemployment, but it treats such shocks as exogenous, not endogenous, phenomena' (ibid., p. 122). It is obvious, as these authors emphasize, that 'there remains a controversy over whether an entirely endogenous business cycle is required, or whether one should be content with a theory which translates certain kinds of shocks into disturbances in which the economy persists below "full employment" for a number of periods' (ibid., p. 126), but then this unavoidably exogenous component of new-Keynesian models differs noticeably from the essentially endogenous nature of macroeconomic instability explored in Minsky's theory and, more generally, in the post-Keynesian approach.

3.2.2 The new-Keynesian reinterpretation of Minsky

Various arguments can be opposed to the fundamentalist conclusions listed earlier. To begin with, it is possible to refute the argument that, because they retain the rational expectations hypothesis, new-Keynesian economists stand completely apart from authors belonging to other Keynesian schools. In fact new-Keynesian economists rely on the rational expectations hypothesis not by analytical necessity but rather because this concession to new classical economics does not impair the main results they achieve. For Greenwald and Stiglitz, 'individuals do not have perfect foresight or rational expectations concerning the future. The events which they confront often appear to be unique, and there is no way that they can form a statistical model predicting the probability distribution of outcomes' (1987, p. 131). Nevertheless, the rational expectations hypothesis is one these authors agree to make, for the following reason. As already mentioned, the new classical school 'obtains results similar to old classical economics, not because it has added a new set of insights, derived from rational expectations, but because it has retained an old set of assumptions, concerning perfect markets and market-clearing', among which the most important one is that agents have access to identical information (1992, p. 70). Rejecting this assumption, common to all standard neoclassical models, is what is crucial to the theoretical results achieved by new-Keynesian economists. In particular the assumption of asymmetric information appears, in the eyes of new-Keynesians, to be the *sine qua non* for there to be a financial constraint on investment.

In the framework chosen by these authors decision-making is subject to probabilistic risk. However the asymmetric distribution of information gives rise to a kind of uncertainty that can be labelled 'endogenous' insofar as outcomes depend on actions undertaken inside the model by the better-informed agents. This approach obviously contrasts with the post-Keynesian view that the main problem raised by information is the ignorance that agents actually share regarding the future outcomes of their present decisions. As a general rule new-Keynesian economists pay only lip service to 'Keynesian uncertainty', since it represents an extreme form of the 'exogenous' uncertainty that Kreps defines as one where 'the probabilities of the states do not depend on the act chosen' by the economic agent (1990, p. 101).

Therefore, even though new-Keynesian economists do not deny the existence of exogenous uncertainty, they identify it with simple probabilistic risk. Such risk concerns situations where it is possible to know – or at least to discover – the entire set of outcomes as well as the probability of realization of each individual outcome. It is then always possible to build probability distributions to describe present and future events. Exogenous uncertainty is brought into the setting in a 'weak' form by introducing a stochastic shock affecting, for instance, the output level. As argued by Dymski:

> 1. This shock can be understood accurately as generated by a stable probability distribution. 2. All agents have ready, costless knowledge of this distribution (or it is equally costly for all agents to learn about it), independent of each agent's previous actions and endowment. 3. The probability of the shock is independent of any agent's actions. 4. The uncertainty created for individual agents by the stochastic shock is eliminated within the economy as a whole, via either aggregation across agents or repeated draws through time (1993, p. 84).

In order to measure the consequences of such a conception, Dymski goes on to study the impact of introducing weak exogenous uncertainty into a standard model of optimization.[23] It comprises two types of agents, 'owners' (lenders) and 'entrepreneurs'. In the presence of weak exogenous uncertainty, that is, of a stochastic shock affecting their output level, entrepreneurs simply maximize their expected utility. Dymski shows that, in this type of risky environment model, financial structure – lending and borrowing – has no effect on the first best optimum of the model. The essential explanation of such a result is that:

> the use of subjective probabilities eliminates any effects of uncertainty per se on decision making. The uncertain technology is made certainty equivalent by parameterizing its behavior. Obviously, the assertion that agents know the possible states of the world and the likelihood of each assumes these agents are operating in a stable decisional environment. Implicitly, decisions are made repetitively, so that prior experience serves as an error-correction mechanism. The firm under probabilistic risk thus uses realizations to make ex ante uncertain outcomes predictable in the limit (ibid., p. 85–6).

This very simple reasoning helps us to understand why, in the new-Keynesian theoretical setting, exogenous uncertainty in its weak form cannot account for the fact that agents may be subject to financial constraints.

The impact of weak exogenous uncertainty is entirely different whenever asymmetric information is introduced into the same kind of standard model. As Dymski shows, 'endogenous uncertainty alone is sufficient for financial structure to matter' (ibid., p. 86). In contrast weak exogenous uncertainty has only a marginal influence – of quantitative but not qualitative nature – on the equilibrium attained in a 'pure' asymmetric information environment (that is, without exogenous uncertainty).[24] In sum, when one identifies, as new-Keynesians do, exogenous uncertainty with probabilistic risk, only asymmetric information allows us to lay down the theoretical foundations for an analysis that highlights the pivotal role played by financial structure on the evolution of economic activity.

As already mentioned, new-Keynesian models of business cycles also rely on asymmetric information in order to obtain results presenting marked similarities with Minsky's findings: financial variables are a fundamental propagating factor of financial crises and, hence, of economic depressions; that the system may adjust, even in the long run, is an idea that is discarded. In short, new-Keynesian economics offers strong endogenous foundations for the explanation of the tendency exhibited by macroeconomic fluctuations to self-amplify and persist.

These analogies between the two approaches appear to be particularly clear when one of the essential aspects of Minsky's analysis of fluctuations is considered: his financial theory of investment. With regard to this point, the new-Keynesian approach in terms of asymmetric information allows us to specify the theoretical foundations of two key concepts of Minsky's theory of investment: the lender's risk and the borrower's risk.

We have seen that Minsky characterizes the lender's risk as a increase in the marginal supply price of investment. Thus, the cost of investment includes not only the price for the purchase of capital goods, but also the capitalized value of financial costs. More precisely, Minsky notes that the lender's risk gives rise in loan contracts to higher interest rates, more guarantees and restrictive covenants. At first glance such behaviour firmly resembles the risk aversion of suppliers of external funds. However, in a neoclassical context with perfect information, diversification allows lenders to reduce such risk by taking measures in order to be only weakly exposed to the risk attached to each individual loan. As for the borrowers, an infinitely elastic supply of external finance is available to them in the financial market at a determined interest rate. Individual businesses will therefore undertake all investment projects whose net present value is positive, without having to calculate what proportion of internal and external funds would be required to finance them. Within this setting, and in accordance with the first Modigliani–Miller proposition, financial structure and investment would therefore be independent.

Such conclusions evidently no longer hold in the informational environment retained by the new-Keynesian economists. The asymmetric character of information, and the related phenomena of adverse selection and moral hazard, explains the link that exists between the financial structure of a firm and the amount it invests. In the first place, the cost of external resources a firm has to face is greater than the opportunity cost associated with the reliance on internal funds. This cost includes a premium whose purpose is to compensate lenders for the risk they incur when they finance poor projects. This premium creates a preference for internal funds, because businesses might not invest in projects that would require borrowing or the issuing of new shares, while a sufficient amount of internal finance would have enabled them to do so. In the second place, we have seen that the presence of asymmetric information is likely to lead to credit rationing because of the inability of lenders to recognize those businesses that have good projects. This induces lenders to allocate funds to borrowers emitting observable signals, such as businesses pledging large enough amounts of collateral. Hence, the obvious relationship between investment decision-making and financial structure.

It is important to note that this outcome is independent of the degree of risk characterizing an investment project. If the project is risky, but the information regarding the distribution of incomes that is available to borrowers and lenders is symmetrical, the project will be financed, as lenders fund all projects exhibiting a positive expected net present value. As we mentioned earlier, diversification is the way to overcome problems related to risk aversion. This is what is meant by Fazzari and Variato, for whom 'risk alone does not explain why financial structure is important for investment in the sense that inadequate finance will prevent firms from undertaking otherwise desirable projects. One needs asymmetric information that motivates defensive behavior on the part of lenders' (1994, p. 358). Accordingly, in an environment with asymmetric information, the independence between real and financial decisions assumed by neoclassical economists is rejected and real investment is not exclusively determined by exogenously-given preferences and technology. In a situation of asymmetric information, two firms with identical investment opportunities from a technological viewpoint may make different investment decisions, depending on their financial structure.

Beyond the shared dismissal of the standard theory of investment and the analogous findings as to the connection between investment decisions and financial structure, the essential question is whether the more recent and more formalized approach proposed by new-Keynesian economists has contributed to supporting in a way that is decisive the views initially put forward by Minsky. Some authors have answered this question in the affirmative. Their contribution highlights the theoretical incompatibility between, on the one hand, the identity of information among individuals assumed by the standard theory and Minsky's notion of the lender's risk, on the other. Thus, Fazzari and Variato argue that for the lender's risk to arise when borrowers and lenders have identical information regarding the profitability of investment 'implies that either the borrower wants to go ahead with a money-losing deal or the lender systematically forgoes what he knows are money-making opportunities' (ibid., p. 359). Conversely, theory based on asymmetric information, such as new-Keynesian theory, explains why it may be rational for a business to ask for resources to finance an investment project and just as rational for a potential lender not to respond to his or her demand and resort instead to credit rationing.

Similar conclusions apply to Minsky's borrower's risk. This kind of risk has hardly any relevance in a neoclassical environment since, as already mentioned, if the borrower's risk is founded on the risk aversion of entrepreneurs, it can be diminished thanks to diversification. As regards this point, the approach developed by new-Keynesian economists leads to conclusions that differ dramatically from those obtained by neoclassical theory in a perfect information setting. Accordingly new-Keynesian analysis provides a better understanding of the borrower's risk: although utility maximizing agents are perfectly aware of the advantages derived from risk diversification, not to diversify is an optimal reaction to asymmetric information, and not something that is arbitrarily assumed. As we have seen, asymmetric information implies that external finance is not a perfect substitute for internal finance. External resources when available are more expensive. Therefore, in order to carry out profitable investment projects, businesses can feel obliged to commit a greater amount of their own funds, either as a direct source of finance, or as collateral to improve their access to external resources. A commitment of this nature compels entrepreneurs to forgo diversification opportunities when their desire is to invest, but alloting greater amounts of one's own resources to the acquisition of specific fixed capital goods raises one's exposure to risk. As was emphasized in the previous chapter, it is precisely on these grounds that new-Keynesian models of business cycles centre their analysis on the link that exists between equity constraints and bankruptcy costs.[25] The role of this – strictly financial and therefore non-technological – relationship is one of the factors limiting the expansion of investment. Thus, renewal of theoretical foundations has shed new light on this factor, thereby allowing a restatement of Kalecki's increasing risk principle and of Minsky's borrower's risk.

A priori the analysis in terms of asymmetric information, as developed by the new-Keynesian economists, offers a reinterpretation of the behaviours associated with both the lender's and the borrower's risk, which underpin Minsky's financial theory of investment, and provide them with microeconomic foundations. Moreover, with regard to Minsky's original conception, it provides a restatement that can be justified on the grounds that financial constraints affecting investment are related to information and market structures *per se*, to 'inherent characteristics of decentralized market production' (Fazzari, 1992, p. 127) and not to the use agents make of existing information and markets. We have seen that, in Minsky's analysis of investment decisions, agents' subjective assessment of their investment opportunities is contingent on their dependence on external financing. However, as pointed out by Dymski (1993a, p. 79), this conception violates an important assumption of modern microeconomic theory, one Kreps labels the 'Harsanyi doctrine' (1990, p. 111), according to which 'any difference in subjective probability assessments must be the result of differences in information'. Accordingly, subjective probability assessments must not be sensitive to the degree of exposure of cash flows to risk. From this standpoint it seems then that, in Minsky's approach, the capacity of investors to perceive the true state of investment opportunities is distorted by their financial situation. This is what Bernanke (1983), a supporter of the new-Keynesian view, means when he argues that Minsky's analysis assumes irrationality of agents. Bernanke considers that, in Minsky's demonstration, agents are irrational because they make systematic errors when they assess the real state of the world.[26]

In addition new-Keynesian theory, which 'seeks to adapt microtheory to macrotheory', acknowledges Lucas's criticism (1976), applying to traditional Keynesian theories of fluctuations, that these macroeconomic approaches of business cycles are incompatible with the premises of microeconomic theory. Besides, as noted by Mishkin, new-Keynesian economics offers the advantage, when compared with Minsky's analysis, of providing a precise definition of the financial crisis, depicted as 'a disruption to financial markets in which adverse selection and moral hazard problems become much worse, so that financial markets are unable to efficiently channel funds to those who have the productive investment opportunities' (1992, p. 117). In sum, these various remarks, associated with the theoretical compatibility underlined by Fazzari, tend to support the idea that Minsky's theory could be (advantageously) restated with the help of the analytical tools developed by the new-Keynesian economists.

3.2.3 Minsky's specificity preserved

In Minsky's analysis the confrontation between a money supply that tends to lose its elasticity and a demand for money that tends to become gradually more rigid during the ascending phase of the business cycle leads to an endogenous increase of the interest rate.[27] However, this increase is not the only outcome. In general it is accompanied by the development of a quantity constraint that involves the amount of finance that becomes actually available. Attributable to the lender's risk, this constraint is independent of the action of the interest rate. It induces bankers to limit the availability of finance once it has reached a certain level, thereby creating a form of rationing. As Minsky argues, 'although some risks faced by lenders are expressed in observable increases in interest rates, as leverage increases and the confidence in future cash flows decreases, this observed rise in interest rates is not the full picture of the rise in financing costs' (1986a, p. 123). Some agents will then be subject to quantitative constraints insofar as there will be no interest rate that will make banks more willing to grant them more loans.

Minsky's suggestion that investment might be subject to financial quantitative constraints when information is not perfect raises the question as to whether there might exist some relationship between his analysis of banking and the analyses in terms of credit rationing developed by new-Keynesian economists. This question is all the more legitimate because Minsky's position as regards the results obtained by this school of thought is one of comparative approval, since it even leads him to suggest that 'a convergence between the new and the post-Keynesian economics can be expected, and the result is likely to be fruitful' (Ferri and Minsky, 1989, p. 123).

Minsky thus stands quite apart from those authors whose extreme fundamentalist position leads them to reject entirely the contributions of new-Keynesian economics. One of the main reasons for this repeal on the part of some post-Keynesian authors is that the essential assumption made by the new-Keynesians, namely that agents are subject to asymmetric information, appears to involve only a minor deviation from the traditional neoclassical analysis.[28] Minsky's position is not quite so clear-cut: he considers that simple observation of financially sophisticated economies shows on the contrary that problems of asymmetry of information are essential and are empirically meaningful. In these economies agents (in particular entrepreneurs and bankers) specialize in the activities in which they have a specific informational advantage. As argued by Fazzari and Variato, if one considers the 'relevant' information set as the set of data likely to influence an agent's economic choices, 'each individual will "know" a subset of this information. It would be a great surprise if everyone "knew" exactly the same thing. When different agents know different things, information is asymmetric' (1994, p. 360).

In Minsky's representation, as in new-Keynesian economics, the exception is then not asymmetry but rather symmetry of information and therefore, undeniably, 'asymmetric information is both general and fundamental in an economy in which there are differences across agents' (ibid.). When asymmetric information prevails, lenders have access to complete information as to the projects that they finance only inasmuch as investors reveal it voluntarily. However both new-Keynesian economists and Minsky insist that in a world where 'each participant in such negotiations has private information as well as its own market power' bankers never see a pro forma they do not like, since there is an incentive for borrowers to exaggerate the quality of their investment projects (Minsky, 1989a, p. 177). That is why both Minsky's banks and new-Keynesian lenders are 'rational sceptics' with regard to the information provided by borrowers. As expressed by Minsky, 'it is the duty of the "banker"...to be skeptic – to reveal the shaky or heroic assumptions and also the unwarranted inferences' (1992, p. 23). In the two approaches scepticism leads to the emergence of a set of institutional arrangements whose purpose is to protect the interests of lenders: collateral (or net worth), restrictive covenants, interest rate increases and premiums on external finance that increase its price in proportion to the opportunity cost of self-finance.[29]

In this perspective asymmetric information cannot merely be considered as a minor imperfection of otherwise smoothly performing systems or as an arbitrary or *ad hoc* assumption, as it is respectively asserted by post-Keynesian and neoclassical economists in support of their critique of the informational Keynesianism proposed by new-Keynesian economists. On the contrary, in view of our previous remarks, asymmetric information seems to be an inherent characteristic of market economies. Taking it into account shows that similarities do exist between the new-Keynesian analysis of credit rationing and Minsky's analysis of banking activity. For authors such as Fazzari (1992) the new-Keynesian explanation of credit rationing provides an adequate reinterpretation of Minsky's analysis of the lender's risk and, more generally, of his theory of banking.

However, a careful analysis of Minsky's works shows that this assertion is open to debate. It does not take into account the essential distinction between the decision-making environment retained by the new-Keynesians and the one chosen by Minsky. The approach Minsky develops clearly fits in with post-Keynesian fundamentalism, as it considers that the concepts of expectations, uncertainty and ignorance are at the heart of Keynes's contribution to economic theory. That is why, in contrast to the new-Keynesians who extensively develop models that depart as little as possible from the premises of neoclassical theory, Minsky unambiguously rejects the axioms considered as fundamental features of new classical economics.

The first axiom he rejects is the one depicting an economic world oblivious of history and 'crucial decisions'. Instead Minsky's world is one of complex decision-making where fundamental uncertainty, in the sense of Keynes, dominates and where decisions, once taken, can exhibit over time a strong dose of indeterminacy. It is such an environment of strong uncertainty that must be considered, Minsky believes, in order to provide a relevant description of the way agents behave in the credit market: 'because both bankers and their borrowers are aware of time, they recognize that their current decisions are made in the face of uncertainty' (1986a, p. 118). This has obviously little to do with the exogenous uncertainty, the probabilistic risk favoured by the new-Keynesians. Indeed like Knight for whom 'Uncertainty must be taken in a sense radically distinct from the familiar notion of Risk' (1921, p. 19), Minsky insists that 'the risks bankers carry are not objective probability phenomena; instead they are uncertainty relations that are subjectively valued' (1986a, p. 239).

As we have seen, the environment considered by the new-Keynesians is one characterized by risk, into which they also introduce asymmetric information. This gives rise to a fundamental change in the nature of financial ties and creates a relationship between investment and financial structure. It is asymmetric information and not risk (or exogenous uncertainty) that abolishes the neutrality of financial decisions. Notwithstanding this, there remains a difficult question that Minsky raises: in the presence of fundamental uncertainty – rather than of mere probabilistic risk – is asymmetric information essential to obtaining a financial constraint that affects investment?

In the risky environment described by the new-Keynesian, agents' decisions are subject to stochastic processes that are sufficiently regular for them to be accounted for using statistical tools. Things are radically different in the world of Keynesian uncertainty considered by Minsky. As already mentioned, in this environment decision-makers are confronted with 'crucial decisions'. As a result statistical tools are of little use: a significant time interval separates the decision from its outcome; the project under scrutiny takes place in an environment that changes over time; the course of events is costly if not impossible to reverse once the decision has been taken. Consequently, the introduction of Keynesian uncertainty calls into question each of the four eatures associated with probabilistic risk and has some important implic₂ ions for the behaviour of economic agents. Indeed, as restated by Dym ki, when one considers an environment of fundamental uncertainty,

> (a) stochastic variation is not governed by stable probability distributions; (b) agents lack costless information providing insight into the 'true' state of affairs in the economy; (c) agents cannot always determine the extent to which their own actions are responsible for the outcomes they experience; (d) it is impossible to preclude the possibility of systemic risk, because the economy has no parameters. (1993b, p. 50).[30]

When we consider these four features simultaneously, our understanding of exogenous uncertainty is radically transformed. The economy no longer follows a natural trajectory over time: the apparent stability of the dynamics is due to a complex set of historical and institutional factors and to the capacity of thwarting systems to adjust and to stabilize market behaviours.[31] The knowledge of agents, in particular knowledge that is applicable to crucial decisions, is built and no longer just given.

In this uncertain decision-making environment, the possibility of reinterpreting Minsky's analysis in terms of an approach based on asymmetric information is thus seriously undermined. In particular, the mere existence of Keynesian uncertainty is sufficient to generate credit rationing, without it being necessary to refer to the notion of asymmetric information. As emphasized by Dymski, in an environment of strong uncertainty, the choices made by agents depend both on their opinions about the possible outcomes of uncertain processes and on the consequences of their anticipated errors (1993a). However 'these assessments could both differ between the owner and the entrepreneur borrower, because no objective or subjective standard for the stochastic truth exists' (ibid., p. 98). To make his point, Dymski provides a simple illustration of how rationing can arise in the market for loans when uncertainty prevails (ibid., pp. 95–9). He assumes that at a given point in time, a lender's appraisal of the probability of success of a particular entrepreneur becomes more pessimistic (a high level of output is considered less likely), whereas the attitude of the entrepreneur himself does not change. Under these circumstances, the lender assigns a lower value to the probability of success, α, and the entrepreneur a greater value. In a situation of fundamental uncertainty, as opposed to an environment that is merely risky, reasons for expectations to differ are numerous: divergent interpretation of past experience, different methods of assessment, etc. In all cases lenders, because they appraise α differently, estimate the 'warranted' demand for loans to be lower, for all given levels of the interest rate, than the entire demand coming from entrepreneurs. The amount of credit that is granted will therefore be considered by the latter as rationed insofar as it is lower than their actual demand for credit. Besides, as this rationing is due to opinions of agents that differ, owing to a complex and changing environment, there exists no simple way of reducing it.

Minsky's analysis fits in particularly well with this type of reasoning. For him it is important to define the particular kind of rationality that would prevail then. It must take into account the existence of asymmetric information. Nonetheless, this does not mean that the environment should be described as one of probabilistic risk, as in new-Keynesian theory. Minsky's opinion is akin to the one voiced by Dymski, for whom:

> Clearly, allowing for asymmetric information in a Keynesian uncertain environment will not involve simply transplanting variables directly from the probabilistic-risk context in which they have been developed. Information asymmetry will not, as in New-Keynesian models, involve two parties knowing different portions of a pregiven truth; instead, both will have manufactured different truths, and one side will not agree – or have access to – the truth of the other side. In sum, making use of asymmetric information does not imply acceptance of the methodological conventions of neoclassical economics. The fact that asymmetric information can be assimilated into general equilibrium frameworks is irrelevant for whether asymmetric information, appropriately interpreted, is consistent with Keynesian uncertainty (1993b, p. 53).

Naturally the overruling character of strong uncertainty induces Minsky to reject a second axiom accepted by new-Keynesian economists, namely that the rationality of economic agents can be depicted by the standard hypothesis of rational expectations. In Minsky's model considering strong uncertainty leads neither to Lucas's conclusion that we are in the presence of 'economic reasoning of no value', nor to radical indeterminacy of behaviour. In line with the works developed by post-Keynesian authors in this area, Minsky's economic agent is driven by 'rational spirits' of a different nature.[32] This form of rationality finds strong theoretical underpinnings in Keynes's writings on probabilities and in the rationality of a conventional kind studied previously. It is precisely this form of rationality that characterizes Minsky's analysis of the behaviour of banks in the money market and on the loans market. Like Kregel for whom 'since expectations are partly formed on the basis of the operation of the economy and partly on the imagination of agents, they are composed both of endogenous and exogenous elements' (1995, p. 218), Minsky describes the behaviour of banks as based on 'objective' endogenous variables and on aspects determined in a conventional or 'subjective' fashion. As Minsky explains, 'an increase in debtors who find it difficult or impossible to fulfill their commitments on debts will induce bankers to be skeptical of new proposals for debt financing, even as nonfulfillment of debt contracts by business decreases available bankers' funds' (1986a, p. 118). To this objective factor influencing the formation of banks' expectations, there is an added subjective component. It implies that realized outcomes (for example, the quantity of loans that has been repaid) can induce banks to modify their decisions as to the amount of credit to be granted, independently of how these outcomes fit in with their expectations. This means in particular that, even if results merely confirm the banks' expectations, it is likely that, encouraged by increased confidence in their forecasting methods, they will make more loans. Accordingly, the longer the period during which the debt to equity ratio of the economy remains at a certain level without provoking a financial crisis, the more banks are likely to raise their estimates of the maximum level of indebtedness (in proportion to the value of assets both they and potential borrowers hold) to which it is prudent to agree.[33]

In conclusion, the contributions made by new-Keynesian economists cannot entirely account for the way Minsky describes the behaviour of agents, in particular their financial behaviour. This is due to the differences in the decision-making environments within which the two approaches are embedded. As opposed to many other post-Keynesian authors, Minsky does consider problems that arise between agents in situations of asymmetric information. Nevertheless, these problems occur in a world of fundamental uncertainty, one that has little to do with an environment of probabilistic risk. Such uncertainty implies a form of rationality that contrasts with the rationality presumed by new-Keynesian economists.

The differences between the analyses of Minsky and the new-Keynesians are greater still when we turn to another key aspect of the former's approach, namely the institutional dimension of his theory of fluctuations. This question is the subject of the following chapter.

NOTES

1. See Woodford's model examined earlier.
2. Keynes, *The Collected Writings*, XIV, p. 152 and *The General Theory* (CW VII, 1973, p. 162).
3. This is what Keynes is led to conclude on many occasions, in *The General Theory* (CW VII, 1973, Chapter 12, p. 151, but also in Chapter 13, p. 170 and in Chapter 22, p. 317).
4. For a more detailed analysis, see Dangel (1988).
5. Orléan (1988, p. 236). As illustrated by the often cited beauty contest, *The General Theory*, (CW VII, 1973, p. 156).
6. Ferri and Minsky (1989) p. 131.
7. Ibid.
8. Keynes (CW VII, 1973, p. vii). While it is most generally recognized that both economists considered it was important to distinguish between risk and uncertainty, there is less agreement as to whether their conceptions of uncertainty were similar. See Hoogduin (1987) and Schmidt (1996).
9. As Davidson (1991) notes, the review of the literature by Machina (1987), which provides an extensive survey of theories of choice under uncertainty, reflects the traditional view on this issue. While Machina does refer to models of subjective probability, he never mentions the existence of other analyses of uncertainty that could also be added to the 'probabilistic tool box' of traditional theory.
10. Some post-Keynesian authors such as Lavoie (1985b, pp. 499–500) consider cruciality rather than the uniqueness of a decision – as in Knight for example – as being what alters the economic environment in the future. Crucial decisions are, in fact, very common (e.g. investment involves such decisions). As Davidson notes (1982–83, p. 192), the uniqueness of an event in a finite realization could simply mean that the event has a very low probability.
11. See the passage from Keynes's *Quarterly Journal of Economics* article cited above.
12. This is emphasized by Arena (1989).
13. See Keynes's appraisal of the works of Ramsey in *The Collected Writings*, X, pp. 338–9.
14. Keynes writes the probability relation thus defined as $a|h = \alpha$.
15. For a detailed analysis of this problem, also see Arrous (1982).
16. Hicks (1979, p. 114).This contrasts with the traditional formulation of this axiom that states that, given a certain information set, of two propositions, either one is more probable than the other, or they are equally probable.
17. Such an interpretation is developed by Lawson (1985).
18. Keynes (CW VII, 1973, p. 173). It is necessary to point out that the notion of 'weight' raises the very delicate problem of the determination of the point in time at which a decision is taken. In fact Keynes excludes the idea of a maximum weight that would correspond to the existing set of available information, to express this idea in the language of rational expectations. Rather, Keynes argues that it is not possible to equate the cost of additional information with an increase in weight in the same way that traditional theory relates an increase in information with an increase in certainty: 'There clearly comes a point when it is no longer worthwhile to spend trouble, before acting, in the acquisition of further information, and there is no evident principle by which to determine how far we ought to carry our maxim of strengthening the weight of our argument' (CW VIII, 1973, p. 83).

19. See Keynes's analysis in Chapter 12 of *The General Theory*.
20. But not, however, by all of these authors. Greenwald and Stiglitz (1993) in particular seem to support the post-Keynesian perspective concerning this point. For these authors 'increased flexibility of wages and prices might exacerbate the economy's downturn in case of shocks'.
21. For a good illustration, see Stiglitz (1992).
22. Greenwald and Stiglitz (1987, p. 127). This remark also applies to the model of fluctuations built by Greenwald and Stiglitz and examined earlier. Though we have pointed out that this model can yield endogenous chaotic dynamics, this possibility is merely mentioned by the authors and not studied in detail. They focus instead on the nature and on the role played by shocks in generating fluctuations of economic activity.
23. See the detailed analysis of the model in Dymski's article (1993a, pp. 84–6).
24. See the complete demonstration (Dymski 1993a pp. 86–94).
25. See in particular the important role played by these bankruptcy costs in Greenwald and Stiglitz's model examined earlier.
26. For a more complete analysis of this issue, see Dymski (1993).
27. This point will be analysed in more detail later.
28. Concerning this point, see in particular Dymski and Pollin (1993); Davidson (1992), Van Ees and Garretsen (1993).
29. See Minsky (1986a, pp. 187–93).
30. For Dymski systemic risk appears when 'the *ex post* average experience of all agents vis-à-vis some stochastic event may diverge from the average anticipated *ex ante*' (1993b p. 50). For a detailed analysis see Dymski (1993 a, pp 97–8).
31. See below.
32. See in particular Kregel (1987) and Davidson (1982–83). The phrase 'rational spirits' has been coined by Kregel (1987).
33. This is an additional argument supporting the existence of an increasing stair-like money supply curve as in Minsky's analysis (see Minsky, 1957, and our analysis of this question below). The horizontal segments of the curve can then be interpreted as corresponding to the periods during which banks raise the indebtedness ratios they judge acceptable and do not hesitate to resort to liability management to respond to borrowers' demands for funds. As soon as the acceptable indebtedness threshold ratio is reached, banks might decide to make use of quantitative credit rationing or to increase the interest rate, which explains the increasing portions of the curve.

7. Institutional Dynamics

1 INTRODUCTION

As with many contemporary business cycle theories, the assumptions underpinning non-linear new-Keynesian models are considered as invalidated only by the refutation of the predictions that can be derived from them, in accordance with M. Friedman's methodological principles (1953). As Boyer argues, making this sort of methodological choice implies that

> in general, it does not seem that certain characteristics are taken into account although they are essential and ultimately determine macroeconomic dynamics. It is possible, of course, to reason on the basis of false premises ... but it is better for the physicist and engineer to work on sound assumptions. To the extent that the macroeconomist would rather be more like the physicist than the mathematician, it is essential to take into consideration the consequences of institutions in microeconomic and macroeconomic terms alike (1993, p. 20).

This type of critique does not apply to post-Keynesian macroeconomics. Unlike the theories we have just referred to, post-Keynesian analysis of macroeconomic disequilibria is characterized by the importance it ascribes to institutions. These institutions take the form of arrangements (involving the goods, labour and financial markets), of contracts expressed in money terms concerning immediate or future payments. The existence of these institutional arrangements, specific to monetary economies of production, implies that money is not merely some arbitrarily chosen *numéraire* or accounting device. Holding money increases agents' liquidity, i.e. their ability to meet their contractual commitments when the latter fall due. In addition money allows agents, confronted with the radical uncertainty typical of the environment in which the most important economic decisions are taken, to hold their savings in the form of cash (for a period that is *a priori* undefined) rather than in the form of consumer or investment goods. Thus, in the type of economy considered by post-Keynesian analysis 'the holding of money is a valuable choice' (Davidson, 1991, p. 139). As this choice, one which consists in adopting a 'wait and see' attitude (including in the long run), leads to an increased preference for liquidity, and to a drop in effective demand for goods resulting from productive activity, it has harmful consequences at the macroeconomic level (Kregel, 1980). In an economy where institutional arrangements – and in particular the monetary institutions – influence the rational behaviour of agents, an equilibrium may be reached and maintained where unemployment prevails. Under these circumstances it is necessary to set up institutional mechanisms and public policies capable of stimulating effective demand whenever the private sector displays a propensity to produce a lack of effective demand (Davidson and Davidson, 1996).

When compared with Minsky's analysis, it also seems that both new-Keynesian models of financial instability and non-linear models of Keynesian inspiration neglect an essential aspect of the financial instability hypothesis, an aspect we propose to label 'institutional dynamics.' When this institutional dimension is taken into consideration, Minsky's business cycle theory is interpreted as the combination of two intertwining kinds of dynamics: 'financial' dynamics, at the origin of economic instability, and 'institutional' dynamics, the effect of which is to offset and stabilize the naturally explosive amplitude of economic fluctuations.

In Minsky's theory of fluctuations two types of institutional agents exert a crucial influence on the dynamics of market economies: financial institutions, on the one hand, and public authorities, on the other.

2   THE BEHAVIOUR OF BANKS AND FINANCIAL INSTABILITY

Minsky's analysis of the behaviour of banks rests upon two main foundations. In the first place, and in agreement with most post-Keynesian economists, Minsky adopts a clearly endogenous monetary approach: 'if the [analyst's] priors are that the monetary mechanism is a main player in the determination of investment and through investment the level of aggregate demand then the monetary supply is endogenously determined in the financing processes: the Keynesian vision goes along with the endogeneity of money' (1991b, p. 209). This vision consists in considering that: 1) the supply of money is not independent of its demand; 2) there exists a particular relationship between commercial banks and the central bank. It is thus assumed that the latter adopts an accommodating attitude, meaning that it responds passively to the liquidity needs of the former.

In the second place, Minsky's position regarding the determination of the interest rate is somewhat paradoxical, as it consists in conciliating the endogenous character of money supply with the endogenous character of the interest rate, arguing that 'the financing needs of the investment boom raise interest rates' and that a rising inelastic demand will lead to a rise in the observed price unless supply is infinitely elastic at the existing price ... For a variety of reasons ... the supply of finance from banks eventually becomes less than infinitely elastic. This means that after favorable conditions for investment are sustained over time, the cost of financing investment as it is being produced increases (1986a, p. 195).

As is easily understood, this aspect of Minsky's analysis of banking is important for the coherence of his theory of business cycles. It is only by proving that the interest rate is both procyclical and endogenous that the second principle of the financial instability hypothesis – the endogenous emergence of macroeconomic instability in the financially sophisticated economies that he focuses on – can be considered as robustly founded.

The elements central to Minsky's analysis of endogenous money were defined some forty years ago, in his very first article, 'Central Banking and Money Market Changes' (1957a). This article offers an interpretation of the endogeneity of money that describes the money supply as a function that captures the intricate relationships which unfold in the money market between the central bank and the commercial banks. Careful reading of this contribution helps to provide a clear picture of Minsky's complex analysis of endogenous money supply. Reference to the 1957 article shows that it is grounded upon two main elements: first, an analysis that highlights the entrepreneurial and innovative behaviour of commercial banks, with the effects such behaviour has on the determination of the money market interest rate; second, an explanation of how financial innovation, bank liquidity, and the endogenous interest rate are interrelated.

2.1 Active Commercial Banks and Rejection of a Completely Exogenous Interest Rate

In 'Central Banking and Money Market Changes', Minsky begins by analysing the case where the central bank is implementing a restrictive monetary policy (1957b, pp. 171-3). Monetary authorities apply a policy of this kind when they fear that economic expansion might generate inflation, a policy that causes an increase in the interest rate, owing to 'a vigorous demand for financing relative to the available supply' (ibid., p. 163). Two possibilities are considered. The first consists in reasoning within a stable institutional environment, one where 'a tight money policy will be effective and the interest rate will rise to whatever extent is necessary in order to restrict the demand for financing to the essentially inelastic supply... This can be represented as a positively sloped curve between velocity and the interest rate' (ibid., p. 172). Institutional stability is not, however, Minsky's main focus. At the beginning of the 1950s changes began affecting the money market, as the markets for Federal funds and for repurchase agreements emerged and expanded. For Minsky these evolutions simply reflected the existence of a form of institutional instability governed by the profit-seeking and innovative behaviour of commercial banks.

Minsky's view of the status and the behaviour of banks proves to be quite isolated within Keynesian fundamentalism. The fact that the behaviour of banks is guided essentially by the permanent quest for profit opportunities lessens to a great extent the distinction between banks, other financial institutions and non-financial agents. Thus, a sharp contrast appears here with the position defended by the proponents of the 'circuit' theory of money, according to whom the existence of an unambiguous distinction between banks and firms, based on a 'hierarchy' of functions, is the key idea (Lavoie, 1985a, pp. 67–8). For Minsky this dichotomy between banks and financial institutions has no foundation. Indeed, 'the line between commercial banks, whose liabilities include checking deposits, other depository thrift institutions, miscellaneous managers of money (like insurance companies, pension funds and various investment trusts), and investment bankers is more reflective of the legal environment and institutional history than of the economic function of these financial institutions' (1986a, p. 223). For similar reasons the distinction between financial institutions and non-financial agents does not seem crucial to him: 'banks and bankers are not passive managers of money to lend or to invest; they are in business to maximize profits. They actively solicit borrowing customers, undertake financing commitments, build connections with business and other bankers, and seek funds' (ibid., pp. 229–30).

Interestingly, this aspect of Minsky's theory is reminiscent of the approach developed in 'Commercial Banks as Creators of Money' (1987), an article where Tobin contrasts the 'old view' on banking with the 'new view'. Like Minsky, Tobin and the supporters of the new view make no clear distinction between banks and other financial institutions, or between what Gurley and Shaw call the 'monetary system' – comprising the commercial banks and the Fed – and the 'other financial intermediaries' (1956, pp. 260–1). All these financial agents are 'financial intermediaries' whose main and characteristic function is to 'satisfy simultaneously the portfolio preferences of ... borrowers [and] lenders' (Tobin, 1987, p. 274). Another important resemblance between banks and other financial institutions is related to the Marshallian behaviour adopted by all financial intermediaries. As with 'nonfinancial industries', their supply will go on increasing as long as 'the marginal returns on lending and investing ... will not exceed the marginal cost to banks of attracting and holding additional deposits' (ibid., pp. 277 and 281). Thus, in the absence of reserve requirements, 'expansion of credit and deposits by the commercial banking system would be limited by the availability of assets at yields sufficient to compensate banks for the costs of attracting and holding the corresponding deposits' (1987, p. 279). Accordingly, it is the regulatory restrictions (reserve requirements and interest rate ceilings) imposed only upon banks rather than the monetary nature of their liabilities that underpin the relation between reserves and deposits, as determined by the customary money multiplier. However, as noted by Tobin, even in presence of such regulatory constraints, the simple money multiplier does not necessarily apply to all increases of reserves: the level of deposits and of bank assets is in fact also influenced by 'depositor preferences' as well as by the 'lending and investing opportunities' offered to banks (1987, pp. 279–81).

Thus, Minsky's analysis of banking, by attenuating the distinction between commercial banks and other financial intermediaries, and between money and other financial assets, but also by underscoring the entrepreneurial behaviour of banks, is akin to the one developed by the new view. However, the two approaches also display differences. Even though Tobin argues that changes in depositors' preferences can affect the lending capacity of banks, he does not seem to fully size up the role played by banks' active management of assets and liabilities as a way of, first, untightening the regulatory quantitative constraints to which they are subjected and, second, simply carrying out their profit-seeking activity. On the contrary, and like Schumpeter (1951a), Minsky insists that the search for market power is a fundamental determinant of innovation. Banks are entrepreneurial firms whose innovations allow greater profits: 'in a capitalist economy, the purpose of activity is to make money. For business, making money means making profits. Every business-person worthy of hire knows that market power facilitates making money. As Joseph A. Schumpeter emphasized, innovation is a source of market power; it yields a transitory monopoly position' (Minsky, 1986b).[1] New financial instruments, new financial procedures and new financial institutions are thus created by innovators who receive monopoly rents that disappear as innovations diffuse.

The process described in the 1957 article unfolds as follows. Rising interest rates act as a signal which private market operators interpret as new profit opportunities. Higher interest rates imply that greater opportunity costs affect the excess reserves held by commercial banks. Their incentive is therefore to lend these reserves to the Federal funds market. Besides, the Federal funds rate is always lower than the discount rate, Minsky observes (1957a, p. 164). This is a circumstance banks short of reserves will take advantage of, as will non-bank financial institutions, such as government bond houses, induced to make borrowings by issuing repurchase agreements that non-financial firms acquire. This is made all the easier because high interest rates will lead such firms to move away from non-interest-bearing demand deposits and seek more profitable ways of investing their money.[2] Thus the increase in interest rates creates an environment propitious to the emergence and the development of institutional innovations.

An important outcome of such innovations is that they increase the velocity of money and thereby the quantity of money supplied to potential borrowers.

Two main factors explain the relationship that develops between the rise in velocity and the increase in the quantity of money. In the first place, greater reliance by banks on the market for Federal funds allows a larger volume of demand deposits for a given amount of central bank money: 'a given volume of reserves now supports more deposits' (Minsky, 1957a, p. 171). In the second place, the innovative process described earlier implies that the assets held by commercial banks undergo two important changes: 1) the proportion invested in short-term government securities, such as Treasury bills, diminishes as higher rates persuade non-financial firms to increase their holdings of such assets; and 2) lending to government bond houses also declines as these agents now collect a large amount of funds from non-financial firms through issues of repurchase agreements. As a result, for a determined volume of demand deposits, a larger amount of bank loans is granted to firms (ibid.) Why Minsky identifies these various changes, affecting the balance sheets of banks and brought about by the innovative process, with an increase in bank reserves thus becomes clear, as well as why both velocity and the quantity of money increase when economic activity expands (ibid., p. 170).

These changes that concern the money market thus create institutional instability, which gives rise to rightwards shifts in the interest rate–velocity curve. An upward-stepped money supply curve obtains, similar to the one represented in Figure 7.1. The increasing portions of the curve depict the effect of a restrictive monetary policy on the interest rate when the institutional environment remains stable. However, such increases do not last indefinitely, as an increase in the interest rate (for instance, from r_0 to r_1) creates profit opportunities, money market innovations and thus institutional instability, as described by the curve shift from I to II. A plateau, a–b, appears, which characterizes the period during which institutional innovation is spreading.

During this period the impact on the interest rate of a restrictive monetary policy is completely counteracted, while the velocity of circulation and the supply of money appear to be infinitely elastic. As stressed by Minsky, in such a context the effectiveness of monetary policy based on the surveillance of monetary aggregates weakens. As a result, in order to fight inflation, the central bank has no other choice than to act directly on the liquidity of commercial banks. It will therefore try to diminish reserves to an extent that is great enough to compensate for the increase in velocity. This reaction to the profit-seeking and innovating behaviour of commercial banks will have the effect of pushing up interest rates even more, thus recreating the conditions for the whole process to recur. Hence the succession over time of the increasing and horizontal portions of the curves represented in Figure 7.1.

It is interesting to stress here the particular features of the money supply curve. They afford a good understanding of the complexity of Minsky's reasoning and of its originality within post-Keynesian theory. Let it be recalled that the debate on the endogeneity of the money supply is essential, as it constitutes the focal point of the post-Keynesian critique of the neoclassical synthesis. The post-Keynesians consider that the assumption

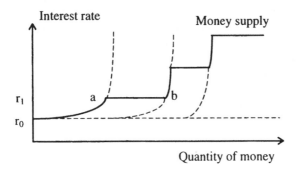

Figure 7.1 Institutional dynamics and interest rate

made by the neoclassical synthesis that the central bank has the ability to determine the quantity of money in the economy must be rejected. Many of the authors (Kaldor, 1982, Moore, 1988) who have delved into the question have been led to conclude that assuming the endogeneity of money amounts to substituting a horizontal line for the vertical curve drawn by authors belonging to the synthesis, as represented in Figure 7.2.

This 'horizontalist' view, as opposed to the 'verticalist' view of the synthesis, is the manifestation of its proponents' willingness to emphasize the monetary authorities' capacity to set the (short-term) interest rate, but in no way the quantity of money (Moore, 1988). In the post-Keynesian monetary production economy, the quantity of money is to a large extent determined by the demand for credit by entrepreneurs and is thus influenced by the level of effective demand. In other words it is the animal spirits of entrepreneurs that play the key role in the dynamics of money. In this matter the horizontalists adopt a radical position, since their reasoning leads to the assertion that any increase in the demand for money will increase the equilibrium amount of money, without any effect on the interest rate. The money supply is endogenous and adapts both completely and passively to the demand for money. On the contrary, interest rates are determined exogenously by the central bank. In short, one can qualify post-Keynesian horizontalism as an approach in which the money supply is endogenous and the interest rate exogenous.

The originality of Minsky's analysis with regard to the horizontalist conception appears clearly: the upward stepped money supply curve resulting from his theory contrasts sharply with the horizontal curve of Figure 7.2. This difference reflects a substantial divergence in the interpretation of the relationship between the central bank and the commercial banks. For Minsky the way commercial banks react to profit opportunities and to the policy conducted by the central bank prevents the latter from setting the interest rate at the level it deems desirable. The evolution of this rate depends strongly on

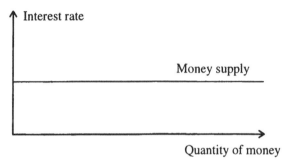

Figure 7.2 The 'horizontalist' view

the succession of phases of institutional stability and instability induced by the active behaviour of the commercial banks. The horizontalist conception of the money supply is thus rejected in Minsky's interpretation, which makes room for an interest rate that is not entirely exogenous even though the money supply is endogenous. In addition, the interest rate behaves procyclically: its increase simply reflects the dynamic process that takes place under the influence of the innovations of commercial banks confronting the restrictive reactions of the central bank when the economy expands.

Nevertheless, within the setting described so far, the determination of the interest rate continues to contain an exogenous component, inasmuch as rises in the interest rate (the increasing portions of the curve in Figure 7.1) are the consequence of restrictive policies applied by the central bank. Complete endogeneity of the interest rate, capable of generating a genuinely endogenous instability in the economic system, requires the introduction of additional ingredients into the analysis.

2.2 Liquidity, Financial Structure and the Endogenous Interest Rate

The aim of this subsection is to show that Minsky's analysis offers an entirely endogenous explanation of the variations of the interest rate throughout the economic cycle. This explanation rests upon three main ideas that are present in the seminal article of 1957: a rational tendency towards greater liquidity of the economy; an extension of liquidity preference; and the role of financial structure.

2.2.1 A rational tendency towards greater illiquidity

The main idea underpinning Minsky's demonstration is that the institutional innovations induced by the profit-seeking behaviour of commercial banks do not simply involve a greater velocity of money and an increase in the supply of finance. In fact, the institutional innovative process also exerts a negative influence on the liquidity of the economy. In other words, the innovative process described earlier is likely to lead to a situation where the economy becomes less liquid although the quantity of money is rising. As Minsky writes, 'the reverse side of the coin to the increase in velocity is that every institutional innovation which results in both new ways to finance business and new substitutes for cash assets decreases the liquidity of the economy' (1957a, p. 173). This evolution is mainly due to the particular form of rationality that Minsky's banks exhibit when decisions are taken within an environment of radical uncertainty. As noted earlier, such rationality rests upon objective bases, but also on more conventional or subjective grounds. This means that, even if actual outcomes only confirm banks' expectations, it is likely that, on account of their increased confidence in the way they are forming their expectations, banks will augment their lending and contribute to making the economy less liquid. Reduced liquidity of the economy is in fact caused by the deterioration of the financial structure of borrowers and lenders, as manifested in the rise in the debt-to-net-worth ratio (ibid., p. 174). Moreover profit-seeking by both financial and non-financial agents implies decreased liquidity of holdings. On the one hand, it leads to the substitution in commercial banks' portfolios of private debt for government securities. It reflects, on the other hand, the replacement of deposits in firms' portfolios by government debt and, at a later stage, of government debt by repurchase agreements issued by government security houses. This evolution in financial behaviour will lead banks to modify interest rates, in a way that is entirely endogenous, as a result of two phenomena: namely, an enlargement of the scope of liquidity preference and a deterioration of financial structure.

2.2.2 Greater liquidity preference

With the effects of institutional innovation the economy becomes subject to a greater risk of illiquidity, which in turn leads to greater liquidity preference. As stated by Minsky, 'economic units ... desire more liquidity. A tendency to use savings to liquidate debt and hence to increase the ratio of net worth to debt will arise' (ibid.). To understand the impact of increased liquidity preference, it is necessary to observe that it is not equivalent to a larger demand for money. Reliance here on the distinction established by Wray

(1992) is very helpful. According to Wray an increase in liquidity preference (the desire to exchange illiquid assets for more liquid ones) is actually the opposite of demanding more money, that is, demanding more funds because spending is expected to augment. Applied to Minsky's analysis of banking, this means that an increase in liquidity preference should be understood as not having the same effect on the interest rate as a greater demand for money. In fact, as seen previously, not only are banks eager (because of profit opportunities), they are also able (thanks to liability management) to respond to borrowers' larger demand for money.[3] To the contrary, it is unlikely that banks will as easily agree to raise their supply of money in a context of enhanced liquidity preference. For Minsky, as for many other post-Keynesian authors, such an increase in liquidity preference is associated with a reduction in anticipated profits, an environment that does not encourage commercial banks to develop their assets or to augment their supply of finance.[4] In fact, a situation of 'generalized liquidity preference' arises, since it concerns not only households and firms, but also banks. Although it might be assumed that borrowers would share the same expectations as banks and, as a result, would reduce their demand for money, Minsky reminds us that there is in fact an 'inelastic demand for finance', due in particular to the existence of investment projects displaying very long gestation periods and thereby requiring the roll-over of debt for the repayment of principal.[5]

The confrontation between a supply of money that is inclined to diminish under the influence of the preference by banks for greater liquidity and a demand for money that tends to become more inelastic during the ascending phase of the business cycle provides a first explanation of the endogenous variation of the interest rate in Minsky's analysis.

2.2.3 Financial structure and banking conditions

Independent of any variation in liquidity preference, a second aspect, the indebtedness of the economy, also plays a fundamental role in the determination of the interest rate. In fact, as argued by Minsky as early as in 1957, the increase of the debt ratio is likely to exert an upward pressure on the financial conditions granted to borrowing agents (1957a, p. 174). To understand this, account must be taken of the way the financial structures of both borrowers and lenders evolve.

In Minsky's analysis, the evolution of the borrowers' financial structure affects the lender's as well as the borrower's risk.[6] As was expounded in Part One, when he refers to the lender's risk, Minsky clearly alludes to Keynes's definition in Chapter 11 of *The General Theory*. However, whereas Keynes relates the lender's risk to the decision to invest and to the comparative uncertainty of long-run expectations, Minsky also considers different types of financial structure.[7] Indeed, notwithstanding the amount that can be self-financed, investment of whatever level involves issuing debt. The greater the size of its investments, the higher the risk that a business will default, which is reflected in the financial conditions applied by banks. To that effect 'some risks faced by lenders are expressed in observable increases in interest rates, as leverage increases and the confidence in cash-flows decreases' (1986a, p. 193). Other effects of the increase in the lender's risk are that it can give rise to loans of shorter maturity, or loans of smaller amounts, or to restrictions in dividend payouts.

While the lender's risk can be clearly observed in loan contracts, Minsky notes that the relationship between financial structure and financial conditions also takes a more subjective appearance, in the form of the borrower's risk. Here again the author acknowledges his indebtedness to Keynes (CW VII, 1973, p. 144). Yet, reference to the principle of increasing risk first brought to light by Kalecki (1937) is even more clear. Indeed, in Minsky's approach the borrower's risk is the manifestation that, beyond the amount that can be self-financed, investment implies financial costs that are inescapable, whereas the cash flows generated by production are unquestionably uncertain. Therefore 'the borrower's risk will increase as the weight of external or liquidity diminishing financing increases' (1986a, p. 191). Then, because a bank loan is to a large extent granted on the basis of the debtor's expected profits, the bank's risk increases in line with the borrower's risk. It is therefore likely that an increase of the borrower's risk will lead, as with a greater lender's risk, to an endogenous rise in the interest rate charged on bank loans.

The relationship between the liability structure of borrowers and the financial conditions imposed upon them is an essential aspect of Minsky's explanation of interest rate determination. It is also one that is well known, as it underpins his financial theory of investment. Nonetheless, a second aspect of his analysis, one that is not quite so familiar, deserves to be examined. It concerns the effect on the interest rate of changes affecting the balance sheet structure of banks. Here again we refer to the 1957 article where Minsky shows that even if 'loans make deposits', implying that the quantity of newly granted loans is equal to that of new deposits, development of the activity of banks reduces their liquidity. As mentioned before, competition among banks leads them to increase their indebtedness in proportion to the amount of their equity, reserves and safe assets (such as government securities). How banks undergo the process of balance sheet fragilization is explained in Chapter 10 of *Stabilizing an Unstable Economy*, which Minsky devotes to banking (1986a, pp. 223–253). He shows very simply that the profit-seeking behaviour of banks leads them to reduce deliberately their equity-to-assets ratio when their activity is expanding. That is because even a small reduction in this ratio is likely to lead to large increases in the rate of profit as well as to a rapid increase in the size of the banks' total assets. Expansion thus encourages them to engage in financial operations involving high leverage.[8]

Conversely, when the economy is slowing down, banks will seek to increase their equity-to-assets ratio in order to protect their shareholders against possible losses resulting from the default of borrowers. Thus, as a result of competition, the equity-to-assets ratio of commercial banks is subject to change during the business cycle, inasmuch as its evolution tends to be countercyclical. This has two implications.

First, banks that have be financially more fragile because of high leverage may become confronted with steadily increasing refinancing costs, owing to the 'collegiate surveillance' exerted by banks and other institutions operating in the money market (1986, p. 240). As is likely, banks that face growing borrowing costs in the money market will be inclined to pass them on to the rates they charge, thereby endogenously contributing to the higher interest rates on bank loans.

Second, increased leverage of banks is also at the heart of a second kind of upwards pressure exerted on banks loans. The reason, already noted by Minsky in 1957, is that 'the chances of insolvency and illiquidity [of commercial banks] increase simultaneously', which persuades them to demand higher interest rates in order to compensate for the increasing risk associated with the greater size of their assets (1957a, p. 174). Minsky thus proposes a enlarged view of the lender's risk since, in the present case, it no longer refers only to the borrower's financial structure, but also to the bank's.

Again, Minsky manifests his differences with other post-Keynesian theorists. Indeed, in the horizontalist approach commercial banks are extraordinarily passive, both in the money market where the interest rate is fixed exogenously by the central bank and in the market for loans where they respond automatically to borrowers' demands. In this approach commercial banks do not exert any significant influence on prices and quantities in the markets where they operate. In contrast, Minsky's commercial banks recover a more active role in the determination of prices and quantities both in the money market and, as has just been seen, in the loans market. The important result obtained here is that the endogeneity of the money supply is no longer synonymous with the passivity of commercial banks. What becomes possible (and necessary) then is an analysis of the business cycle focusing on banking, precisely the choice Minsky made some forty years ago.

The dynamics involving financial institutions is one of the two aspects of the institutional dynamics contained in Minsky's analysis of economic fluctuations. The second aspect concerns the behaviour and the role of institutions controlled by the public authorities, which we examine next.

3 INSTITUTIONAL THWARTING SYSTEMS

In Minsky's theory institutional factors such as public authorities' interventions affect the nature of the business cycle in a way that is ambivalent. On the one hand, they act as 'thwarting systems' whose purpose is to counteract and contain the naturally explosive amplitude of economic fluctuations. On the other hand, they themselves can change into and become factors of instability and inefficiency.

In what follows we shall see that the ambivalence of institutional factors is something Minsky drew attention to in his early works, more precisely in the late 1950s. Our argument is developed in two main steps. First, on the basis of Minsky's contribution, we investigate the actual contents of his analysis of fluctuations where he takes into account the institutional context that governs relationships between economic agents. Second, we examine the reasons why he believes the stabilizing effects of a given institutional structure are not immutable. Because institutional arrangements will give rise to reactions on the part of private agents, they must necessarily undergo endogenous change in order to remain effective.

3.1 Thwarting Systems or the Need 'To Stabilize an Unstable Economy'

For Minsky the various institutional mechanisms that are present in contemporary market economies play a central role in the unfolding of economic fluctuations. Their function is to slow down and adjust the dynamic process at the origin of the economy's endogenous and 'incoherent' behaviour. This amounts to introducing every now and then new initial conditions into the system, which modifies the behaviour of markets and alters the parameters affecting economic agents' decisions. Considering change in economic activity in this way is interesting on more than one count. First, it is reminiscent of and supplements a certain type of business cycle model developed in the 1950s. Second, it provides a relevant theoretical framework for the analysis of the role of the stabilizing institutional mechanisms that are present in financially sophisticated economies.

3.1.1 Reinterpreting growth models with ceilings and floors

The business cycles model proposed by Minsky in the late 1950s drew heavily on the models of multiplier and accelerator interaction developed several years before by Hicks and Goodwin.[9] These two authors were well aware both of the inherent limits of linear macroeconomic models of the type proposed by Samuelson and the fundamentally non-linear nature of economic activity. This is why their business cycle models incorporated constraints, the role of which was to act as boundaries to expansion or depression.

In view of the obvious kinship between these buffer-growth models and Minsky's approach, it is helpful to restate briefly the main assumptions underlying these models and look back on the way they generate economic fluctuations. However, in order to bring to light the effects of institutional mechanisms, these models are presented here in a form that differs slightly from the one initially proposed by their authors and still found today in the standard textbooks on macroeconomic dynamics. Our presentation, which is the one utilized by Minsky himself, consists in highlighting the influence of initial conditions (and their variations) on the movement of the time series generated by constrained linear models. It has the advantage of making it clear that the shape of the time-paths obtained in these models is the outcome of a dynamic process that goes through a series of stages. In each stage the values taken by the economic variables serve as the initial conditions for the determination of their values at the next stage. A dynamic process is then called 'unconstrained', in Minsky's terminology, when the initial conditions of each stage are generated endogenously by the process itself (Ferri and Minsky, 1992). By contrast, any process wherein the initial conditions of the next stage differ – under the influence of factors exogenous to the process – from those that the process would have generated naturally are said to be 'constrained'. In this kind of approach, non-linearity therefore appears in the form of functions defined piecemeal, the specificity of which is to undergo variations when new initial conditions are defined.

On these grounds we can examine the general behaviour of the models where the multiplier and the accelerator interact. These are usually composed of a consumption function of the form, $C_t = aY_{t-1}$ (a standing for the average and marginal propensity to consume), and of an induced investment function of the form, $I_t = b(Y_{t-1} - Y_{t-2})$ (where b represents the accelerator). When introduced into the equilibrium condition, $Y_t = C_t + I_t$, these relations yield a second-order difference equation:

$$Y_t = (a+b) Y_{t-1} - bY_{t-2} \qquad (7.1)$$

Equation (7.1) means that when the value of the reaction coefficients a and b and the values of the initial conditions, Y_{t-1} and Y_{t-2}, are known, it is possible to determine recursively any solution Y_n to the system. In addition, we know that the second-order difference equation (7.1) solves for:

$$Y_t = A_1 U_1{}^t + A_2 U_2{}^t \qquad (7.2)$$

where U_1 and U_2 are the roots of the associated characteristic equation $U^2 - (a+b) U + b = 0$, and A_1 and A_2 are constants depending on the value of parameters a and b and on the initial conditions.[10]

Solving equation (7.2) yields different types of dynamics, depending on the value of the parameters, namely: (a) monotonic convergence of the income level towards a stable level (if the roots are real and of absolute values less than unity); (b) damped fluctuations, the system being stable and converging towards the long-term equilibrium level by values that are alternately less than and greater than the equilibrium output level (if the roots are complex and their modulus is less than unity); (c) explosive fluctuations, the amplitude of fluctuations of national output around the long-term equilibrium level increasing in each period (if the roots are complex and their modulus is greater than unity); (d) instability in the form of monotonic divergence or regular explosive growth, the national product diverging increasingly from its equilibrium level (if the roots are real and greater than unity in absolute value).

Unlike Samuelson's (1939) analysis, which investigates the whole range of solutions set out above, Hicks (1950) concentrates exclusively on parameter values that, when combined, give either accelerated growth, or amplified fluctuations – cases (c) and (d). Hicks therefore situates his approach in a configuration such that both roots U_1 and U_2 are greater than unity, with $U_1 > U_2 > 1$. He further assumes that the economy exhibits a maximum growth rate, a ceiling, which we shall denote g. Therefore, $Y_t = Y_0 e^{gt}$ when the ceiling is effective. In addition, the dominant root U_1 is very much greater than the growth rate of the ceiling income. Finally, both roots U_1 and U_2 are such that $U_1 > U_2 > g > 1$.

Under these assumptions the economy evolves in the following way. Let us suppose that the economy is initially so defined that it generates two consecutive incomes Y_0 and Y_1 $(Y_1 > Y_0)$ such that: both these incomes are less than their corresponding ceilings; $U_1 > Y_1/Y_0 > U_2$. These initial conditions determine positive coefficients A_1 and A_2, A_2 being much greater than A_1, because U_1 is assumed to be much greater than g.[11] Then equation (7.2), which characterizes the dynamics of the system or rather its unconstrained dynamics, yields an explosive-type evolution over time. However, after a certain time, let us say in period n, income reaches a higher value than the ceiling corresponding to that period. At that point, the constraint becomes binding and the realized income is no longer determined by equation (7.2). For two successive periods income is determined by equation:

$$Y_1 = gY_0 \qquad (7.3)$$

This takes us back to a situation where $Y_1/Y_0 = g < U_2$. The prominent feature here is that the sign of the coefficient A_1 of dominant root U_1 solving equation (7.2) becomes negative. This change in sign indicates the start of the rebound of the path against the ceiling, that is, the turning point of the cycle.

A cumulative depression process follows and the economy henceforth undergoes a downturn that is guided essentially by the negative term of increasing absolute value, $A_1(U_1)^t$.

This explosive downward movement of income can only slow down if there is a lower limit, a floor, to counter the process generated by the unconstrained dynamics, analogous to the ceiling examined above. As in Hicks's model, the floor may consist in a maximum value being set for the firms' divestment. When this maximum value is attained, the realized value Y_t is different from that obtained with equation (7.2). A new equation determines the change taking place in the economy. It features a negative and comparatively large coefficient A_2 and a positive and comparatively small coefficient A_1. As in the previous case there comes a point where the cycle reverts. A new expansion phase arises, which is initially moderate and then explosive. It continues until the economy rebounds again on the ceiling, as described previously. And so on.

When we compare the general form of Hicks's model with that of the models proposed by Minsky in the late 1950s, the two approaches look very much alike. In both cases the authors have opted to take non-linearities into account by introducing constraints on booms and slumps, in the form of floors and ceilings. These models are therefore capable, as we have just seen, of generating persistent fluctuations by building on the unstable solution of the Samuelson model.

Behind this apparent similarity, however, the interpretation of two economists differs, insofar as they do not attribute the same meaning to the constraints that stabilize the dynamics of the economy. In Hicks's model, common sense justifies the existence of these constraints: real investment cannot be negative, hence the existence of a floor, determined by the growth of autonomous investment and the size of investment due to depreciation. In addition, output, consumption and investment are limited by the available amounts of natural resources and labour, as well as by the size of the gains in productivity. Hence the existence of a ceiling.

Things are very different for Minsky. He of course does not deny the influence of such constraints on the level of economic activity. Nevertheless, he does not think they are essential for explaining the cyclical dynamics observed in market economies. He argues that floors and ceilings reflect primarily the set of institutional mechanisms set up by public authorities in order to confine the amplitude of economic fluctuations within reasonable limits. This is why Minsky terms these institutional arrangements 'thwarting systems.'

The original idea Minsky develops is therefore that the main purpose of these thwarting systems is to modify the initial conditions governing time series during phases of explosive expansion or cumulative depression. As mentioned earlier, these new initial conditions have the effect of inverting the sign of the dominant root of the oscillator model solution equation. As a result the movement of the economy eventually slows down and reverts down and reversing. Depression (or deflation) is thus converted by an institutional-type floor into a moderate and then explosive recovery, which in turn runs up against an institutional ceiling. The time series observed is then the outcome of incessant rebounds of the economy between ceilings and floors generated by institutional thwarting mechanisms existing in the economy.

Minsky's constrained linear model is interesting in more than one respect. First, unlike Samuelson's oscillator-type unconstrained linear model, it accounts for the complexity of change affecting capitalist economies over time. Evolution takes the form of 'steady growth (when $U_1 > g > U_2$), cycles (when $U_1 > U_2 > g > 1$), booms, or depressions when $g > U_1$)' (1959, p. 134). In other words, Minsky's model 'exhibits the features of chaotic models, including the sensitivity of the time series that is generated to initial conditions' (Ferri and Minsky, 1989, p. 138). Second, unlike usual constrained linear models, which ignore institutional thwarting systems, this model accounts for the effect of institutional change and interventions by public authorities on economic dynamics.[12] In Minsky's model the dependence of the floors and ceilings on policy and institutional arrangements can be made quite precise.

The 'incoherence' of economic trajectories – in particular the occurrence of explosive, amplified change leading to either very large values (even infinite) or even to negative values of economic magnitudes – inherent in unconstrained linear models can thus be countered by setting up institutional thwarting mechanisms. Under these circumstances, 'business cycles can result either from the values of the "U's" being complex, from regular interventions that contain the economy between "floors and ceilings" if the "U's" are greater than one, and from introductions of energy from outside if the "U's" are less than one' (Ferri and Minsky, 1989, p. 137).

In Minsky's approach, stabilizing economic activity, that is, setting new initial conditions in order to contain the amplitude of time series, is essentially the concern of the government, via its fiscal policy, and of the central bank, through its role as lender of last resort.

3.1.2. 'Big government', lender of last resort and stabilizing economic activity

Minsky views budget deficits and interventions by the central bank as lender-of-last-resort as extremely effective instruments for stabilizing economic fluctuations. Even if full employment is not achieved, these instruments help limit the drop in income and in liquidity during economic recessions and during the onset of a financial crisis.

Let us consider the role of budget deficits first. In Minsky's theory, investment is the essential determinant of economic activity. Investment is largely influenced by aggregate profits (realized or anticipated).[13] It follows, he argues, that 'a main aim of policy is to constrain the variability of profits' (Fazzari and Minsky, 1984, p. 107). Now, Minsky reminds us that in a closed economy aggregate profits are equal to the sum of investment and of budget deficit, as is expressed by Kalecki's accounting identity (1971). Consequently, a deficit, by upholding aggregate demand when private investment flags, establishes a lower limit, a floor, for profits, wages and current production prices.[14] In other words, 'policy will be stabilizing if a shortfall of private investment quickly leads to a government deficit, and a burst of investment quickly leads to a budget surplus' (Fazzari and Minsky, 1984, p. 107). Such stabilization of actual and expected profits is crucial to ensuring the continuity of the economic system. It is utilized in particular to maintain the viability of debt structures and therefore the level of private investment. In fact 'once rational bankers and business men learn from experience that actual profits do not fall when private investment declines, they will modify their preferred portfolios to take advantage of the stability of profits' (Minsky, 1992, p. 12).

Thus the presence of a 'big government' whose fiscal policy is very sensitive to variations in overall profits improves the stability of the economy. Nonetheless, isolated policy of this sort may prove insufficient in periods of economic turmoil. True public deficits partly offset the reduction in profit flows resulting from a fall in investment and maintain current production prices and consumer goods prices. However, during an economic crisis deficits cannot directly counteract the drop in another type of price, one that is essential in Minsky's investment theory, the price of capital assets. This price is dependent upon the amount of money in circulation, but also on more subjective variables such as liquidity preference, the debt level that is judged acceptable or the profits economic agents expect.[15] It is necessary to turn then, as a supplementary step, toward a second type of institutional thwarting mechanism, the role of the central bank as lender of last resort.[16]

The main purpose of this type of intervention is to offset debt-deflation phenomena or the different forms of financial instability that market economies have been experiencing, especially since the middle of the 1980s. In the case of the UnitedStates, which Minsky gives precedence to, one obviously thinks of the financial market crash of October 1987, the Federal Savings and Loans Insurance Corporation (FSLIC) debacle and the collapse of the junk bond market. Through their sheer scale and the difficulties experienced in correcting them, these different examples indicate that the stability of the current financial system cannot be based exclusively on government fiscal policy.

For Minsky these phenomena also emphasize the need for an extended interpretation of the role of lender of last resort. This is why he distinguishes three aspects of this type of intervention (Minsky, 1986a). First, when funds are lacking in the money market (a situation generally synonymous with substantial falls in the value of the claims agents exchange for liquidity), the central bank must intervene by increasing the amount of money in circulation. Second, during the financial restructuring period that follows a crisis, the central bank must take care to favour recourse to long-term rather than short-term borrowing by acting accordingly on interest rates. Finally, the central bank is responsible for guiding the development of the financial system, both through regulations and banking system surveillance, in order to restrain speculative banking (excessive reliance on liability management in particular).

There is no denying that, in the last twenty years, the endogenous aspect of central bank policy has been considerably reinforced, in accordance with the approach advocated by Minsky, and in contrast to the claims of the monetarist school.[17] Its function as lender-of-last-resort has extended constantly to new institutions and new instruments.[18] At the end of the 1960s the Fed intervened to sustain the municipal bonds market. In 1970 it acted in order to avoid the collapse of the commercial paper market. In the 1980s it stepped in during the foreign debt crisis, the Continental Illinois bankruptcy crisis and the financial market crash. In each of these events the Fed (believed, as it was, to be following a monetarist policy) provided liquidity and was compelled to validate to some extent many risky financial practices.

The insistence on institutional constraints thus marks a sharp opposition between Minsky's approach and the market-oriented economic behaviour portrayed by current business cycle theories of neoclassical inspiration. The idea highlighted by Minsky is that the institutions found in modern economies give rise to regulatory mechanisms that hinder the internal dynamics resulting from the free operation of markets. Accordingly, each kind of institutional structure will have the effect of yielding realized values (asset values and income flows) that differ from those generated by unconstrained internal dynamics. In particular, the central bank intervenes almost daily in the money and financial markets as lender of last resort. The main purpose of its interventions is to avoid outcomes generated by markets today becoming, if this is undesirable, the initial conditions that will govern tomorrow's dynamics. Thus, when the central bank intervenes in the money market to shore up a failing financial institution or to stabilize the foreign exchange market, then the levels of the interest rate, asset prices or exchange rates will differ from the values resulting from the operation of the markets alone.

3.2 The Ambivalence of Institutional Thwarting Systems

The line of argument developed in the previous section seems to imply that the economy will operate smoothly in the long run, as long as the regulating structure set up by the public and monetary authorities remains effective. In fact the impact of an intervention structure is not immutable: its capacity to stabilize the amplitude of economic fluctuations and to constrain market agents to undertake only moderately risky actions varies greatly over time. Minsky writes: 'because profit-seeking agents learn how a regulatory structure operates and because regulation means that some perceived opportunities are not open to exploitation, there are incentives for agents to change their behaviour to evade or avoid the constraints' (1992a, p. 17). This means that some institutional interventions and mechanisms that were initially stabilizing may turn into factors of instability and inefficiency. To be persuaded of this, one need only recall the Savings and Loans debacle and the powerlessness of the FSLIC when confronted with problems of financial instability in the 1980s. Looking back, this example shows that regulation and an initially effective intervention arrangement can begin to backfire if decision-makers at the policy and institutional level do not take adequate account of the behaviour of market participants in response to the institutional changes they are up against.

This interaction between market dynamics and institutional dynamics appears to be a key element in Minsky's theory of cycles. As mentioned earlier, this question is examined in 'Central Banking and Money Market Changes', an article in which Minsky analyses both the complex interactions taking place in the monetary market between private banks and the central bank and the ensuing institutional dynamics. A dynamic process unfolds then, notably when the economy is expanding, involving commercial bank innovations and reactions in the form of restrictive monetary policy that can undermine the stability of the economic system.

The same type of analysis applies when examining the origin and main consequences of recent financial innovations. Securitization of bank assets is a good example of such financial innovations.[19] A securitized asset is a claim on the cash flows generated by portfolios of financial assets that may be mortgages, automobile paper and credit card debts. As a general rule a financial institution creates the portfolio that will be securitized, provides the bridging facility, sells the securities (generally to pension funds, investment funds and insurance companies) and chooses a trustee to represent the interests of the security holders.

The great expansion of securitization, notably in the United States, has certainly been related to factors that are independent of actions taken by monetary authorities, such as technological progress and its lowering effect on transaction costs, the deterioration of the quality of banks' balance sheets in the wake of the LDCs' debt crisis or the collapse of the real estate market in certain regions of the United States.[20] However securitization also appears to be a response of private financial institutions to certain actions taken by the monetary authorities, such as the pressure exerted by the Fed on banks, in order that they increase their capital ratios, or restrictive monetary policies, causing market interest rates to rise well above the regulated rates on deposits.

In theory, securitization of bank assets is based upon the standard microeconomic risk analysis according to which asset diversification and the holding of liquid assets protect investment portfolios against sudden reductions in value due to the failure of individual borrowers. The problem is that during the securitization process the institution that ensures the placement of the securities knows that it will only hold the securitized loan for a limited time (several weeks or several months). Therefore, the incentive for lenders to make a careful appraisal of each loan is strongly reduced. Besides, once the individual features of a loan, including the risk of default, are tied in with those of hundreds or thousands of other loans in a securitized claim, they become blurred. In fact, the investor will rely entirely on the guarantees provided by Federal agencies and on the pooling of risks to maintain his flow of income. If, however, the risk of default on one of the loans underlying the securitized claim can in a period of prosperity be considered independent of the risk on the other loans, when a widespread recession occurs, such an assumption obviously no longer holds. This is aggravated by the fact that aggressive competition among banks (and savings banks) during the previous economic expansion will have led to a systematic reduction in the safety standards applied to lending.

In the same connection Minsky stresses that one of the main consequences of the financial innovation process is to persuade profit-seeking financial institutions to increase the riskiness of their portfolios.[21] He begins by recalling that markets for futures and options can be used for speculation as well as for hedging. In addition he explains that risk 'unbundling', as permitted by such financial innovations as securitization of bank loans, off-balance operations and swap contracts can facilitate the acceptance of greater risk, not by the financial entities that are the most efficient, but by those that are already in a poor situation and are striving, regardless of the cost, to increase their rate of return.

The greater risks taken by institutions already in distress are perfectly illustrated by the quality deterioration of the loan portfolios of the American Savings and Loans Associations (S&Ls).[22] These institutions had already encountered serious problems when interest rates increased at the end of the 1970s and beginning of the 1980s. Once the regulation limiting the diversification of portfolios to long-term mortgage loans had been lifted in 1982, a large number of S&Ls invested in very speculative operations in order to improve their financial performance. In spite of the financial innovations that allowed them to hedge interest rate risk and to reduce default risk (including the use of asset securitization), losses of S&Ls soared. The reduction of inflation and of interest rates between 1982 and 1984 caused a general decrease of prices and incomes from oil, agriculture and real estate in regions dependent on these activities. This led to generalized repayment defaults. The cash flows that supported the payment commitments of many S&Ls diminished in very great proportions. An outbreak of losses due to non-profitable assets, added to those created by interest rate volatility, contributed to the worsening situation of these institutions. In 1987 ten per cent of S&Ls were insolvent and a third had undergone large losses (Campbell and Minsky, 1987, p. 261). In early 1989, despite six years of sustained economic growth, the tangible net worth of 400 S&Ls was a negative 2 billion dollars (Thomas, 1989).

The spectacular growth of the junk bonds market followed a similar course.[23] References by Minsky to this phenomenon remain quite elliptic. His interest is indirect and he states that this growth was mainly supported by the financial needs of companies engaged in LBOs. According to Minsky, these 'takeovers are a technique by which indebtedness adjusts to the erosion of felt risk' (1986b, p. 350). They contributed, with the expanded influence of pension funds, mutual funds and insurance companies, to the development of 'money manager capitalism' (Minsky, 1989b). In this form the management of money is performed by professionals whose goal is to obtain a maximum short-term return on their portfolio, that is, to maximize the combination both of short-term cash flows, in the form of dividends and interest, and of capital gains. Accordingly, managed money is closely related to the Keynesian pattern of speculation: the appreciation or the depreciation of asset prices can dominate over the search for large long-term global returns. Money manager capitalism thus focuses on the value (prices and positive variations in prices) of financial assets and in particular of shares. Therefore, money managers pressure corporate managers to act in a way that will sustain the market value of their shares (ibid.). The viability of this type of capitalism is, however, contingent on the absence of any serious depression. During prosperity experimenting with new portfolio managing techniques is readily encouraged. Nonetheless, the situation that ensues is obviously one of merely short-lived tranquillity. Because the new portfolio management techniques actually increase the likelihood of crises occurring and the probability of depression setting in, they threaten the system's survival. For Minsky the October 1987 crash is a perfect illustration of the dangers entailed by this form of capitalism: 'We might characterize the crisis of 19 and 20 October [during which] money managers were trying to sell securities [while] the block traders were both reluctant and increasingly unable to take positions as the first financial crisis of the new capitalism of "managed money'" (ibid., pp. 395 and 398).

Therefore, Minsky's analysis of innovation departs from the traditional interpretation of the phenomenon, well summarized in the following statement and significant of the state of mind that prevailed in the 1980s:

> On balance, however, the innovations have been almost certainly beneficial for the system as a whole. These different types of risks have been almost certainly beneficial for the system as a whole. The different types of risks involved in the various instruments have been unbundled. This should increase the efficiency of the financial system, since each element of a deal can be provided – and the associated risk taken – by the financial entity that can do so most efficiently. The increase in the number of separate risks should not, in itself, increase the total risk for the system as a whole (Watson *et al.*, 1986).

It is thus not surprising that, in spite of the ongoing accelerated rhythm of financial innovation, economists and public authorities did not correctly appraise the problems it generated in terms of increased instability. This did not escape Minsky who wrote: 'In recent years, we have seen many institutional changes in banking and finance. These changes have been permitted even though the authorities have no theory enabling them to determine where the changes taking place in financial practices tend to increase or to decrease the overall stability of the financial system' (1986a, p. 45). For all the reasons listed above, Minsky considers that such an attitude eventually leads to serious problems, since the global effect of the financial innovation process is to accentuate the fragility of the financial structure: 'the introduction of financial layering in finance, together with the invention of new instruments designed to make credit available by tapping pools of liquidity, is evidence, beyond that revealed by the financial data itself, of the increased fragility of the system' (ibid., p. 87). These problems are to a large extent inherent in the intervention of monetary authorities, much as the difficulties encountered by organizations such as the FSLIC in the US. They are not, however, an argument in favour of laissez-faire, nor do they imply rejecting institutional thwarting systems. On the contrary they suggest that 'intervention cannot be frozen in time but must adapt as institutional and usage evolution takes place; successful capitalism requires both a structure of regulation and a sophisticated awareness of the way profit-seeking drives the evolution of structures and behaviour' (1992, pp. 17–8). In other words, while 'thwarting systems are analogous to homeostatic mechanisms which may prevent a system from exploding', they are more than just that (Ferri and Minsky, 1992, p. 89).

As a result, any incapacity on the part of public authorities to interpret correctly the change in economic environment and, more particularly, to take account of the impact of their interventions on the behaviour of private agents, can impair the smooth flow of macroeconomic dynamics. Three types of difficulties are liable to arise. First, the data drawn from time series generated by an actually explosive system, but constrained by interventions and by the institutional mechanism, may give the impression that they result from a naturally stable dynamic process.[24] This may lead to detrimental decisions at the policy level. In a setting of this kind, economists and policy-makers may mistakenly infer that the system is endogenously stable and thus that institutional thwarting mechanisms are useless. Once the problems of macroeconomic instability have seemingly been eliminated, the public authorities may be encouraged to apply policies aimed at, for example, the improvement of the microeconomic efficacy of the system. In the area of finance the study of contemporary market economies shows that such policies usually take the form of deregulation and of slackening of the rules applicable to agents involved in the money and financial markets, notably in assets and liabilities management. The periods of great financial instability experienced by western countries and by Japan in the early 1990s and, more recently, the financial crisis affecting the Asian markets exemplify the adverse effects produced by this quest for microeconomic effectiveness and its baneful impact on the stability of the system as a whole. These events have provided a harsh reminder that, as Minsky predicted, inflexible and short sighted action by the public authorities may result in the weakening of the stabilizing mechanisms set up in the past, thereby creating an environment exposed to the outburst of financial crises.

Second, Minsky emphasizes that the large injections of liquidity associated with interventions by the government and the monetary authorities are inflationary, as purchasing power is injected more quickly into the economy than new production is created.[25] The fragility of the system, inasmuch as it calls for anti-deflationary intervention, is thus at the heart of an inflationary bias in the economy. The problem is that in financially sophisticated economies it is difficult to avoid overshooting when fighting inflation. Cost inflation acts on the current production price level. As Kregel (1992) shows, monetary policy appears to be an unwieldy instrument for the control of inflation. It may aggravate recession and lead to increased unemployment. However, monetary policy appears more effective in preventing speculative inflation of capital asset prices. This can be achieved by acting directly on variables such as the interest rates and on the financial system's liquidity, which contributes directly to determining these prices. Nevertheless, the effect of restrictive monetary policy on the price dynamics of assets remains difficult to predict: in an uncertain environment, capital asset prices also depend to a large extent on volatile expected profits. Consequently, any attempt by the monetary authorities to hold down the rise in prices in capital markets (for instance, by increasing the interest rate) may very well produce a downwards revision of expectations, which may, in turn, cause disruption to these markets.

Third, it is clear that even if measures carried out by public authorities can help fight financial instability in the short run, they do not necessarily impel the economy towards a situation of both full employment and stability. Their interventions also validate existing, fragile, financial structures and thus leave unsolved or even amplify the problems associated with such structures. This is so because rational agents will tend to adopt increasingly risky financial behaviour, based on incurring large amounts of debt. In turn this will create greater financial fragility at the macroeconomic level. Such behaviour is encouraged because the potential costs associated with risky financial practices on the part of private agents are to a very large extent socialized: the public authorities (the government and the central bank) rather than the individual agents are left with the burden of absorbing the costs that result from the increase of the budget deficit or the intervention of the central bank as lender of last resort.

4 CONCLUSION TO PART THREE

Confronting recent models of the financial instability hypothesis with the two central – but often underestimated – aspects of Minsky's theory, that is, the behaviour of agents in situations of uncertainty and the role played by institutions in the evolution of market economies, highlights the limitation of these models, despite their high degree of mathematical sophistication. This confrontation also indicates new directions for research that remain to be explored by economists seeking to formalize Minsky's approach correctly.

We have underlined the deficiencies of the models founded on the premises underlying new-Keynesian economics. They mainly concern the aversion displayed by the authors belonging to this school to departing from the standard probabilistic framework, the one that is congruent with the rational expectations hypothesis. This position is hardly compatible with Minsky's analysis of certain forms of behaviour, notably those governing the relations between lenders and borrowers, which appear to be rational only when uncertainty of the kind defined by Keynes prevails.

In addition, the inclusion of the role of institutional mechanisms calls into question the results produced thanks to the non-linear models of endogenous financial cycles. Indeed Minsky's theory does not simply describe the cycle as a mechanical phenomenon, as a succession of phases of the following sort: increase of financial fragility $\rightarrow$ financial crisis $\rightarrow$ gradual return to more safe and sound finance. This is so because as a rule financial crises thwarted by institutional mechanisms do not develop all their effects (debt-deflation, widespread bankruptcies, disappearance of the agents with the most fragile financial structures, etc.). As a consequence the natural tendency towards increased financial fragility is temporarily slowed down, but is in no way reversed. On the contrary, greater fragility takes the form of a sustained trend, permanently transforming the fundamentals of the economy and the behaviour of agents. Then, because the economy becomes increasingly fragile in the long run, it becomes necessary to increase the frequency and scale of actions undertaken by the public authorities in order to prevent the emergence of instability, until a time comes where the crisis can no longer be contained.

Thus, in the financially sophisticated economies that Minsky scrutinizes, the natural tendency to generate periods of great instability may be partly offset by thwarting systems. Nevertheless, such systems cannot lead to stable full employment equilibrium. Downward instability (debt-deflation) tends, under the influence of the institutional thwarting mechanisms set up by the public authorities, to turn itself into increased instability, characterized by a sustained trend of excessive borrowing, increased interest rates and persistent inflationary pressure.

NOTES

1. The reference to Schumpeter under whose supervision Minsky began writing his dissertation, is not explicit in the 1957 article. Nonetheless, in later works, Minsky repeatedly stresses the influence of Schumpeter on his own analysis of banking behaviour.
2. As Minsky explains, non-financial firms became the main source of finance for government bond houses in the middle of 1956.
3. Up to a certain point: see next paragraph.
4. See for instance, Minsky (1975, pp. 76 and 123), Wray (1988 and 1990).
5; Minsky (1986a, p. 195). Consequently, the demand for money will be less elastic inasmuch as the economy exhibits greater financial fragility.
6. See the analysis developed in Part One.
7. Here what Minsky most certainly has in mind is Kalecki's increasing risk principle (Kalecki, 1937). The influence of Kalecki appears even more distinctively below, when we deal with the borrower's risk.
8. 'The impact of increased leverage on bank profits is impressive: if a bank that makes 0.75 percent on assets decreases the ratio of capital to assets to 5 per cent from 6 percent, the profit rate on book value will be 15.0 percent rather than 12.5 percent. If such an increase in leverage takes place over several years, the profit rate will rise each year. With a constant dividend on book value ratio, this implies that the growth rate mandated by retained earnings will rise from 7.5 to 10 percent.' (Minsky, 1986a, p. 237).
9. See Minsky (1957b, 1959), Hicks (1950), Goodwin (1951).
10. If m is the effective growth rate of income, then for any two successive dates chosen as initial conditions, $Y_1 = mY_0$. This therefore gives (since $Y_1 = A_1U_1 + A_2U_2$ and $Y_0 = A_1 + A_2$): $A_1 = (m-U_2) + (U_1-U_2)Y_0$ and $A_2 = (U_1-m)/(U_1 - U_2)Y_0$ Assuming that values a and b are such that $U_1 > U_2 > 1$ (i.e. in the case of explosive time series in an unconstrained system), it follows that: $U_1 > U_1 > m$, therefore $A_1 < 0$ and $A_2 > 0$; whereas $U_1 > m > U_2$ implies that $A_1 > 0$ and $A_2 > 0$.

11. See footnote 10. This characteristic implies that during the early periods (t small), the weight of U_2 is predominant in determining the dynamic evolution, whereas during subsequent periods, it is the root U_1 that tends to dominate. It ensues that the income growth rate converges towards U_1 when t tends towards infinity.
12. Such as Hicks's model examined earlier, but also Goodwin's 1951 model, based on a non-linear accelerator.
13. See in particular Minsky (1986a, Chapters 7 and 8).
14. For an analysis of the relationship between profits and the setting of wages and current production prices, see Ferri and Minsky (1984), and Minsky (1986a, Chapter 7).
15. Cf. Minsky (1975, 1986a).
16. In the US, the central bank includes not only the Federal Reserve system but also the different deposit insurance institutions.
17. On this point, see the useful paper by Friedman (1992).
18. See Wojnilower (1987).
19. See for instance Minsky (1991b).
20. For a more detailed analysis of the reasons for the securitization boom, see Wojnilower (1985, 1987).
21. Campbell and Minsky (1987). See also Carter (1989).
22. See Campbell and Minsky (1987) and Minsky (1992b).
23. In 1987, the volume of new issues of junk bonds reached 14 times the levels of 1982 and represented 23.2 per cent of the total issues of corporate debt, as compared to 5 per cent in 1982.
24. See Blatt (1978).
25. See Friedman (1992). This is a problem that Minsky has often raised: the necessity for the Federal Reserve to act as lender of last resort may often be incompatible with its other objectives, in particular with keeping the inflation rate down.

Conclusion

A key feature of contemporary market economies is the existence of interrelationships between finance, investment and economic fluctuations. Analysing them requires the careful study of numerous and often intricate questions, a task to which Minsky devoted a lifetime's work as an economist. His main achievement was the conception and elaboration of the financial instability hypothesis. This notion embraces three important aspects: a financial and dynamic dimension; a particular view of the behaviour of economic agents in situations of uncertainty; and an institutional dimension.

Underlying the financial dynamics implied by the financial instability hypothesis we find Minsky's financial theory of investment, associated with his analysis of financial fragility and endogenous instability. This aspect of his analysis is fundamental for two reasons. First, it is what makes Minsky's approach specific and original when compared with traditional macroeconomic analyses. Second, it is the chief feature of his work to attract the attention of recent writers.

To begin with, two essential features are characteristic of Minsky's conception of financial dynamics: the rejection of neoclassical macroeconomics, in particular the conclusions of both the Keynesian neoclassical synthesis and the new classical school; the attempt to conceive a monetary theory differing from traditional post-Keynesian monetary analysis, notwithstanding his agreement with the main underlying principles of the latter. Thus, when he constructs his two-price model, Minsky insists on the uncertainty of future streams of income, on the value attached to liquidity and on the impact on investment of the variations in the interest rate applied to loans, thereby remaining very close to traditional post-Keynesian authors. However the two-price approach used by Minsky is not in itself very original. Many authors, including Wicksell and Fisher, but also Keynes himself and Tobin, have relied on it to explain business cycles. The originality of Minsky's analysis of financial instability lies in having also used and updated key concepts borrowed from various theoretical constructs, such as Kalecki's principle of increasing risk, Fisher's notion of debt-deflation, Keynes's distinction between the supply price and the demand price in *A Treatise on*

Money and between the prices of capital assets and debt instruments in *The General Theory*.

In fact, Minsky's analysis of financial dynamics is original on two counts. It is founded upon a specific view of the relation between finance and investment, and it contains a particular approach to economic fluctuations.

First, Minsky's investment function differs sharply from the one developed within the Modigliani-Miller and Jorgenson neoclassical approach. Minsky denies the neutrality of financial structure with regard to investment. Instead, choices concerning financial structure are essential determinants of investment. So is financial market behaviour. Thus Minsky provides a revival of the financial variety of Keynesianism developed by authors such as Gurley and Shaw. However, based as it is on the careful study of the financial negotiation that takes place between lenders and borrowers, Minsky's approach is more elaborate. Accordingly, the rate of interest and the variations (whether expected or not) of the quantity of money play an important role in the determination of economic activity, but they are no longer the most important variables, whereas they are for the Keynesians of the neoclassical synthesis and for the monetarists à la Lucas. The main variables are, instead, those that describe financial structure and influence the quantity of investment, such as actual and acceptable debt-to-equity ratios and indicators measuring the respect for debt repayment obligations. Emphasis on the role these variables play in the determination of capital asset prices is also one of the essential aspects that distinguish Minsky's analysis from the investment theories of Keynes, Tobin and traditional post-Keynesians.

Second, with regard to the analysis of business cycles, his particular position within the Keynesian school gave Minsky the incentive to develop an analysis of economic phenomena that went well beyond the simple criticism of the different approaches of neoclassical inspiration. As opposed to many post-Keynesians, Minsky proposes a general vision of the way a 'financially sophisticated' market economy works. His approach to financial relations is one where the profit-seeking behaviour of rational economic agents is likely to generate endogenous dynamic phenomena of economic and financial instability.

The financial dynamics Minsky outlines in his contributions is probably the aspect of his work that has most strongly inspired authors in recent years, in particular those who have endeavoured to build models describing the relations between finance, investment and economic fluctuations. On the whole, these models have produced interesting results. First of all, they have brought convincing support to the, still, minority view according to which the nature of economic fluctuations is both endogenous and financial. In addition, the reliance on sophisticated mathematical tools and on concepts developed within approaches unrelated to the Keynesian fundamentalist school has helped to simplify and sometimes to clarify some aspects of Minsky's theory.

However, these models can only account for some of Minsky's insights. Our insistence on the deficiencies of these works indicates new and promising directions for economists eager to find relevant ways of modelling the phenomena connected with financial instability.

Exploring these new paths would require the careful and preliminary study of the two additional dimensions of the financial instability hypothesis. As mentioned above, they concern the analysis of behaviours in situations of uncertainty and the role of institutional factors. These two aspects have been less studied and exploited by the commentators of Minsky's works and by the authors of recent models of financial instability than the financial dynamic dimension, yet they strongly influence the relation between finance, investment and economic fluctuations in the financially sophisticated economies Minsky considers.

Minsky's analysis of behaviour in situations of uncertainty is to some extent an extension of the approach proposed by the new-Keynesians. As opposed to other post-Keynesian authors, Minsky believes that asymmetric information does exert some influence on the behaviour of agents, in particular of those operating in capital markets. However, the existence of this kind of imperfection cannot be considered as a necessary condition for there to be credit rationing or, more generally, constraints of some sort in the financial markets. The essential reason for this, as we have seen, is that financial arrangements are set up within a decision-making environment where asymmetric information and fundamental uncertainty do in fact coexist. Fundamental uncertainty, which has nothing to do with the 'weak' exogenous uncertainty (or probabilistic risk) retained by the new-Keynesians, induces banks to adopt, independently of any effect of asymmetric information, a whole range of behaviours that go far beyond the rationing of the demand for loans in the credit market. Indeed, when 'strong' uncertainty prevails, the adoption of behaviours that are based upon a particular form of rationality, where conventions and animal spirits play an important role, implies that agents do not act as do the robot-like decision-makers of the rational expectations theory. Other behaviours and other variables have to be considered: the level reached by the agents' indebtedness, the ratios of indebtedness that are judged acceptable, changes in the 'state of confidence', the liquidity preference of banks and the related appearance of financial and endogenous instability. All these aspects are excluded from the outset by the new-Keynesians, willing as they are to depart as little as possible, when making assumptions and when choosing analytical tools, from standard microeconomic analysis. There is, therefore, a large amount of material available here for further research with a view to improving the assumptions made by the authors of the recent models of financial instability and in particular those built on the basis of the concepts of asymmetric information and sunspots.

As mentioned earlier, the third dimension of the financial instability hypothesis is institutional. Economic fluctuations in Minsky's approach are brought about by the way both public and private financial institutions work.

Minsky's contribution to the theory of financial institutions is twofold. First, his approach to financial intermediation offers prospects for the renewal of the Keynesian analysis of banking. By focusing his analysis on banks, Minsky stands clearly apart from the horizontalists whose positions are still widely shared by post-Keynesian theorists of the endogenous money supply. Numerous theoretical influences have inspired Minsky's analysis of banking. His ability to integrate the contributions of authors as different as Keynes, Schumpeter or Kalecki within a single consistent setting has allowed him to investigate certain aspects that are often lacking in even recent Keynesian analyses of banking: financial innovation, fundamental uncertainty, increasing risk, the financial structure and the liquidity preference of banks.

His second contribution is more fundamental still, as it concerns the theoretical validity of his analysis of the business cycle considered as a whole. Careful scrutiny of Minsky's approach of endogenous money has brought to light the pivotal role played by the analysis of banking within his theory of economic instability. Taking banks and their behaviour into account has enabled him to lay the foundations for an original approach to economic fluctuations, differing from both Keynesian macroeconomics and recent theories of business cycles. Organized around the study of the dynamics of financial relationships, his approach shows that the rational profit-seeking and innovative behaviour of banks produces both endogenous changes in the supply of loanable funds – affecting both prices and quantities – and endogenous financial instability. The behaviour of banks, an aspect that is often neglected by commentators on Minsky's approach, thus appears to be one of the most important ingredients of the financial instability hypothesis. It therefore deserves to be taken into account in all of its complexity by theorists interested in the relation between finance, investment and economic fluctuations.

The analysis of the dynamics involving public institutions also appears to be an essential aspect of Minsky's contribution to the analysis of business cycles. Indeed, for more than two centuries, there have been two opposing conceptions of the evolution of economic activity. In his memorial to Wesley Mitchell, Schumpeter distinguishes between those economists who consider that 'the economic process is essentially non-oscillatory and that the explanation of cyclical as well as other fluctuations must be sought in particular circumstances (monetary or other) which disturb that even flow' and those who believe that the 'economic process itself is essentially wave-like – that cycles are the form of capitalist evolution'.[1]

The analysis developed by Minsky, while it does not call this distinction into question, shows that it must nevertheless be reconsidered if the institutional factors that characterize market economies today are to be embodied explicitly into business cycle analysis. In fact there is scope within contemporary analyses of economic fluctuations for a third family of business cycle theories. Fitting somewhere in between the purely exogenous conceptions (developed within new classical economics) and the endogenous explanations (at work in non-linear models of cycles), it would depict the economic process as fundamentally oscillatory but not cyclical in essence. This third approach could make room both for steady growth and regular business cycles as possible transient features of economic time series, but in addition it would not exclude the emergence of the potentially 'incoherent' (or chaotic) dynamics resulting from the behavioural interaction of economic agents. Under these circumstances the transformation of potential incoherence into realized incoherence would be mainly dependent upon the various kinds of institutional thwarting systems at work in the economic system.

This sort of approach would have the merit of renewing the treatment of the relationships that arise between institutions and economic activity. In new classical economics it is assumed that governmental institutions can only disturb the operation of markets that otherwise clear through the interplay of supply and demand. For their part the Keynesians of the IS-LM synthesis consider economic policy as totally exogenous. In contrast, the analysis based on Minsky's approach shows that the public authorities (the government and the central bank) react in an endogenous fashion to the behaviour of private agents. They thus participate in creating genuinely institutional dynamics that interacts with the real dynamics and the financial dynamics of the economy and modifies the unconstrained outcomes (that occur in the absence of thwarting systems) of these last two. The essential consequence of the permanent interaction between institutions and market behaviour is that the economic system never reproduces itself in exactly the same form. In this context the establishment of adequate institutional thwarting mechanisms becomes extremely complex and requires increased awareness on the part of the public authorities. Such awareness is necessary, as the stabilization processes set up at a certain point in time may prove to be highly destabilizing at some later date.

Finally, Minsky's analysis shows that the institutional changes imposed by the public authorities on the initial conditions of a dynamic process generate constrained time series, in other words, truncated business cycles. This also happens when stabilizing mechanisms set up previously have the effect of guarding for a comparatively long period against a financial crisis or a deep depression. In this case stability is destabilizing: private agents tend to become less risk averse and to adapt their profit-seeking behaviour to existing institutional arrangements, which gradually undermines the stabilizing capacity of these arrangements and amplifies the effects of the crisis when it eventually breaks out. The extent of the problems raised by the bailing out of the Savings and Loans Associations in the United States and the more recent difficulties experienced by the central banks and by the International Monetary Fund in containing the Asian crisis are painful evidence of this fact. They also indicate strongly that there is a need for more work to be done to improve our understanding of how investment, finance and economic fluctuations are interrelated, in particular by investigating further into the institutional dimension of business cycles and pursuing the work initiated by Hyman P. Minsky.

NOTES

1.   Schumpeter (1951b, p. 252).

References

Aglietta, M. (1995), *Macroéconomie Financière*, Paris, La Découverte.

Arena, R. (1989), 'Keynes après Lucas, quelques enseignements récents de la macroéconomie monétaire', *Economies et Société*, April-May, Série MO, 7, 13-42.

Arena, R. and Torre, D. (1992), 'Introduction', in R. Arena and D. Torre (eds), *Keynes et les Nouveaux Keynésiens*, Paris, PUF.

Arnold, V.I. (1984), *Catastrophe Theory*, New York, Springer.

Arrous, J. (1982), 'Keynes et les probabilités: un aspect du fondamentalisme keynésien', *Revue Economique*, September, 839-61.

Arrow, K. and Hahn, F. (1971), *General Competitive Analysis*, San Francisco, Holden-Day.

Azariadis, C. (1981), 'Self-fulfilling prophecies', *Journal of Economic Theory*, 25, 380-96.

Azariadis, C. and Guesnerie, R. (1986), 'Sunspots and cycles', *Review of Economic Studies*, 58, 725-37.

Azariadis, C. and Guesnerie, R. (1991), 'Sunspots equilibria in sequential markets models' in W. Hildenbrand and H. Sonnenschein (eds), *Handbook of Monetary Economics*, Elsevier Science Publishers B. V.

Baumol, W. and Benhabib, J. (1989), 'Chaos: Significance, mechanism, and economic applications', *Journal of Economic Perspectives*, 3, 77-106.

Benassy, J.P. (1984), 'A non-walrasian model of business cycle', *Journal of Economic Behavior and Organization*, 5, 77-89.

Bernanke, B. (1983), 'Nonmonetary effects of financial crises in the propagation of the Great Depression', *American Economic Review*, 73, June, 257-76.

Bernanke, B. and Gertler, M. (1989), 'Agency costs, net worth, and business fluctuations', *American Economic Review*, March, 14-31.

Bernanke, B. and Gertler, M. (1990), 'Financial fragility and economic performance', *Quarterly Journal of Economics*, 87-114.

Besanko, D. and Thakor, A. (1987), 'Collateral and rationing: sorting equilibria in monopolistic and competitive credit markets', *International Economic Review*, October, 671-89.

Bester, H. (1985), 'Screening versus rationing in credit markets with imperfect information', *American Economic Review*, September, 850-5.

Blanchard, 0. (1979), 'Backward and forward solutions in economies with rational expectations', *American Economic Review*, **69**, 114-8.

Blatt, J.M. (1978), 'On the econometric approach to business cycle analysis', Oxford Economic Papers, **32**, 469-79.

Blaug, M. (1978), *Economic Theory in Retrospect*, 3d. rev. ed., Cambridge, Cambridge University Press.

Boyer, R. (1993), 'La crise de la macroéconomie contemporaine: une conséquence de la méconnaissance des institutions?', in P. Malgrange and L. Salvas-Bronsard (eds), *Macroéconomie, Développements Récents*, Paris, Economica.

Brossard, O. (1998), 'L'instabilité financière selon Minsky: l'incertitude et la liquidité au fondement du cycle?', *Revue Economique*, **49**, 2, 407-35.

Calomiris, C. and Hubbard, R. (1989), 'Price flexibility, credit availability, and economic fluctuations: evidence from the United States, 1894-1909', *Quarterly Journal of Economics*, **54**, 429-52.

Calomiris, C. and Hubbard, R. (1990), 'Firm heterogeneity, internal finance, and credit rationing", *Economic Journal*, March, 90-104.

Calomiris, C., Hubbard, R. and Stock, J. (1986), 'The farm debt crisis and public policy', *Brookings Papers on Economic Activity*, 441-79.

Campbell, C. and Minsky, H.P. (1987), 'How to get off the back of a tiger or, do initial conditions constrain deposit insurance reform?', paper presented at the Conference on Bank Structure and Competition: proceedings, Federal Reserve Bank of Chicago, 253-67.

Cantor, G. (1883), 'Grundlageneiner allgemein Mannichfaltigheitslehre', *Mathematische Annalen*, **21**, 545-91.

Carter, M. (1989), 'Financial innovation and financial fragility', *Journal of Economic Issues*, September, 779–93.

Cass, D. and Shell, K. (1983), 'Do sunspots matter? ', *Journal of Political Economy*, **91**, 193-227.

Chan, Y. and Thakor, A. (1987), 'Collateral and competitive equilibrium with moral hazard and private information', *Journal of Finance*, June, 345-63.

Chang, W. and Smyth, D. (1971), 'The existence and persistence of cycles in a non linear model: Kaldor's 1940 model re-examined', *Review of Economic Studies*, **38**, 37-44.

Clower, R. (1967), 'A reconsideration of the micro foundations of monetary theory', *Western Economic Journal*, **6**, 1-9.

Crotty, J. (1986), 'Marx, Keynes, and Minsky on the instability of the capitalist growth process and the nature of government economic policy', in S. Helburn and D. Bramhall (eds), *Marx, Schumpeter, and Keynes: a Centenary Celebration of Dissent*, Armonk, New York, M.E. Sharpe.

Crotty, J. (1990a), 'Owner-manager conflict and financial theories of investment stability: a critical assessment of Keynes, Tobin and Minsky', *Journal of Post Keynesian Economics*, **12**, 519-42.

Crotty, J. (1990b), 'Keynes on the stages of development of the capitalist economy: the institutional foundation of Keynes methodology', *Journal of Economic Issues*, September, 761-80.

Dangel, C. (1988), 'La théorie monétaire de J.M. Keynes: l'hypothèse de séparabilité de la demande de monnaie', *Recherches Economiques de Louvain*, **54**, 4, 439-58.

Dann, L. and Mikkelson, W. (1984), 'Convertible debt issuance, capital structure change and financing-related information: some new evidence', *Journal of Financial Economics*, June.

Danzinger, S., Van der Gaag, J., Smolensky E. and Taussig, M., (1982-83), 'The life cycle hypothesis and the consumption behavior of the elderly', *Journal of Post Keynesian Economics*, Winter, 208-27.

Davidson, P. (1978), *Money and the Real World*, London, Macmillan.

Davidson, P. (1980a), 'The dual-faceted nature of the Keynesian revolution: money and money wages in unemployment and production flow prices', *Journal of Post Keynesian Economics*, Spring, **2**(3), 291-307.

Davidson, P. (1980b), 'Post Keynesian economics: solving the crisis in economic theory', in I. Kristol and D. Bell (eds), *The Crisis in Economic Theory*, New York, Basic Books, 151-73.

Davidson, P. (1982-83), 'Rational expectations: a fallacious foundation for studying crucial decision-making processes', *Journal of Post Keynesian Economics*, Winter, 182-98.

Davidson, P. (1987), 'Sensible expectations and the long run non-neutrality of money', *Journal of Post Keynesian Economics*, Fall, 146-53.

Davidson, P. (1991), 'Is probability theory relevant of uncertainty? A Post Keynesian perspective', *Journal of Economic Perspectives*, **5**(1), Winter, 129-43.

Davidson, P. (1992), 'Would Keynes be a New Keynesian?' *Eastern Economic Journal*, Fall, 449-63.

Davidson, P. and Davidson, G., *Economics for a Civilized Society*, London, Macmillan, 1996.

Davis, E.P. (1992), *Debt, Financial Fragility and Systemic Risk*, Oxford, Clarendon Press.

Day, R. (1982), 'Irregular growth cycles', *American Economic Review*, **72**, 3, 406-14.

Day, R. (1987), 'Chaos and cycles', Lecture Note for the Workshop on Alternative Approaches to Macroeconomics, Sienne, November.

Day, R. and Shafer, W. (1985), 'Keynesian chaos', *Journal of Macroeconomics*, **7**, 277-95.

Day, R. and Shafer, W. (1987), 'Ergodic fluctuations in deterministic economic models', *Journal of Economic Behavior and Organization*, **8**, 339-61.

Delli Gatti, D., Gallegati, M. and Gardini, L. (1990), 'Real accumulation and financial instability: a model of profit flows, debt commitments and capital asset prices', *Studi Economici*, **41**(2), 101-26.

Delli Gatti, D., Gallegati, M. and Gardini, L. (1992), 'A non-linear model of the business cycle with money and finance', *Metroeconomica*, **1**, 1-32.

Delli Gatti, D., Gallegati, M. and Gardini, L. (1993a), 'Complex dynamics in a simple macroeconomic model, with financing constraints', in G. Dymski and R. Pollin (eds), *New Perspectives in Monetary Macroeconomics, Explorations in the Tradition of Hyman Minsky*, Ann Arbor, The University of Michigan Press, 51-76.

Delli Gatti, D., Gallegati, M. and Gardini, L. (1993b), 'Investment confidence, corporate debt and income fluctuations', *Journal of Economic Behavior and Organization*, **22**, 161-87.

Diamond, D. (1965), 'Government debt in a neoclassical growth model', *American Economic Review*, December, 1126-50.

Dow, S. and Earl, P. (1982), *Money Matters*, Oxford, Martin Robertson.

Dymski, G. (1992), 'A "new view" of the role of banking firms in keynesian monetary theory', *Journal of Post Keynesian Economics*, **14**, 3, Spring, 311-20.

Dymski, G. (1993a), 'Asymmetric information, uncertainty, and financial structure: "New" versus "Post" Keynesian microfoundations', in G. Dymski and R. Pollin (eds) (1993).

Dymski, G. (1993b), 'Keynesian uncertainty and asymmetric information: complementary or contradictory?', *Journal of Post Keynesian Economics*, **16**, 1, Fall, 49-54.

Dymski, G. and Pollin, R. (1992), 'Hyman Minsky as hedgehog: the power of the Wall Street paradigm' in S. Fazzari and D. Papadimitriou (eds).

Dymski, G. and Pollin, R. (eds) (1993), *New Perspectives in Monetary Macroeconomics, Explorations in the Tradition of Hyman Minsky*, Ann Arbor, The University of Michigan Press.

Eichner, A. and Kregel, J.A. (1975), 'An essay in Post Keynesian theory: a new paradigm in economics', *Journal of Economic Literature*, December, 1293-312.

Fazzari, S. (1992), 'Keynesian theories of investment and finance: Neo, Post and New', in S. Fazzari and D. Papadimitriou (eds).

Fazzari S. and Minsky H.P. (1984), 'Domestic monetary policy: if not monetarism, what?', *Journal of Economic Issues*, 18, 101-16.

Fazzari, S. and Papadimitriou, D. (eds) (1992), *Financial Conditions and Economic Performance: Essays in Honour of Hyman Minsky*, Armonk, New York, M.E. Sharpe.

Fazzari, S. and Variato, A.M. (1994), 'Asymmetric information and Keynesian theories of investment', *Journal of Post Keynesian Economics*, **16**, 3, 351-69.

Fazzari, S., Hubbard, R. and Petersen, B. (1988), 'Financing constraints and corporate investment", *Brookings Papers on Economic Activity*, **1**, 141-95.

Feingenbaum, M. (1978), 'Quantitative universality for a class of non linear transformations', *Journal of Statistical Physics*, **19**, 1, 25-52.

Ferri, P. and Minsky, H.P. (1984), 'Prices, employment and profits', *Journal of Post Keynesian Economics*, Summer, 489-99.

Ferri, P. and Minsky, H.P. (1989), 'The breakdown of the IS-LM Synthesis: implications for Post-Keynesian economic theory', *Review of Political Economy*, July, 123-41.

Ferri, P. and Minsky, H.P. (1992), 'Market processes and thwarting systems', *Structural Change and Economics Dynamics*, **3**, 1, 79-91.

Fisher, I. (1907), *The Rate of Interest*, New York, Macmillan.

Fisher, I. (1932), *Booms and Depressions*, New York, Adelphi.

Fisher, I. (1933), 'The debt-deflation theory of great depressions', *Econometrica*, October, 337-57.

Flaschel, P. (1985), 'Some stability properties of Goodwin's growth cycle. A critical elaboration', *Zeitschrift für Nationalökonomie*, 44, 63-9.

Flavin, M. (1984), 'Excess sensitivity of consumption to current outcome: liquidity constraints or myopia?', *NBER Working Papers*, 1341.

Franke, R. and Semmler, W. (1992), 'Expectation dynamics, financing of investment, and business cycles', in D. Papadimitriou (ed.), *Profits, Deficits and Instability*, London, Macmillan.

Friedman, B. (1992), 'Risks in our high-debt economy: depression or inflation?', in S. Fazzari and D. Papadimitriou (eds).

Friedman, B. and Laibson, D. (1989), 'Economic implications of extraordinary movements in stock prices', *Brookings Papers on Economic Activity*, **2**, 137-71.

Friedman, M. (1953), *Essays in Positive Economics*, Chicago, University of Chicago Press.

Friedman, M. (1968), 'The role of monetary policy', *American Economic Review*, **58** (1), March, 1-17.

Gabisch, H. and Lorenz, W. (1989), *Business Cycle Theory: a Survey of Methods And Concepts*, 2nd ed., New York, Springer-Verlag.

Gertler, M. and Hubbard, R. (1988), 'Financial factors in business fluctuations', in *Financial Market Volatility*, Kansas City, Federal Reserve Bank of Kansas.

Gleick, J. (1987), *Chaos: Making a New Science*, New York, Viking.

Goodwin, R. (1951), 'The non-linear accelerator and the persistence of business cycles', *Econometrica*, **19**, 1, 1-17.

Goodwin, R. (1967), 'A growth cycle' in C.H. Feinstein (ed.), *Socialism, Capitalism and Economic Growth*, Cambridge, Cambridge University Press.

Grandmont, J.M. (1986), 'On endogenous competitive business cycles', *Econometrica*, **53**, 3, September, 995-1045.

Grandmont, J.M. and Laroque, G. (1976), 'On temporary keynesian equilibria', *Review of Economic Studies*, 43, 3-12.

Grandmont, J.M. and Malgrange, P. (eds) (1987), *Non Linear Economic Dynamics*, Orlando, Academic Press.

Greenwald, B. and Stiglitz, J. (1986), 'Externalities in economies with imperfect information and incomplete markets', *Quarterly Journal of Economics*, **105**, February, 87-114.

Greenwald, B. and Stiglitz, J. (1987), 'Keynesian, New Keynesian and New Classical Economics', *Oxford Economic Papers*, **39**, 119-32.

Greenwald, B. and Stiglitz, J. (1992), 'Methodological issues and the New Keynesian economics', in A. Vercelli and N. Dimitri (eds), *Alternative Approaches to Macroeconomics*, 38-86.

Greenwald, B. and Stiglitz, J. (1993a), 'New and old Keynesians', *Journal of Economic Perspectives*, **7**, 1, Winter, 23-44.

Greenwald, B. and Stiglitz, J. (1993b), 'Financial market imperfections and business cycles', *Quarterly Journal of Economics*, February, 77-114.

Greenwald, B., Stiglitz, J. and Weiss, A. (1984), 'Informational imperfections in the capital market and macroeconomic fluctuations', *American Economic Review*, May, 194-99.

Guckenheimer, J. and Holmes, P. (1983), *Nonlinear Oscillations, Dynamical Systems, and Bifurcations of Vector Fields*, New York, London, Academic Press.

Guesnerie, R. (1987), 'Stationary sunspot equilibria in an n-commodity world', in J.M. Grandmont and P. Malgrange (eds).

Gurley, J. and Shaw, E. (1955), 'Financial aspects of economic development', *American Economic Review*, September, 515-38.

Gurley, J. and Shaw, E. (1956), 'Financial institutions and interrelationships', *Journal of Finance*, **11**, May.

Hahn, F. (1977), 'Keynesian economics and general equilibrium theory: Reflections on some current debates', in G.C. Harcourt (ed.), *Microeconomic Foundations of Macroeconomics,* London, Macmillan.

Hall, R. and Jorgenson, D. (1967), 'Tax policy and investment behavior', *American Economic Review*, **57**, 391-414.

Hall, R. and Mishkin, F. (1982), 'The sensitivity of consumption to transitory income: estimates from panel data on households', *Econometrica*, **50**, 461-81.

Hansen, A. (1964), *Business Cycles and National Income*, New York, Norton.

Hawtrey, R. G. (1919), *Currency and Credit*, New York, Longman.

Hawtrey, R. G. (1926), 'The trade cycle', *Economist*, reprinted in *Reading in Business Cycle Theory*, Irwin, 1951, 330-49.

Hawtrey, R. G. (1928), *Trade and Credit*, New York, Longman.

Hicks, J.R. (1950), *A Contribution to the Theory of the Trade Cycle*, Oxford, Clarendon Press.

Hicks, J.R. (1979), *Causality in Economics*, New York, Basic Books.

Hirsch, M. and Smale, S. (1974), *Differential Equations, Dynamical Systems, and Linear Algebra*, New York, Academic Press.

Hodgman, D. (1961), 'The deposit relationship and commercial banks behaviors', *Review of Economics and Statistics*, August, 257-8.

Hoogduin, L. (1987), 'On the difference between the Keynesian, Knightian and "Classical" analysis of uncertainty', *de Economist*.

Hubbard, R. and Kashyap, A. (1990), 'Internal net worth and the investment process: an application to U.S. agriculture', NBER Working Paper, 3339.

Jaffee, T. and Russell, T. (1976), 'Imperfect information, uncertainty, and credit rationing', *Quarterly Journal of Economics*, November, 651-66.

Jaffee, T. and Stiglitz, J. (1990), 'Credit rationing' in *Handbook of Monetary Economics*, Vol. II, B. Friedman and F. Hahn (eds), Amsterdam, Elsevier Science Publishers B.V.

Jarsulic, M. (1986), 'Growth cycles in a Classical-Keynesian model', in W. Semmler (ed.), *Competition, Distribution and non-linear cycles*, New York, Springer-Verlag.

Jensen, M. (1988), 'Take overs: their causes and consequences', *Journal of Economic Perspectives*, II, 21-48.

Jevons, W. (1884), *Investigations in Currency and Finance*, London, Macmillan.

Jorgenson, D. (1963), 'Capital theory and investment behavior', *American Economic Review*, **53**, 247-69.

Kaldor, N. (1940), 'A model of the trade cycle', *Economic Journal*, **50**, 78-92.

Kaldor, N. (1966), 'Marginal productivity and the macroeconomic theories of distribution', *Review of Economic Studies*, **33**, October, 309-19.

Kaldor, N. (1982), *The Scourge of Monetarism*, London, Oxford University Press.

Kalecki, M. (1937), 'The principle of increasing risk', *Economica*, **4**, November, 440-7.

Kalecki, M. (1971), *Selected Essays on the Dynamics of the Capitalist Economy, 1933-1970*, Cambridge, Cambridge University Press.

Keynes, J.M. (1971), 'A Treatise on Money', reprinted in *The Collected Writings of John Maynard Keynes*, Vol. V and VI, London, Macmillan.

Keynes, J.M. (1972), 'The consequences to the banks of the collapse of money values' reprinted in *The Collected Writings of John Maynard Keynes*, Vol. IX, London, Macmillan.

Keynes, J.M. (1973), *The General Theory of Employment, Interest and Money*, reprinted in *The Collected Writings of John Maynard Keynes*, Vol. VII, London, Macmillan.

Keynes, J.M. (1973), *Treatise on Probability*, reprinted in *The Collected Writings of John Maynard Keynes*, Vol. VIII, London, Macmillan.

Keynes, J.M. (1973), *The General Theory and After, Part I: Preparation*, reprinted in *The Collected Writings of John Maynard Keynes*, Vol. XIII, London, Macmillan.

Keynes, J.M. (1973), 'The general theory of employment", *Quarterly Journal of Economics*, February 1937, reprinted in *The General Theory and After, Part 2: Defence and Development, The Collected Writings of John Maynard Keynes*, Vol. XIV, London, Macmillan.

Keynes, J.M. (1983), *Economic Articles and Correspondence, Academic*, reprinted in *The Collected Writings of John Maynard Keynes*, Vol. XI, London, Macmillan.

King, R. and Plosser, G. (1984), 'Money, credit and prices in a real business cycle', *American Economic Review*, **74**(3), June, 363-80.

Knight, F.H. (1921), *Risk, Uncertainty and Profit*, Boston, Houghton Mifflin Company.

Kregel, J.A. (1976), 'Economic methodology in the face of uncertainty: the modelling method of Keynes and the Post-Keynesians', *Economic Journal*, June, 220-1.

Kregel, J.A. (1980), 'Markets and institutions as features of a capitalist production system', *Journal of Post-Keynesian Economics*, Autumn, 32-48.

Kregel, J.A. (1982), 'Money, expectations and relative prices in Keynes' monetary equilibrium', *Economie Appliquée*, **3**, 449-65.

Kregel, J.A. (1985), 'Le multiplicateur et la préférence pour la liquidité: deux aspects de la théorie de la demande effective', in A. Barrère (ed.), *Keynes Aujourd'hui, Théories et Politiques*, Paris, Economica.

Kregel, J.A. (1987), 'Rational spirits and the post Keynesian macrotheory of microeconomics', *De Economist*, **4**, 520-32.

Kregel, J.A. (1988), 'Irving Fisher, great-grandparent of the General Theory: money, rate of return over cost and efficiency of capital', *Cahiers d'Economie Politique*, **14-15**, 59-69.

Kregel, J.A. (1992), 'Minsky's "two price" theory of financial instability and monetary policy: discounting versus open market intervention', in S. Fazzari and D. Papadimitriou.

Kregel, J.A. (1995), 'Keynes and the New Keynesian on the rôle of uncertainty and information', in P. Malgrange and L. Salvas-Bronsard (ed.), *Macroéconomie, Développements Récents*, Paris, Economica.

Kreps, D. (1988), *Notes on the Theory of Choice*, Boulder and London, West View Press.

Kreps, D. (1990), *A Course in Microeconomic Theory*, Princeton, Princeton University Press.

Lavington, F. (1921), *The English Capital Market*, London, Methuen.

Lavoie, M. (1983), 'Loi de Minsky et loi d'entropie', *Economie Appliquée*, 2-3, 287-331.

Lavoie, M. (1985a), 'Credit and money: the dynamic circuit, overdraft economics, and Post-Keynesian economics', in M. Jarsulic (ed.), *Money and Macro Policy*, Boston, Kluwer-Nijhoff Publishing.

Lavoie, M. (1985b), 'La distinction entre l'incertitude keynésienne et le risque néo-classique', *Economie Appliquée*, 2, 493-518.

Lavoie, M. (1986-87), 'Systemic financial fragility: a simplified view', *Journal of Post Keynesian Economics*, Winter, IX, 2, 258-66.

Lawson, T. (1985), 'Uncertainty and economic analysis', *Economic Journal*, December, 909-27.

Leland, H. and Pyle, D. (1977), 'Informational asymmetries, financial structure, and financial intermediation', *Journal of Finance*, 371-87.

Lorenz, E. (1963), 'Deterministic non-periodic flow', *Journal of Atmospheric Science*, 20, 2, 130-41.

Lorenz, H. (1989), *Non Linear Dynamical Economics and Chaotic Motion*, Berlin, Springer-Verlag.

Lucas, R.E. (1976), 'Econometric policy evaluation: a critique', in K. Brunner and A.H. Meltzer (eds), *The Phillips Curve and Labor Markets*, Carnegie-Rochester Series on Public Policy, Amsterdam and New York, North Holland.

Lucas, R.E. (1977), 'Understanding business cycles', in K. Brunner and A. Meltzer (eds), *Stabilization of the Domestic and International Economy*, Amsterdam, North Holland.

Lucas, R.E. and Sargent, T.J. (1981), 'After Keynesian Macroeconomics', in R. Lucas and T. Sargent (eds), *Rational Expectations and Econometric Practice*, Minneapolis, The University of Minnesota Press.

Lucas, R.E. in A. Klamer (ed.) (1985), *The New Classical Macroeconomics, Conversations with New Classical Economists and their Opponents*, Wheatsheaf Books, Brighton.

Machina, M. (1987), 'Choice under uncertainty: problems solved and unsolved', *Journal of Economic Perspectives*, 1, 121-54.

Mandelbrot, B. (1983), *The Fractal Geometry of Nature*, San Francisco, W.H. Freeman.

Mankiw, N. (1986), 'The allocation of credit and financial collapse', *Quarterly Journal of Economics*, August, 455-70.

Marshall, A. (1890), *Principles of Economics*, London, Macmillan.

May, R. (1976), 'Simple mathematical models with very complicated dynamics', *Nature*, **261**, 5560, 459-467.

Meyer, J. and Kuh, E. (1957), *The Investment Decision: An Empirical Study*, Cambridge MA, Harvard University Press.

Milde, H. and Riley, J. (1989), 'Signaling in credit markets', *Quarterly Journal of Economics*, February, 101-30.

Minsky, H.P. (1957a), 'Central banking and money market changes', *Quarterly Journal of Economics*, May, 171-87.

Minsky, H.P. (1957b), 'Monetary systems and accelerator models', *American Economic Review*, **47**, 859-63.

Minsky, H.P. (1959), 'A linear model of cyclical growth', *Review of Economics and Statistics*, **41**, 137-45.

Minsky, H.P. (1974), 'Money and the Real World: a review article', *Quarterly Review of Economics and Business*, Summer, 7-17.

Minsky, H.P. (1975), *John Maynard Keynes*, New York, Columbia University Press.

Minsky, H.P. (1977), 'A theory of systemic fragility' in E.I. Altman and A.W. Sametz (eds), *Financial Crisis: Institutions and Markets in a Fragile Environment*, New York, John Wiley and Sons.

Minsky, H.P. (1980), 'Money, financial markets, and the coherence of a market economy', *Journal of Post Keynesian Economies*, Fall, 21-31.

Minsky, H.P. (1982a), *Can 'It' Happen Again?*, Armonk, New York, M.E. Sharpe.

Minsky, H.P. (1982b), 'The financial instability hypothesis: capitalist processes and the behavior of the economy', in C. Kindleberger and J. Lafargue (eds), *Financial Crises: Theory, History and Policy*, Cambridge, Cambridge University Press.

Minsky, H.P. (1986a), *Stabilizing an Unstable Economy*, Yale University Press, New Haven.

Minsky, H. P. (1986b), 'The evolution of financial institutions and the performance of the economy', *Journal of Economic Issues*, **XX**, 2, June, 345-53.

Minsky, H.P. (1988), 'Back from the brink', *Challenge*, January-February, 22-8.

Minsky, H.P. (1989a), 'Comments and Discussion' on B. Friedman and D. Laibson, *Brookings Papers on Economic Activity*, **2**, 173-82.

Minsky, H.P. (1989b), 'Financial crises and the evolution of capitalism: the crash of 1987. What does it mean?', in M. Gottdiener and N. Komninos (eds), *Capitalist Development and Crisis Theory: Accumulation, Regulation and Spatial Restructuring*, London, Macmillan.

Minsky, H.P. (1991a), 'The financial instability hypothesis: a clarification' in M. Feldstein (ed.), *The Risk of Economic Crisis*, Chicago, The University of Chicago Press.

Minsky, H.P. (1991b), 'The endogeneity of money' in E. Nell and W. Semmler (eds), *Nicholas Kaldor and Mainstream Economics: Growth, Distribution and Cycles,* London, Macmillan.

Minsky, H.P. (1992a), 'The structure of financial institutions and the dynamic behavior of the economy', paper presented at the seminar Macroeconomic Dynamics, September, Nice.

Minsky, H.P. (1992b), 'Profits, deficits and economic instability: a policy discussion', in D. Papadimitriou (ed.), *Profits, Deficits and Instability*, London, Macmillan.

Mishkin, F. (1992), 'Anatomy of a financial crisis', *Journal of Evolutionary Economics*, 2, 115-30.

Modigliani, F. and Miller, M. (1958), 'The cost of capital, corporation finance and the theory of investment', *American Economic Review*, June, 261-97.

Moore, B. (1988), Horizontalists and Verticalists: the Macroeconomics of Credit Money, Cambridge, Cambridge University Press.

Muth, J.F. (1961), 'Rational expectations and the theory of price movements', *Econometrica*, July.

Myers, S. (1984), 'The capital structure puzzle', *Journal of Finance*, July, 575-92.

Myers, S. and Majluf, N. (1984), 'Corporate financing and investment decisions when investors have information that investors do not have', *Journal of Financial Economics*, June, 187-221.

Orléan, A. (1988), 'L'auto-référence dans la théorie keynésienne de la spéculation', *Cahiers d'Economie Politique*, 14-15, 229-43.

Pohjola, M. (1981), 'Stable, cyclic and chaotic growth: the dynamics of a discrete-time version of Goodwin's growth model', *Zeitschrift für Nationalökonomic*, 41, 1, 27-38.

Poincaré, H. (1890), 'Sur les équations de la dynamique et le problème de trois corps', *Acta Mathematica*, 13, 1, 1-270.

Radcliffe Committee, (1959), 'Committee on the working of the monetary system', London, HMSO.

Riley, J. (1979), 'Informational equilibrium', *Econometrica*, March, 331-86.

Rogers, C. (1989), *Money, Interest and Capital*, Cambridge, Cambridge University Press.

Rosser, J.B. (1990), 'Chaos theory and the New Keynesian Economics', *The Manchester School*, LVIII, 3, September, 265-91.

Ruelle, D. and Takens, F. (1971), 'On the nature of turbulence', *Communications in Mathematical Physics*, 20, 3, 167-92.

Rymes, T. (1989), *Keynes's Lectures*, 1932-35, Ann Arbor, Mich., University of Michigan Press.

Samuelson, P. A. (1971-72), 'Generalized predator-prey oscillations and economic equilibrium,' in R. C. Merton (ed.), *The Collected scientific papers of P. A. Samuelson*, Cambridge, Vol. III, MIT Press.

Samuelson, P. A. (1939), 'Interactions between the multiplier analysis and the principle of acceleration', *Review of Economics and Statistics*, May, 75-8.

Santomero, A. (1984), 'Modeling the banking firm', *Journal of Money, Credit and Banking*, November, 895-929.

Sargent, T. (1979), *Macroeconomic Theory*, New York, Academic Press.

Saunders, P.T. (1980), *An Introduction to Catastrophe Theory*, Cambridge, Cambridge University Press.

Savage, L. (1954), *The Foundations of Statistics*, New York, John Wiley.

Schinasi, B. (1981), 'A non-linear dynamic model of short-run fluctuations', *Review of Economic Studies*, **48**, 469-656.

Schmidt, C. (ed). (1996), *Uncertainty in Economic Thought*, Cheltenham, UK and Lyme, US, Edward Elgar.

Schumpeter, J.A. (1912), *The Theory of Economic Development*, Oxford, Oxford University Press.

Schumpeter, J.A. (1951a), 'The creative response in economics history', in R. Clemence (ed.), *Essays of J.A. Schumpeter*, Cambridge Ma., Addison-Wesley.

Schumpeter, J.A. (1951b), *Ten Great Economists: From Marx to Keynes*, Galaxy Press, New York.

Schumpeter, J.A. (1954), *History of Economic Analysis*, Oxford, Oxford University Press.

Shackle, G.L.S. (1955), *Uncertainty in Economics*, Cambridge, Cambridge University Press.

Shackle, G.L.S. (1972), *Epistemics and Economics*, Cambridge, Cambridge University Press.

Shackle, G.L.S. (1984), "Comment on the paper by Randall Bausor and Malcolm Rutherford', *Journal of Post Keynesian Economics*, Spring, 388-93.

Shell, K. (1977), 'Monnaie et allocation intertemporelle', CNRS, Seminaire d'Econométrie Roy-Malinvaud, Paris.

Silipo, D. (1987), 'La teoria dell'instabilità del capitalismo: la posizione di Hyman Minsky', *Studi Economici*, 1987, 119-53.

Skott, P. (1989a) 'Effective demand, class struggle and cyclical growth', *International Economic Review*, **30**, 231-47.

Skott, P. (1989b), *Conflict and Effective Demand in Economic Growth*, Cambridge, Cambridge University Press.

Skott, P. (1992), 'On the Modelling of Systemic Financial Fragility', *Aarhus Institute of Economics Mimeo*, February, reprinted in A.K. Dutt (ed.) (1994), *New Directions in Analytical Political Economy*, Aldershot, UK and Brookfield, US, Edward Elgar.

Skott, P. (1995), 'Financial Innovation, Deregulation, and Minsky Cycles', in G. Epstein and H. Gintis (eds), *Macroeconomic Policy after the Conservative Era*, Cambridge University Press, Cambridge

Slovin, M., Johnson, S. and Glascor, J. (1992), 'Firm size and the information content of bank loan announcements', *Journal of Banking and Finance*, **16**.

Smith, A. (1776), *An Inquiry into the Nature and Causes of the Wealth of Nations*, reprinted in E. Cannan (ed.) (1961), London, Methuen.

Srini Vasan, P. (1986), *Credit Rationing and Corporate Investment*, Ph. D., Harvard University, Cambridge.

Stadler, G. (1994), 'Real Business cycles', *Journal of Economic Literature*, December, 1750-83.

Stiglitz, J. (1984), 'Price rigidities and market structures', *American Economic Review*, **74**, 1, 350-6.

Stiglitz, J. (1985), 'Credit markets and the control of capital', *Journal of Money, Credit, and Banking*, **17**(2), 133-52.

Stiglitz, J. (1992), 'Capital markets and economic fluctuations in capitalist economies', *European Economic Review*, **36**, 269-306.

Stiglitz, J. and Weiss, A. (1981), 'Credit rationing in markets with imperfect information', *American Economic Review*, June, 393-410.

Stiglitz, J. and Weiss, A. (1983), 'Incentive effects of terminations: application to the credit and labor markets', *American Economic Review*, December, 912-27.

Stiglitz, J. and Weiss, A. (1992), 'Asymmetric information in credit markets and its implications for macroeconomics', *Oxford Economic Papers*, October, 264-74.

Stutzer, M. (1980), 'Chaotic dynamics and bifurcation in a macro-model', *Journal of Economic Dynamics and Control*, **2**, 253-76.

Taylor, L. and O'Connel, S. (1985), 'A Minsky's crisis', *Quarterly Journal of Economics*, **100**, Supplément, 872-85.

Thomas, P. (1989), 'Reforming savings and loan industry', *Wall Street Journal*, September 28, 1989, A16.

Thomson, J. and Stewart, H. (1987), *Non Linear Dynamics and Chaos*, New York, John Wiley.

Tirole, J. (1982), 'On the possibility of speculation under rational expectations', *Econometrica*, **60**, 1163-81.

Tobin, J. (1952), 'A survey of the theory of rationing', *Econometrica*, **20**, 4, 521-53.

Tobin, J. (1969), 'A general equilibrium approach to monetary theory', *Journal of Money, Credit and Banking*, February, 15-29.

Tobin, J. (1987), 'Commercial banks as creators of money', 1963, reprinted in *Essays in Economics, Volume 1: Macroeconomics*, The MIT Press.

Tobin, J. (1989), Comments on 'Stabilizing an unstable economy', *Journal of Economic Literature*, March, 105-8.

Torre, V. (1977), 'Existence of limit cycles and control in complete Keynesian system by theory of bifurcations', *Econometrica*, **45**, 1457-66.

Van Der Pol, B. (1927), 'Forced oscillations in a circuit with non linear resistance (receptance with retroactive triode)', London, *Edinburgh and Dublin Philosophical Magazine*, **3**, 1, 65-80.

Van Ees, H. and Garretsen, H. (1993), 'Financial markets and the complementarity of asymmetric and fundamental uncertainty', *Journal of Post Keynesian Economics*, **16**, 1, 37-49.

Varian, H.R. (1979), 'Catastrophe Theory and the Business Cycle', *Economic Inquiry*, **17**, 14-28.

Von Neumann, J. and Morgenstern, O. (1953), *Theory of Games and Economic Behavior*, Princeton N.J, Princeton University Press.

Walliser, B. (1985), *Anticipation, Equilibre et Rationalité Economique*, Paris, Calman-Lévy.

Watson, M., Matheson, D., Kincaid, R. and Katler, E. (1986), 'International capital market: developments and prospects', *International Monetary Fund*, Occasional paper 43, February.

Weintraub, S. (1978), *Capitalism's Inflation and Unemployment Crisis*, Reading, Addison-Wesley.

Wicksell, K. (1898), *Interest and Prices*, London, Macmillan.

Williamson, S. (1987), 'Financial intermediation, business failures and real business cycles', *Journal of Political Economy*, **95**(6), December, 1196-216.

Wojnilower, A. (1985), 'Private credit demand, supply, and crunches - How different are the 1980s?', *American Economic Review*, **75**, 351-6.

Wojnilower, A. (1987), 'Financial changes in the United States', in M. de Cecco (ed.), *Changing Money*, New York and Oxford, Basic Blackwell.

Wolfson, M. (1994), *Financial Crises: Understanding the Postwar U.S. Experience*, Armonk, New York, M.E. Sharpe.

Wolfson, M., 'The causes of financial instability', *Journal of Post Keynesian Economics*, **12**, 1990, 333-55.

Wood, A. (1975), *A Theory of Profits*, Cambridge, Cambridge University Press.

Woodford, M. (1985), 'Keynes after Lucas: expectations, finance constraints, and the instability of investment', Mimeo, Columbia University.

Woodford, M. (1986), 'Stationary sunspot equilibria in a finance constrained economy', *Journal of Economic Theory*, **40**, 128-37.

Woodford, M. (1988), 'Expectations, finance and aggregate instability', in M. Kohn and S. Tsiang (eds), *Finance Constraints, Expectations and Macroeconomics*, New York, Oxford University Press.

Woodford, M. (1989), 'Finance, instability and cycles', in W. Semmler (ed.), *Financial Dynamics, and Business Cycles: New Perspectives*, New York, M. E. Sharpe.

Woodford, M. (1991), 'Self-fulfilling expectations and fluctuations in aggregate demand', in N. Mankiw and P. Romer (eds), *New Keynesian Economics*, **2**, Cambridge, , MIT Press 77-110.

Wray, L.R. (1988), 'Profit expectations and the investment saving relation', *Journal of Post Keynesian Economics*, **11**, 131-47.

Wray, L.R. (1990), *Money and Credit in Capitalist Economies: the Endogenous Money Approach*, Aldershot, Edward Elgar.

Wray, L. R. (1992), 'Commercial banks, the central bank, and endogenous money', *Journal of Post Keynesian Economics*, Spring, **14**, 3, 297-310.

Index

Printed and bound by CPI Group (UK) Ltd, Croydon, CR0 4YY

23/04/2025

14660987-0003